MW01618593

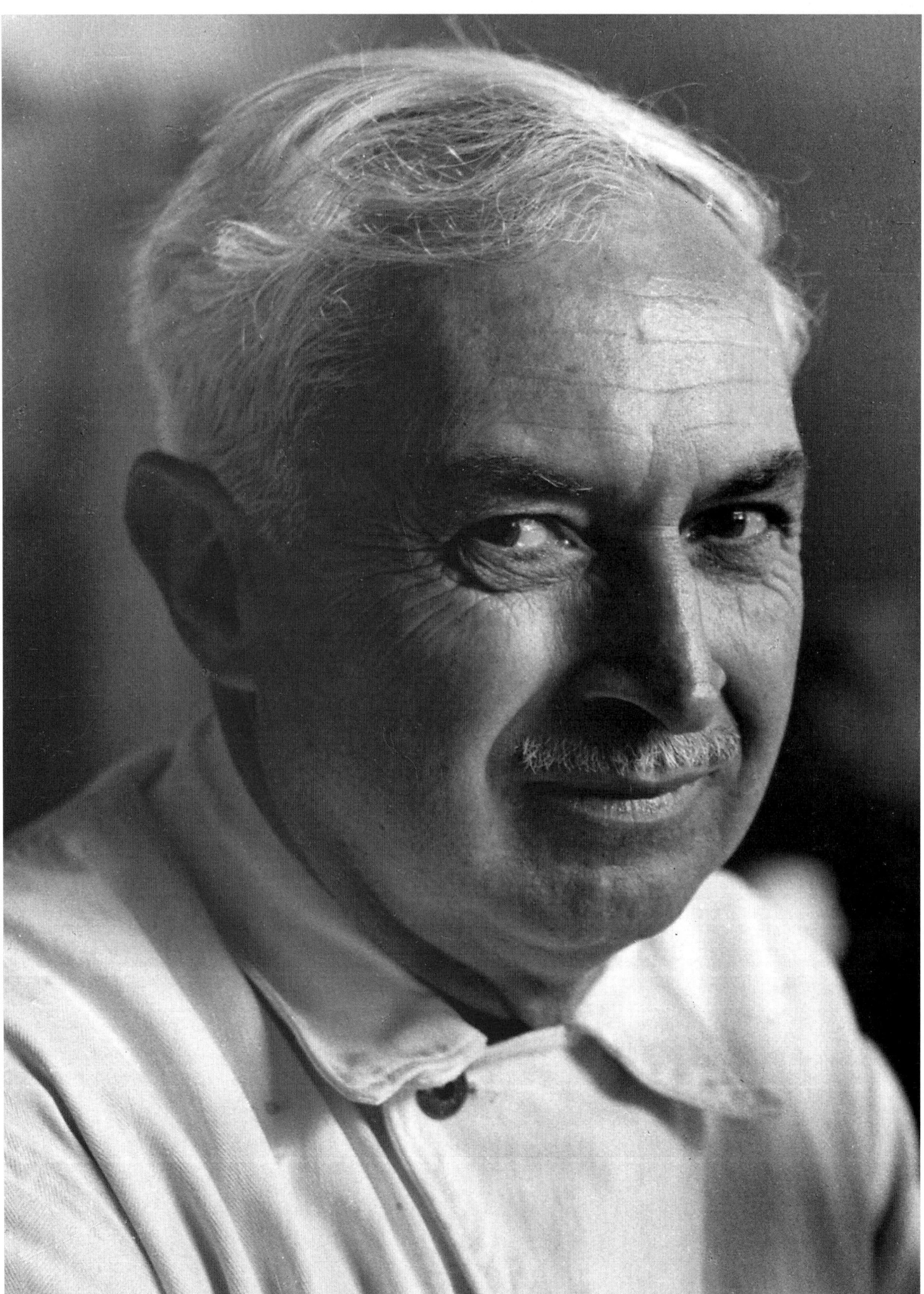

Donal Hord

Transcending the Solid

San Diego Historical Society

with foreword by William H. Gerdts

Published on the occasion of the exhibition *Donal Hord–Transcending the Solid*, shown at San Diego Historical Society, March 19 through October 10, 1999. The exhibition was directed by Jennifer Luksic, Curator of Collections.

Published in 1999 by Kales Press
Carlsbad, California

Kenneth Kales	Designer
Jeff McKinley	Production Coordinator
Leah Roschke	Design Assistant
Carina Woolrich	Photographer (except as noted)
San Diego Historical Society	Archival Photographs

Library of Congress Catalog Card Number: 99-61316
ISBN 0-9670076-0-7

Printed and bound in the United States of America.

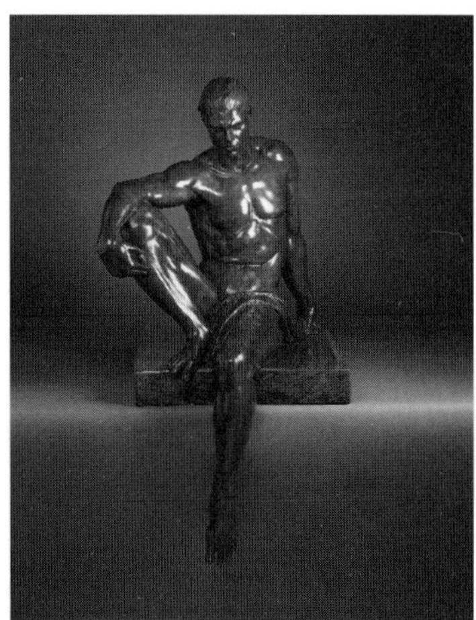

on the front cover: *Young Bather*
title page portrait: Donal Hord, Florence, Italy, 1955
on the back cover: *Guardian of the Waters*

This catalogue is published through a generous gift from the Legler Benbough Foundation in memory of Legler Benbough.

San Diego Historical Society recognizes the long and integral role of Legler Benbough and his family as participants in the history and culture of the city of San Diego.

Underwriters

Legler Benbough Foundation

Steven H. and Alida Brill Scheuer Foundation

Ellen Browning Scripps Foundation

Heller Foundation

Creative Candy Concepts

Cubic Corporation

Northern Trust Bank of California

Outdoor Systems, Inc.

Bente and Gerald E. Buck

Decorative Arts Council of the
San Diego Historical Society

Tom and Nell Waltz

Ned and Kathleen Buoymaster

Anne Evans

Philip M. Klauber

Contents

Preface 11

Foreword 13

Acknowledgements 17

In Memoriam 19

Introduction 23

Biography 25

Exhibition Plates 47

Notes to Exhibition Plates 135

List of Life's Work 137

Chronology 141

San Diego Historical Society 143

Preface

Robert M. Witty
Executive Director
San Diego Historical Society

When I arrived in San Diego in 1961, it seemed that everybody knew, or knew of, Donal Hord. It remained that way until his death in 1966, and some years beyond. But the city grew rapidly, from a small town to one of the nation's largest, and Hord's name became less familiar as thousands of newcomers joined our region each year.

Hord's colossal *Guardian of the Waters* still sits outside San Diego County's beaux-arts Administration building, gracing the waterfront as it has for the past 60 years. And his brooding *Aztec* sculpture, also known as *Montezuma*, remains highly visible on the San Diego State University campus, where students have nicknamed him *Monty*.

Hord sculptures are in many other highly visible places, indoors and out, in Marina Park in downtown San Diego, at Scripps Institution of Oceanography, in the vestibule of the San Diego Public Library, at the San Diego Zoo, Coronado High School and elsewhere.

So it is his name that has become less recognizable, not his work. One of the aims of this exhibition of Donal Hord sculptures is to make the connection between the man and his work, and introduce to the public many of his works from private homes and gardens, private art collections and museums from as far away as Philadelphia and the Franklin D. Roosevelt Library in Hyde Park.

During his lifetime he won international acclaim, and upon his death extraordinary praise, eulogized as "the greatest sculptor in America." But he suffered the curse of working in the remotest corner (from New York), which limited his public fame.

Hord's place in San Diego is secure; he is our eternal artist in residence.

Foreword

William H. Gerdts, Ph.D
Graduate School of the City University of New York

Donal Hord was one of the most eminent American sculptors over a period of about forty years, but since his death in 1966, he has seldom figured in accounts of the nation's sculptural development, outside of those published in his adopted state of California. This lack of national recognition was not true when the artist was at the height of his career; indeed, he figured as one of the eighteen artists selected by Dorothy C. Miller for the exhibition, *Americans 1942*, held at New York's Museum of Modern Art, where Ms. Miller was curator; five stone carvings were included in that display. The following year, Hord became an Associate Member of New York's prestigious National Academy of Design, and was elected a full Academician in 1951. Meanwhile, Hord has been the recipient in 1948 of the Award of Merit from the American Academy of Arts and Letters in New York, an award presented only once in five years for sculpture; two years later he was elected to membership in the American Academy's parent organization, the National Institute of Arts and Letters. And in the 1950s, Hord was the subject of several important articles published in *American Artist* magazine, the first in October, 1950, written by Catherine Sullivan, and a second in September, 1959, written by Janice Lovoos. Hord received international recognition when his bronze *Angel of Peace*, a commission he received in 1956, was installed four years later above the graves in the American Battle Cemetery in Belgium, commemorating those soldiers who lost their lives in the Battle of the Bulge in World War II.

Since then, however, those art historical surveys of America's twentieth century sculpture emanating from the East have tended to overlook Hord and, indeed, his California colleagues, almost completely. Hord is absent from the masterly survey of *Sculpture in America* published by Wayne Carven in 1968, only two years after Hord's death. He was missing from the important examination of *200 Years of American Sculpture*, held at the Whitney Museum of American Art in New York 1976, and likewise from Janis Ekdahl's reference book, *American Sculpture A Guide to Information Sources*, which appeared the following year. The major exception to this oversight was Roberta Tarbell's perceptive inclusion of Hord in the show and catalogue, *Vangard American Sculpture 1913-1939*, held at the Rutgers University Art Gallery in New Brunswick, New Jersey, in 1979, a traveling exhibition which finished up in Oakland, California in April, 1980; Hord's *Veiled Figure* was lent to the display by The Brooklyn Museum.

Tarbell was the first mainstream art historian who placed Hord correctly, not only as a major exponent of the Direct Carving phenomenon, but also by acknowledging the California component of this movement, beginning with the efforts of Ralph Stackpole at the San Francisco Art Institute. She noted, too, the specific impact of Aztec sculpture on Stackpole's art during his 1926 - 1927 travels through Mexico, and, in turn, Stackpole's importance for the sculptural preferences both in methodology and materials, of the California sculptors, Beniamino Bufano, Gordon Newell, Robert Howard, Jacques Schnier, Peter Krasnow, and Hord. Hord, however, received only passing mention by Tarbell, garnering far less attention than any of his fellow Californians.

In California itself, however, Hord has been long recognized as one of the state's preeminent sculptors, going back as far as the important show of *Contemporary American Sculpture* held in 1929 in San Francisco at the California Palace of the Legion of Honor, where the bronze head of *El Cacique*, a Mayan chieftain, borrowed from the Fine Arts Gallery of San Diego, was on view. This work had previously been seen in Los Angeles in 1927 in the annual exhibition of the Painters and Sculptors of Southern California, where Hord showed frequently through 1935. The acquisition of *El Cacique* by the Gallery was recognized in San Francisco's *Argus* magazine in September, 1928, a short-lived publication which offered its readers frequent notice of Hord and, indeed, the development of Direct Carving in California sculpture. Stackpole wrote "Cut Direct" for the *Argus* in May, 1927, an article reproduced in the *Los Angeles Times* on May 22, and he followed this up in the *Argus* that October with a piece on "The School of Cut-Direct in Mexico." That very month, Hord went to study at the Academy of Art in Mexico City, as noted in November in the *Argus*, which, in February, 1929, commented that Hord was reviving the ancient Mexican art of carving in obsidian.

Hord's involvement with Direct Carving in especially resistant materials became the central theme of many subsequent discussions, involving not only obsidian, but also such stones as jade, onyx, porphyry, basalt, granite, and especially diorite, and rosewood, mahogany, and lignum vitae in wood. On his election to the National Academy, Hord listed his *Guardian of the Waters* fountain for the Civic Center in San Diego, and his *Aztec*, at San Diego State College, both in diorite, as two of his three most important works; the fountain was the basis for a major publication on *San Diego Civic Centre Fountain and Donal Hord, Sculptor*, published by the Federal Art Project of Southern California, probably in 1939. His California colleague, Jacques Schnier, included pieces in obsidian and diorite in his 1948 book, *Sculpture in Modern America.* After his death, Hord was discussed by Helen Ellsberg in the December, 1977 issue of the California-based *American Art Review*. Two years later, his mahogany *Sunrise* was included in the show of *Southern California Artists 1890-1940,* held at the Laguna Beach Museum of Art, and Hord was represented again by this work in the exhibit, *100 Years of California Sculpture,* held at the Oakland Museum in 1980. And in 1955, Ilene Susan Fort, in her ground-breaking exhibition at the Los Angeles County Museum of Art, *The Figure in American Sculpture*, accompanied by a comprehensive catalogue, included Hord, along with Bufano and Schnier, among the California sculptors represented.

Hord was thus acknowledged in California far more than in the East. His greatest recognition has come, naturally enough, from his adopted home city of San Diego, where he is not only well represented both in public monuments and in various public collections, but also was a founding member in 1929 of the group of Contemporary Artists of San Diego which held annual exhibitions through 1936; he and James Tank Porter were the two sculptors in the association. Two years earlier, in a September, 1927, article in *San Diego Magazine*, Lyman Bryson noted Hord as a sculptor who "will help make the reputation of Southern California," and in the Fall of 1941 of *Spanish Village Art Quarterly*, Hord himself published his thoughts and methodology on "Hard Stone." A decade after Hord's death, the California First Bank in La Jolla published a well-illustrated catalogue of Hord's sculpture, with reminiscences by Hord's stonecutter-assistant, Homer Dana. In the following decade, Bruce Kamerling, the curator of the San Diego Historical Society, became the keeper of the flame beginning in the Summer of 1985, with the single most significant article on Hord published to date. This appeared in the Society's *Journal of San Diego History,* which included dozens of illustrations of Hord's sculpture, a "Chronology," and a full listing of the artist's projects. Kamerling followed this up with his inclusion of Hord in his study of "Early Sculpture and Sculptors in San Diego" in the *Journal* in the Summer of 1989, and two years later in his catalogue of selection from the Society's collection in *100 Years of Art in San Diego.*

Bram Dijkstra also discussed Hord's sculpture in the 1988 publication, *San Diego Artists*. Though voicing some reservations concerning some of Hord's pieces, Dijkstra held that "The emotional universality, and the psychological tension embedded in these works make them as good as anything ever done by an American sculptor." The time is past due for this to be acknowledged beyond the regional confines of San Diego and California, for Hord was, indeed, a great American artist, as the present exhibition fully establishes.

Acknowledgements

Jennifer Luksic
Curator of Collections
San Diego Historical Society

Bruce Kamerling, Curator of Collections at the San Diego Historical Society from 1977 to 1996, began the research for this text, and I would like to include his acknowledgements for this work:

In addition to the information provided by Florence Hord and Homer Dana, I would like to acknowledge the assistance of two other individuals who shared their knowledge of Hord and his work and helped me with my research: Dorr Bothwell, Hord's first wife and a remarkable human being and talented artist, provided valuable insights into Hord's early years in San Diego. Betty Quayle, a good friend, conducted extensive research on the Hord and Dana family genealogies. She also undertook the lengthy process of organizing Dana's vast photographic record of Hord and his work including transferring all of the original negatives to acid free folders and creating an inventory of the photographs.

I also thank Betty Quayle for locating some of the pieces. Mike Kelly for designing the Web page, which helped us locate "lost" Hord pieces. Tammie Bennett, staff registrar, for ensuring the safety of the objects. Carina Woolrich for photography, and just that right camera angle. The Board of Trustees of the San Diego Historical Society for their support. Will Chandler for insight. Laura Finster for sharing her deepest feelings about Bruce and his dreams. And finally I want to thank the lenders to this exhibition who put their trust in the San Diego Historical Society to do justice to these beautiful works of art.

In Memoriam

Will Chandler

Bruce Alan Kamerling
16 October 1950 - 17 October 1995

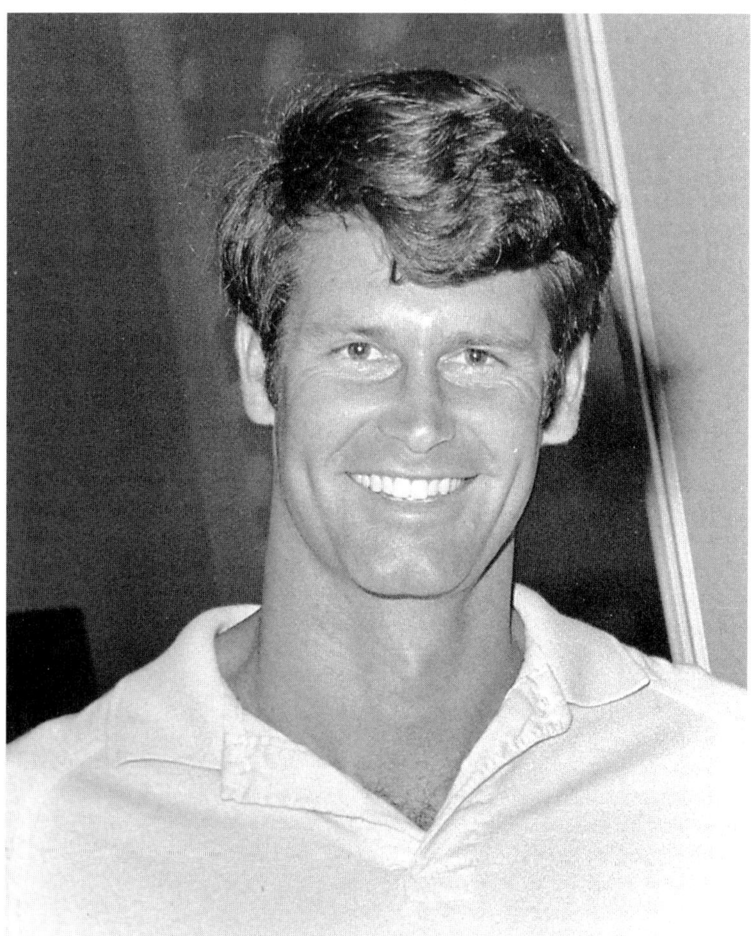

Bruce Kamerling's contributions to art history and to his community are so varied and so plentiful that a brief memoir like this one could easily become a simple listing of his achievements. For me, though, Bruce was a friend and colleague whose encouragement and influence remain the things most missed. The pleasure of his company and his thoughts were such a given in my life for nearly twenty years that I have been slow in learning just how I miss him. When I go inside, there he is, to a degree that softens the pain of his absence and the question of what more we all might have seen had he lived.

What we did get to see is still unfolding. The exhibition which this catalogue commemorates was inspired by and grounded in Bruce's many years of work, begun in the late 1960s when he was still in his teens, on the art and life of Donal Hord, and in his friendship with Hord's assistant Homer Dana, and with Florence Hord, Donal's widow. Bruce created an archive with seemingly endless files of Hord's work, as well as the work of dozens of other San Diego artists, and readily shared his research with other scholars. He was a frequent contributor to the San Diego Historical Society's *Journal of San Diego History*, to Edan Milton Hughe's *Artists in California, 1786-1940*, and to numerous other journals and publications. The artifact collections of the San Diego Historical Society were immeasurably enriched by his efforts and organizational vision. His books on the painter Alfred Mitchell and on the architect Irving Gill will remain essential texts for many years to come.

As a friend, Bruce was delightfully good company. Tall, memorably handsome and unfailingly polite, he had as well a quick and arcane wit, and was capable of summing up absurd moments with naughty puns in Latin that were always funny. But, I most often think of Bruce as both unusually patient and unusually dedicated to his goals. He was very determined not to be constrained by others' limited understanding of him, and he was one of the most industrious people I have ever known. He was so quietly productive that it was easy to assume that the work one witnessed was all that he was busy with at the time.

This was seldom the case. I'd worked closely with him on an exhibition of Irving Gill's designs and on other similar projects before I learned that he was also an accomplished painter and sculptor. Invited to a solo exhibition of his beautiful figural drawings and paintings, I was astounded to realize that he had done these pieces while he was also working full time as Curator of Collections for the Historical Society, sitting through endless meetings as a member of the City of San Diego's Historic Sites Board, researching major articles on San Diego women artists and on San Diego sculptors, and still managing to put in eight hours a week bodybuilding at the gym and to go out dancing on the weekends.

Over the years he also served as President of Save Our Heritage Organization, as volunteer consulting Egyptologist for the San Diego Museum of Man and President of the Lesbian and Gay Historical Society of San Diego. His work and friendship with Mrs. Alfred Mitchell led to his purchase of the Mitchell home from her estate. Designed for the Mitchells by Richard Requa in 1937, it was the perfect residence and studio for Bruce, and he lovingly preserved and restored its historical features. Despite a limited income, through careful study and patient trading-up, he assembled important personal collections of Renaissance and Baroque period prints and drawings, Craftsman and Art Nouveau decorative arts, and a small but choice group of Egyptian Classical and Pre-Columbian artifacts, all of which he took pleasure in donating to several museums before his death.

To a certain extent, I think Bruce's industriousness was impelled by his realization, years before any of his friends knew it, that his time was going to be limited by illness. For all that he was a willing and open friend he was also an intensely private man, and did not want to have to, in his view, waste energy accommodating well-meant expressions of concern from his friends and acquaintances. When his illness finally overtook him and he was unable to do certain everyday things for himself, a circle of his friends were only too glad to help him carry on in whatever ways they could. It was not surprising that when a dozen of these friends came together to organize home care after Bruce's lung surgery in 1993, some of us had never before met.

Neither was it surprising that, to the day he died nearly two years later, Bruce tried to spare us as best he could from the difficulties of his illness. And, in those last two years, despite encroaching respiratory and other illnesses, Bruce willed himself to curate six more exhibitions for the Historical Society, oversee the casting of three more of his bronze sculptures, donate his art and antiquities collections to museums, and to find the ideal buyers for his beautiful house, who would protect its historical interest. The last months of Bruce's life, with all their hardships and pain, remain for me and other friends among the most golden moments of our lives.

Although Bruce's career included much public responsibility, he was almost completely uninterested in status as such. His passion was accomplishment and the kind of authority that comes only from creative hard work and deep-seated knowledge. His generous efforts to resurrect and preserve the achievements of the earliest generations of San Diego artists are a lasting gift that honors and enriches us all.

"A monolith is brought from the quarry...

The stone envelops the idea and must be forced to yield it...Stone teaches one thing to the artist—that agonies and fears and posturing should not be beaten into a boulder that has kinship only with serene eternity. Stone sculpture should not carry a shape foreign to the spirit of timelessness."

Donal Hord

Introduction

Jennifer Luksic

Donal Hord's sculptures have the power to engage almost all of our senses. Hord possessed the ability to take solid materials such as stone and hardwoods and transform them into life-like and textural works. Even the titles of the works suggest movement, sound and temperature. In *Desert Night, the Wind*, a figure plays a flute and dances slowly so that one can almost hear the sound of the wind dancing across the desert sands in an endlessly rhythmic motion.

Each piece Hord created was, in large part, a response to the qualities inherent in the materials he sculpted. Although Hord would make preliminary sketches or clay figures, he rarely used them when creating the work. Instead, the shape of the jade or the grain of the wood provided the template for the piece.

Hord's ability to use the grains of the wood to represent the muscle tissue in the body or the curve of a breast not only demonstrated his great technical skill, but revealed the true genius of his artistry. His later works showed an artist who was as comfortable with the human body as a student of anatomy—an artist who could create a deep sense of emotion in each work of art. The faces portrayed in his sculptures are entrancing: deep set eyes with introspective, peaceful expressions, but not without a touch of sadness.

Two of the most distinctive features of Hord's sculptures, however, are the originality of his imagery and the excellence of his craftsmanship. The imagery came from deep within, and was often inspired by a natural event he had witnessed or perceived. In many ways, Hord could be considered a mystic, able to draw out the spiritual meaning of the natural phenomena around him. He interpreted in three-dimensional form aspects of things which might not be readily apparent to the emotions or intellect of others.

His interest in Central and South American mythology, Chinese art and philosophy, and the indigenous people of Southern California are typical components in his works. A majority of it contains elements of either nature, or impacts of natural events on man. The natural and sensual physicality of his sculptures are balanced by his references to history, literature and mythology. His imagery was not so much based on his training as on his own creative intuition and his ability to express the physical senses through sculpture.

It is surprising that very little has been published on Donal Hord. He received nearly every award a sculptor could achieve and was the first San Diego artist to become a full Academician of the National Academy of Design and a Fellow of the National Sculpture Society. He was a member of the National Institute of Arts and Letters, an Honorary Life Member of the San Diego Museum of Man and a Guggenheim Fellow in 1945 and 1947.

This exhibition catalogue is a synthesis of the late Bruce A. Kamerling's immense amount of research on Donal Hord's life and work. Kamerling's enthusiasm for Hord's work is apparent throughout his notes and files. It has been heartening to discover that all those who have participated in the preparation of this exhibition have shared this enthusiasm. There is much more to Donal Hord than can be included in these pages.

Many of the objects in this exhibition have never been on public display. Many of them were gifts from the artist to our lenders. Some that we had hoped would be in the exhibit are not because, understandably, the owners could not bear to part with them for any length of time. So it is with the work of Donal Hord—his art has become an inseparable part of our everyday lives.

Biography
Donal Hord
1902 – 1966

Born in Prentice, Wisconsin, Donal Hord moved to San Diego when he was just a child and quickly found an affinity with the area. Thus, he considered himself a native San Diegan. The affinity he felt is evident today by his many well-known works which have become synonymous with San Diego culture, such as *Guardian of the Waters* and the *Aztec.*

Childhood

Donal's father, Riley Merton Horr, son of Leonard and Nettie (Barney) Horr, was born in 1877 in Pilot Knob, Adams County, Wisconsin. Donal's mother, L'Aurore (Laura) Beaudin, was born in 1883, in Chippewa Falls, Wisconsin, the daughter of Hubert and Philomena (Duval) Beaudin. Hord's parents married in Prentice, Price County, Wisconsin on December 23, 1899, and Donald, their only child, was born there on February 26, 1902.

His parents' marriage was troubled, which left Donal with painful memories. One he told of was being shut in a cloakroom while his mother played the violin in the ladies' orchestra. She was apparently afraid to leave him with his father. When Donal was six or seven, his mother divorced his father and changed their name to Hord. The story told by friends is that she derived their surname by removing the last "d" from Donald and adding it to his last name resulting in Donal Hord.

Son and mother moved to Seattle in 1914 without any apparent financial assistance from Riley Horr. Money was difficult to come by and Donal earned what he could by moving trash cans for their neighbors and running a paper route. But the long hours, cold wet weather, and an insufficient diet took its toll on him. The twelve-year-old contracted inflammatory rheumatism which settled in his heart and caused permanent damage. The physical effects limited his activities for the rest of his life.

Early Works 1914 - 1925

Donal first began showing an interest in art during his recovery from rheumatic fever. At thirteen, he took lessons in watercolor and produced landscape paintings of the lush Northwest coast. He and his mother moved to Endoline at the southern part of Puget Sound, where he would walk on the beach near the limestone cliffs. It was here that he did his first sculpturing. On the Puget Sound cliffs, he carved an image of a sphinx. A passerby took a picture and gave him the negative which remains in the archives of the San Diego Historical Society.

Later, his father came to Seattle with a doctor who recommended a warmer climate to improve Donal's health. His father, who had remarried, gave Donal a Boston bull terrier puppy and began sending money on a regular basis.

Inspired by his childhood interest in Central and South American legends, Donal named the bull terrier Manco — after the Inca ruler. He dreamed of tropical jungles and read everything he could on the region. When faced with moving her child to a temperate climate, Donal's mother showed him a map and asked where he would like to live. His choice was San Diego. Its proximity to Mexico was the main attraction.

In 1916, Donal was just fourteen when he and his mother arrived on the steamship *Congress*. His first view of the dry hills of Point Loma made him cry; it was not the steaming jungles he had imagined. However, he soon grew to love San Diego. His frequent trips to the nearby desert and love of ancient legend became the inspiration for his work.

San Diego was an exciting place in 1916. The Panama-California Exposition was underway celebrating the city as the first United States port of call for ships traveling through the recently completed Panama Canal. It is likely that Donal visited the Exposition in Balboa Park where he would have experienced the Spanish Colonial architecture, a full-sized Native American pueblo, art exhibits and displays.

After the Exposition, the San Diego Museum, now named the San Diego Museum of Man, was formed to continue exhibiting the assembled art and ethnographic collections. Donal frequently visited the museum and eventually developed friendships with many of the staff. In later years, he would spend many weekends camping in the desert with Malcolm Rogers, Curator and later Director of the Museum of Man. Desert camping would become one of Hord's favorite pastimes.

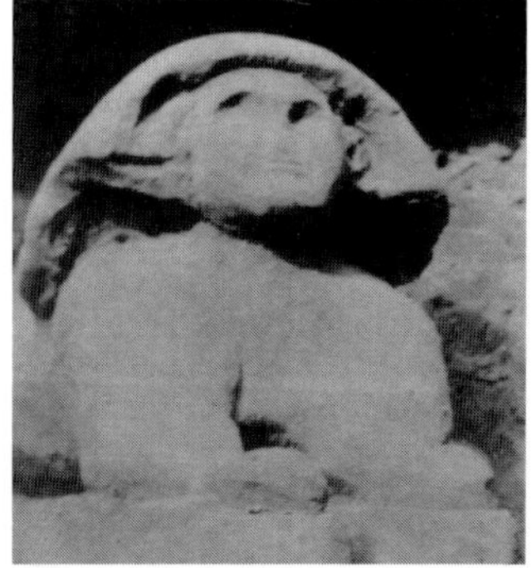

Donal's Puget Sound sphinx, a representation of the ancient art he loved, foretold his own contribution to the art world.

[Bottom left] Donal with Anna Valentien, and classmates Dorr Bothwell, Janet Heldring, Elizabeth Hoops, and unknown in front of the "B" Street School in 1917. [Top] Years later, Donal at 19. [Middle right] In his youth, the desert was his sanctuary and its rejuvenating qualities carried over into his adult life. [Middle left] Hord, Florence Hord, Homer Dana, and George Baker enjoy a desert get-away. [Bottom right] Hord back home at his Pacific Beach studio.

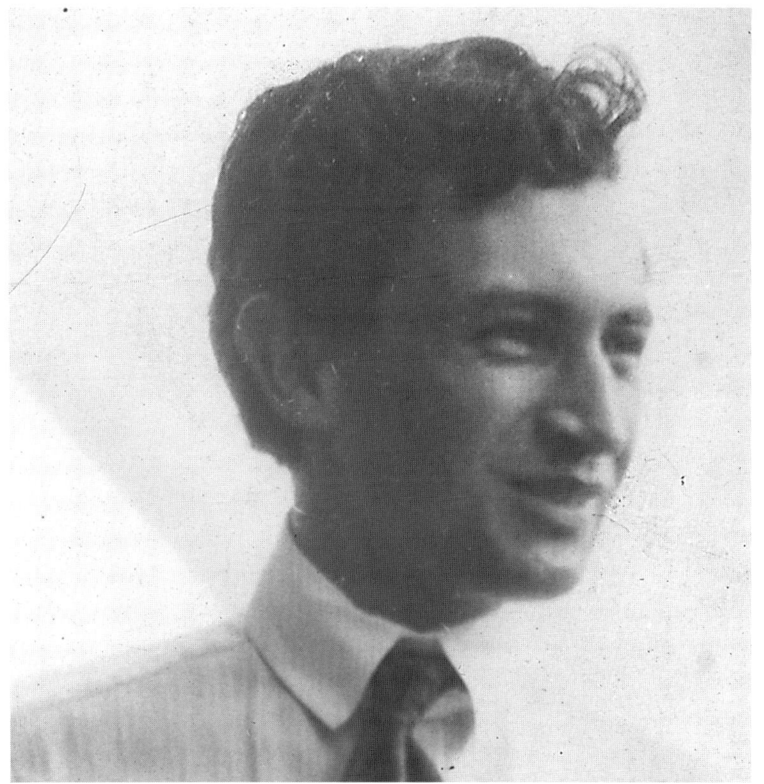

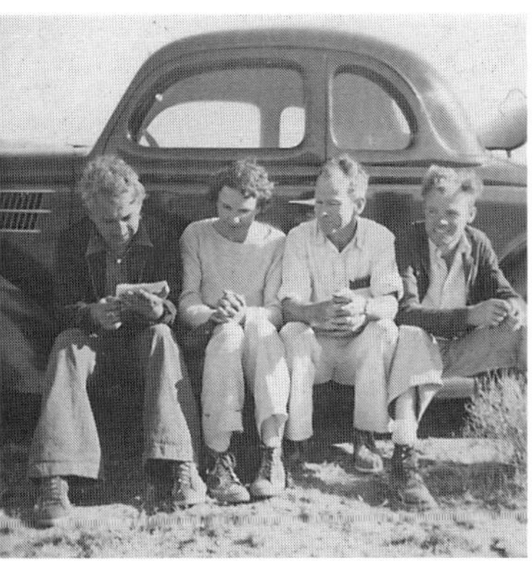

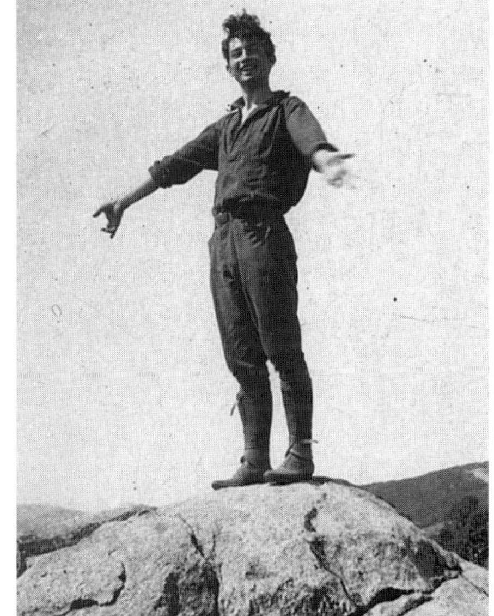

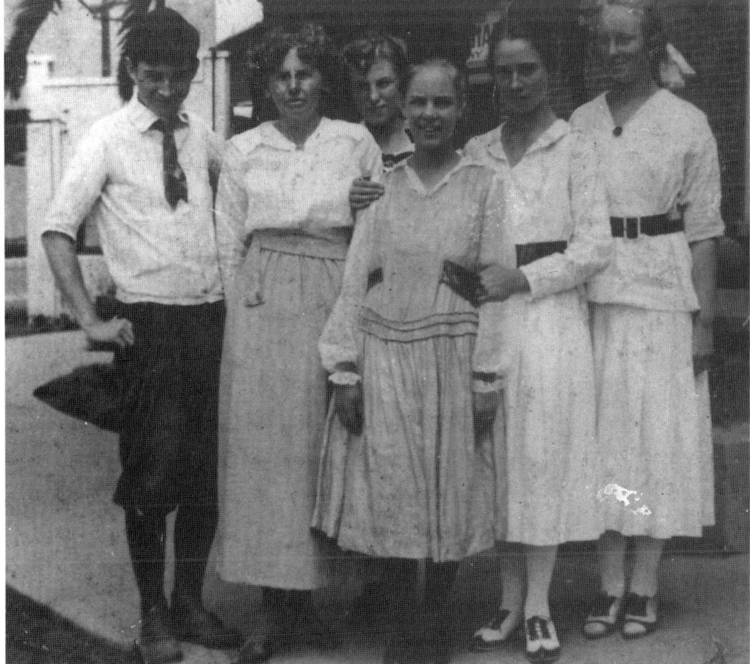

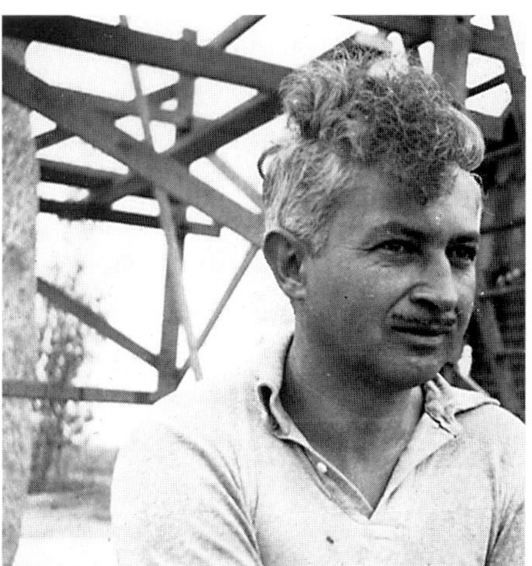

Owing to his heart condition, Donal could not attend school with other children. Instead, he spent his days reading at the San Diego Public Library. He was such a voracious reader that it is told on one occasion he returned a stack of library books he had checked out only the day before. This prompted the librarian to comment that he had only pretended to read them all. Sensitive Donal was deeply hurt and never forgot the incident. It did not deter him however, and he continued to frequent the library. In later years, he became a Friend to the San Diego Central Library and donated to it his life's collection of books and several of his sculptures.

In the fall of 1917, Donal learned that the Evening High School offered crafts classes taught by Anna Marie Bookprinter Valentien. She operated a pottery company in San Diego where she had produced life-size sculptures for exhibition at the 1885 Atlanta and 1893 Chicago Expositions. Adding to her credentials, she had earlier studied sculpture with celebrated European artists Auguste Rodin and Emile Bourdelle.

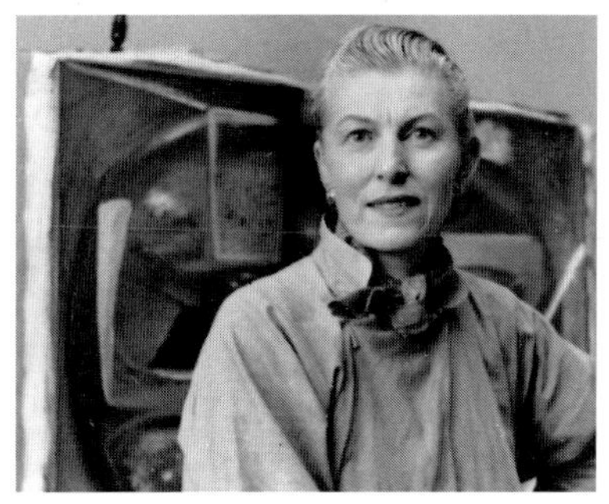

Dorr Bothwell became an accomplished artist in her own right. She is seen here in Paris, 1950.

Hord enrolled as one of Valentien's students along with another budding artist Dorr Bothwell. The two students developed a close friendship and later married, although the marriage was short-lived.

Hord's interests centered on sculpting small figures. As was typical of art instruction at that time, he made copies of plaster casts from Michelangelo sculptures and then worked on these until he could replicate them from memory.

His abiding interest in Pacific Rim cultures, prompted him to begin collecting Asian art. Thomas W. Furlong, a San Diego shopowner who offered Asian imports, became a regular source for Hord's avocation. Hord visited the shop so often that Furlong allowed Hord to pay for his purchases on a lay-away plan of fifty cents a week.

The 1920s were important years for Hord and shaped the direction his life would take. During this time, he began to study art seriously and met his lifelong friend and assistant Homer Dana. From their initial meeting in 1920, Hord and Dana formed a deep bond that was the basis for their forthcoming forty years of collaborative work.

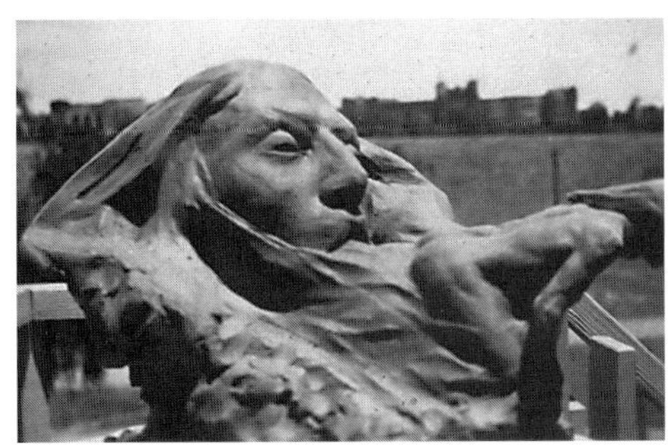

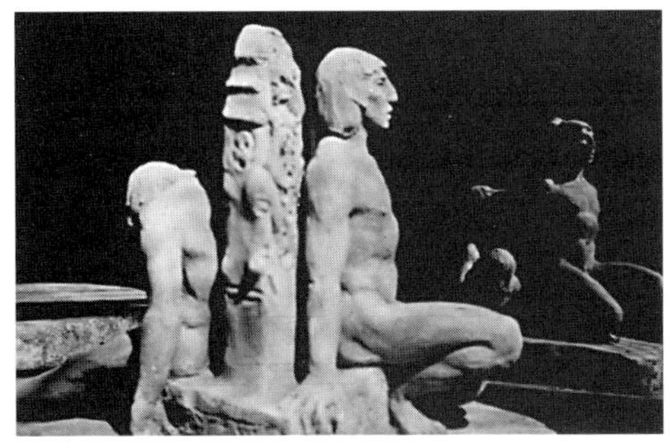

[Top] *Bearded Head* and [Bottom] *Captives* were two of the terracotta pieces fired at Rose Canyon Brickyard in the 1920s.

Born Homer Alan Kautz in Ellensburg, Washington on April 9, 1900, Dana was the third child born to Evalin Dana Everman. When his father died in 1909, his mother sent him to San Diego to attend Madame Tingley's Theosophical School. Ten years later, he joined the Navy, opted for San Diego as his base and adopted his mother's maiden name as his own surname.

Dana and Hord were introduced through Jane Wanless, also a student of Anna Valentien's. Later, Hord saw Dana on a streetcar and from that chance meeting they developed an enduring friendship. They went camping together as Hord's health would allow, exploring first Mission Gorge east of San Diego and later, when Hord purchased a car, the desert beyond.

Hord also explored other art forms. In the 1920s he took a class in short story writing from Emma Lindsay Squire. They would meet at students' homes to read their stories and offer criticism. It was much later though, in 1955, that Hord's writing resulted in a completed full-length novel. Entitled *Dark Horoscope*, the story told of Doña Marina, a guide and interpreter for Cortez during the conquest of Mexico. The manuscript was never published, but remains a part of the San Diego Historical Society archives.

Before meeting Dana, Hord's work consisted of small terracotta pieces fired at the Rose Canyon Brickyard. As the two men's friendship developed, Dana began to pose for Hord's work, including the large reclining figure named *Takquitch*. Dana also began to help him with the creation of sculptures. With Dana's assistance and strength, Hord was able to produce larger pieces.

Santa Barbara School of Arts 1926 - 1929

In 1926, Dana encouraged Hord to study bronze casting with Archibald Dawson at the Santa Barbara School of the Arts. *Art Digest* described Archibald Dawson in 1927 as:

> *a young Scottish artist who has done most delicate and beautiful work in bronze .... He is a member of the Glasgow School of Art, and at present is giving a course of instruction at the School of the Arts in Santa Barbara*

as a visiting teacher. Mr. Dawson gives the following reasons for his point of view with regard to the value of personal work in the actual casting of bronze: "Without an intimate knowledge of the process of casting, a sculptor often works for weeks trying to give qualities in the clay which could be produced simply and with far less labor in the wax stage, or in the bronze stage itself.... The secret of a suitable [craftsmanship] is an intimate knowledge of the medium itself."

Hord learned a great deal from Archibald Dawson. Not only about bronze casting, but also about understanding and manipulating materials. Hord was an outstanding student. In fact, several of his works illustrated the school's advertisements.

Mexico 1929

While in Santa Barbara, Hord pieces received so much notice that New York art patron Mrs. Gould inquired how she might aid the young sculptor. When Hord indicated he wanted to go to Mexico, she obliged. His finances in Mexico were tight; his experiences, however, were rich. In addition to his travels to the Isthmus of Tehuantepec, Veracruz and Mexico City, he completed *Ome-Tochtli*, *Canec*, *Tezcatlipoca* and *Tlaloc*. *Tlaloc* was his first attempt to carve obsidian volcanic glass.

But not all was blissful in Mexico. His work drew sharp criticism from the great muralist Diego Rivera, who referred to some of Hord's sculptures as "pretty toys." The remark stung, but instilled in Hord the determination to produce the finest quality work he could in each endeavor. This commitment to excellence in workmanship and strength of conception eventually engendered the hallmarks of his style.

Philadelphia and New York 1929 - 1930

After returning from Mexico in 1929, he spent a semester at the Philadelphia Academy of Fine Arts with continuing financial scholarships from Mrs. Gould. In Philadelphia, he studied with Walter Hancock and Albert Laesle. It was said that Hancock thought Hord's work so good that he did not think he could teach him anything. Under their tutorship, Hord began carving mahogany reliefs, including *Chumash Fisherman*, *Channel Wind* and *The Spirit of the Whirlwinds*.

Soon after, Dana joined Hord at the Academy. Not as a fellow student, but as a paid model for other student artists. In 1930, the two men moved to New York. When Dana could not find work and grew annoyed with Hord spending all of his time with new girlfriend Erna Obermeyer, Dana returned to San Diego.

Home in San Diego 1930 - 1945

It was not long though before Hord was also San Diego bound. On the way, he stopped to visit his father in South Dakota. To Hord's surprise, he found his father was proud of him and offered financial support for a new studio.

Back in San Diego, he contracted with Willy Andrews to build a 12 by 20-foot studio at his mother's Pascoe Street home. The new studio offered Hord the challenge of working with different materials and developing a greater understanding of their inherent properties to direct his artistic vision.

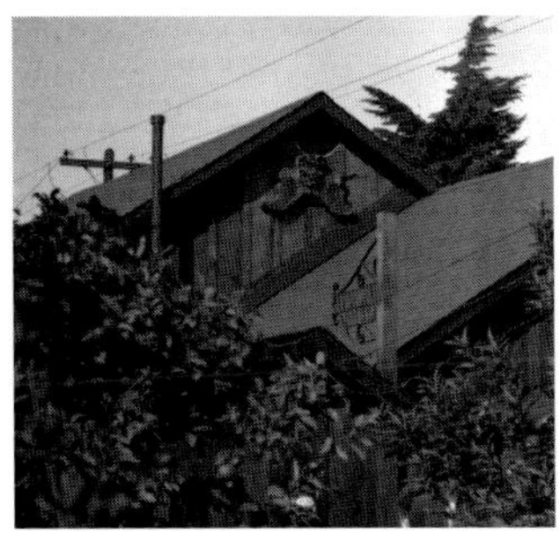

Hord's Pascoe Street studio.

His work in wood was described in 1930 by Hazel Boyer Braun:

Some weeks ago there stood in a studio in San Diego, a slab of mahogany wood, a slab of the life of a grand old tree.... The artist took up his chisel and mallet ... He sought a simple truth that the wood would laugh with him about, because they shared a secret. As the forms evolved along the grain of the wood, inspiration burst into a flame of enthusiasm ....

And in 1932, Reginald Poland, Director of the Fine Arts Gallery of San Diego, wrote:

> *In many ways Donal Hord impresses one with an enthusiastic youthfulness. Scarcely 30 years of age, he already exhibits no indecision, nothing negative, but rather, a bigness of conception and of handling in his carved sculptures indicative of valuable experience and rare wisdom. ... Five years ago he went to the School of the Arts in Santa Barbara. So promising was he, and such good use did he make of his opportunities there, that the school created its first maintenance scholarship in Hord's behalf. The sculptor brings distinction to San Diego in several scholarships which he held as he worked at the Santa Barbara school. And following that, for two years in travel, investigation [...] modeling and carving. For nine months he was in Mexico, and still later in Philadelphia and in New York City... It is not hard to believe Hord when he says that, having a reason for doing a thing is more important than anything else. He is a big enough person to correct his own errors; incidentally he has that saving sense of humor.... [Hord] tries to put into practice two ideas which he has: to make the material used express itself in its own terms, and to keep untouched as much of the material as is possible.*

Hord applied to the Federal Art Project in 1934. Soon after, the good news arrived that he was accepted and placed on the payroll at $75 a month. Dana recalled: "The program only required that you have a job somebody wanted done and the federal government would put the money up for materials."

Hord's first stone carving was for the patio fountain, *La Tehuana*, in Balboa Park's House of Hospitality in 1935. While primarily funded by the State Emergency Relief Act, a program later enveloped by the Works Progress Administration, the piece was also funded by Everett Gee Jackson, a prominent San Diego artist.

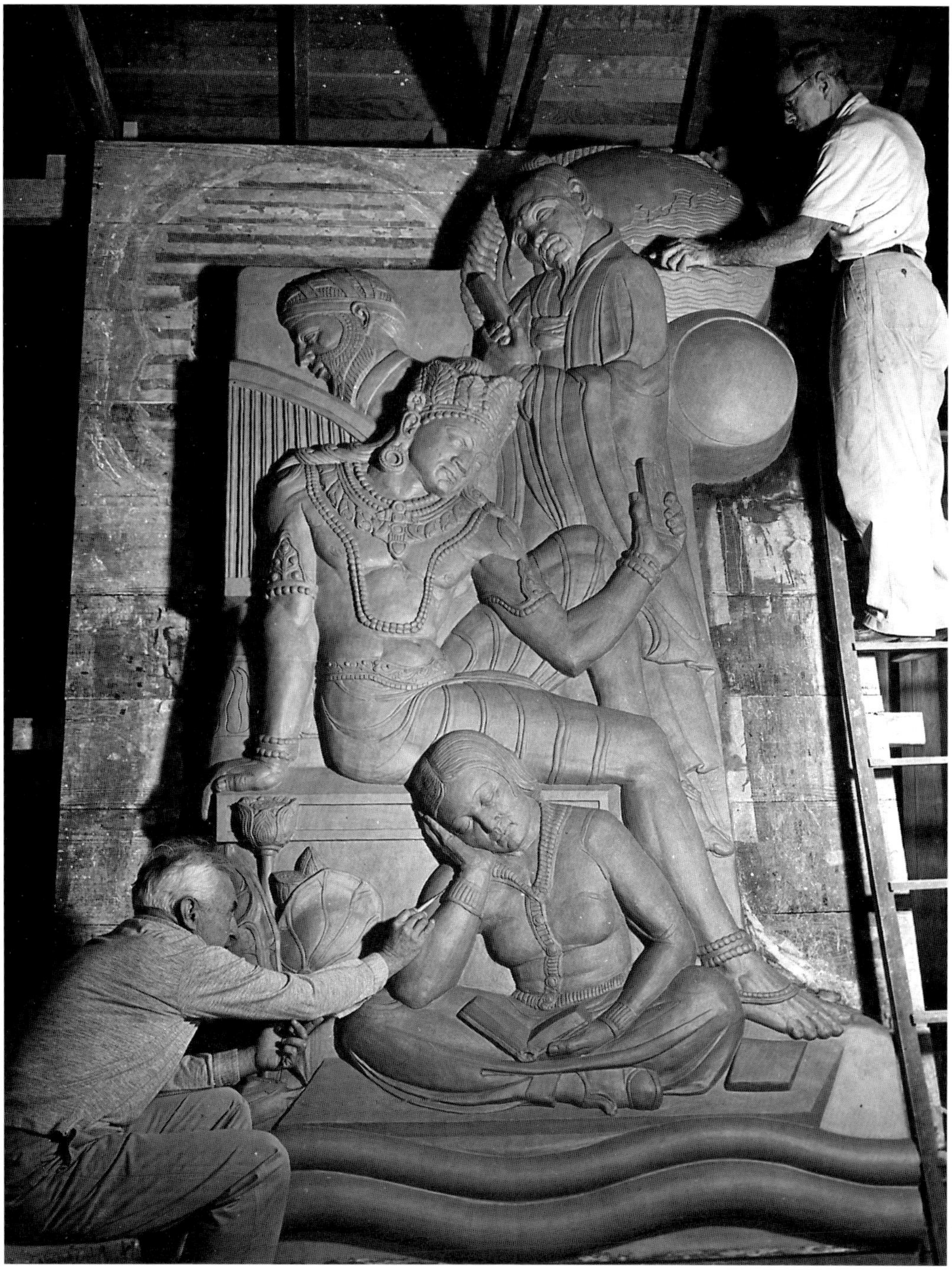

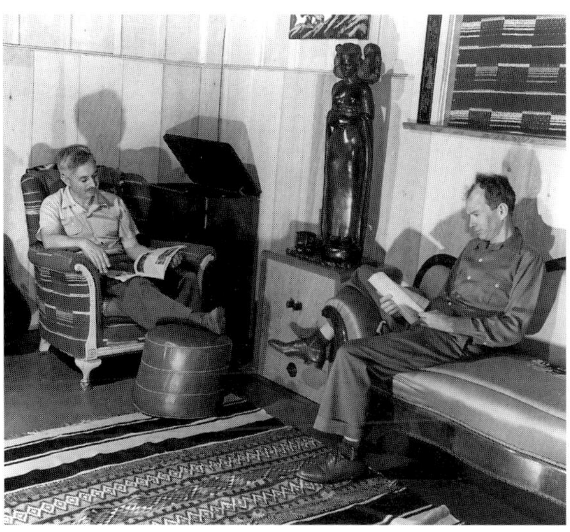

In 1953, Hord was commissioned by the San Diego Central Library to sculpt two bas reliefs entitled *Literature East and West.* [Left] He and Dana enjoyed quiet reading at home in Pacific Beach. *Corn Goddess* is seen on the table between them.

Despite the obstacle that the stone used for the carving was construction grade rather than sculptor's grade, *La Tehuana*, along with the exhibition of *Tropic Cycle*, *Young Maize*, *Mayan Mask*, and *Man with a Sheaf of Wheat*, earned him the "Gold Medal for Sculptural Excellence" at the California Pacific International Exposition.

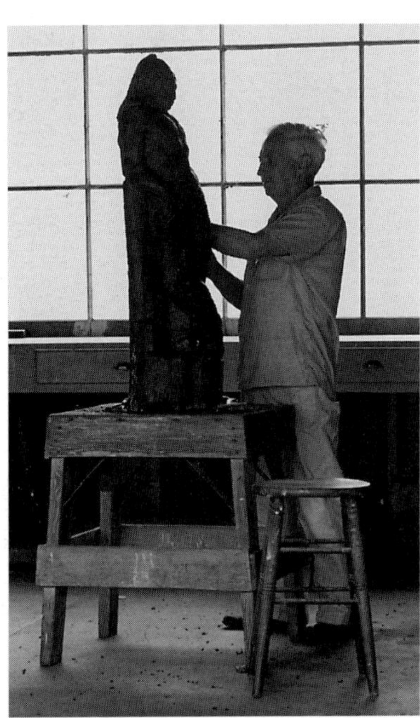

Hord enjoyed the spaciousness of his new Pacific Beach studio. He is seen here working on *El Cargador*.
Photograph by Lawrence Schiller

Hord found after winning several large sculptural commissions, he had outgrown his Pascoe Street studio and moved to what would become his permanent studio in Pacific Beach. The lot gave him room to work on larger pieces such as *Guardian of the Waters, El Colorado* and *Spring Stirring*.

During Hord's time on the federal payroll, he created numerous works for the Federal Art Project which can be seen from San Diego to Los Angeles. The Los Angeles Courthouse, San Diego County Administration Center, San Diego State University, San Diego Public Library, and Coronado High School Library all include his works. The pieces he produced for federal projects do not evoke the kind of living presence that Hord had created in the past or was to create in the future. However, many of those completed during his "time off" display the kind of introspective style with which he was becoming identified.

In 1936, Hord and Dana began the *Aztec*. Funded through the State Emergency Relief Act, Hord underestimated the cost. In order to compensate for this, Everett Gee Jackson, then professor at San Diego State University, suggested that each student contribute a dime to the project. With the students' assistance, Hord was able to finish the figure. It was his first experiment with norite — a black fine-grained granite. The *Evening Tribune* described norite as "harder than steel but brittle like ice."

The block was quarried a few miles west of Escondido. Hord first created a plaster model that he draped with a cloth so that the anatomy of the figure could be seen through the cloth. Unaware of the density of the stone, he and Dana began their work with a brush hammer. After seven months of work, they switched to pneumatic tools. Dana recalls that when they were working on *Aztec* a quarryman said, "Well, I think you're doing very well with the tools you've got. But if you want to get this done in your lifetime, you'll have to get an air hammer and air tools." Dana recounts, "We picked up a service station air compressor, and used it for years and years."

[Next three pages] Hord and Dana sitting in the foreground, gather with government officials around the completed *Aztec*. In the back from left to right are Thyrsis Field, Holger Cahill, Stanton MacDonald, unknown, Joe Danysh, unknown, Arther Ames, and Jean Goodwin.

In 1937, a proud Hord with Dana (left) and George Baker (right) stand in front of the artist's largest sculpture in the United States. The towering *Guardian of the Waters* is seen with its original plaster maquette.

Back at his Pacific Beach studio in 1944, Hord makes the finishing carves on *Desert Night, the Wind*.

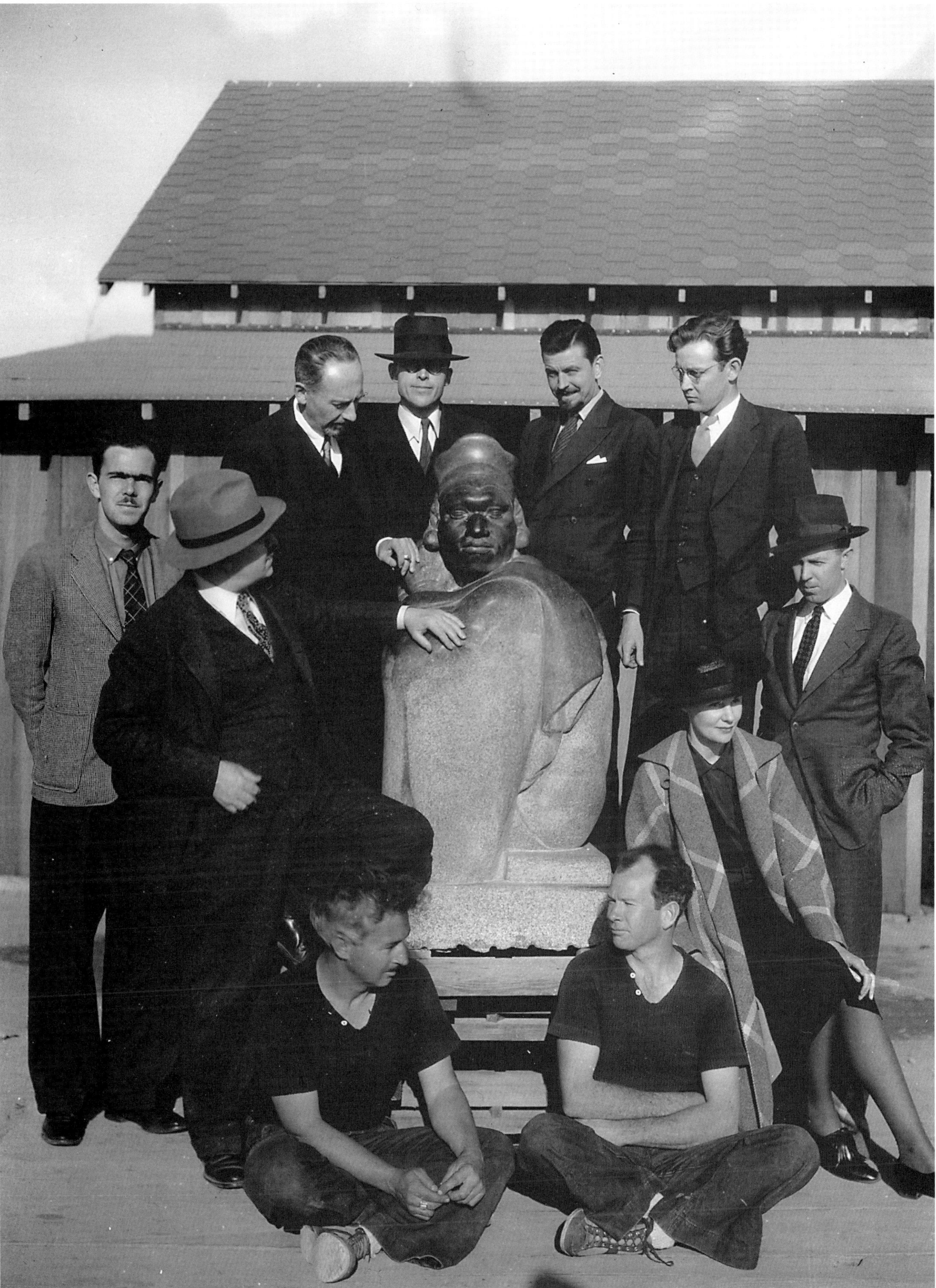

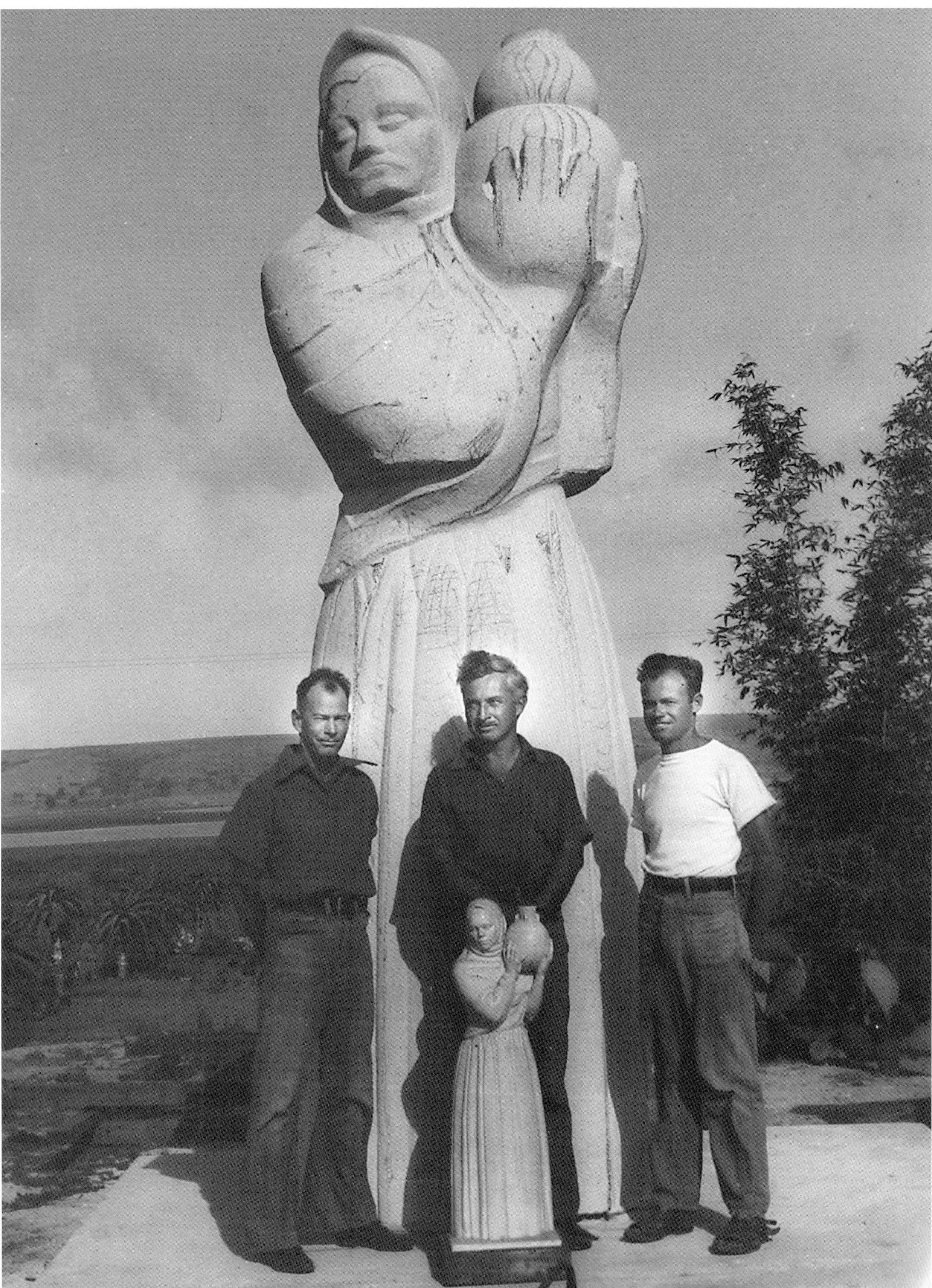

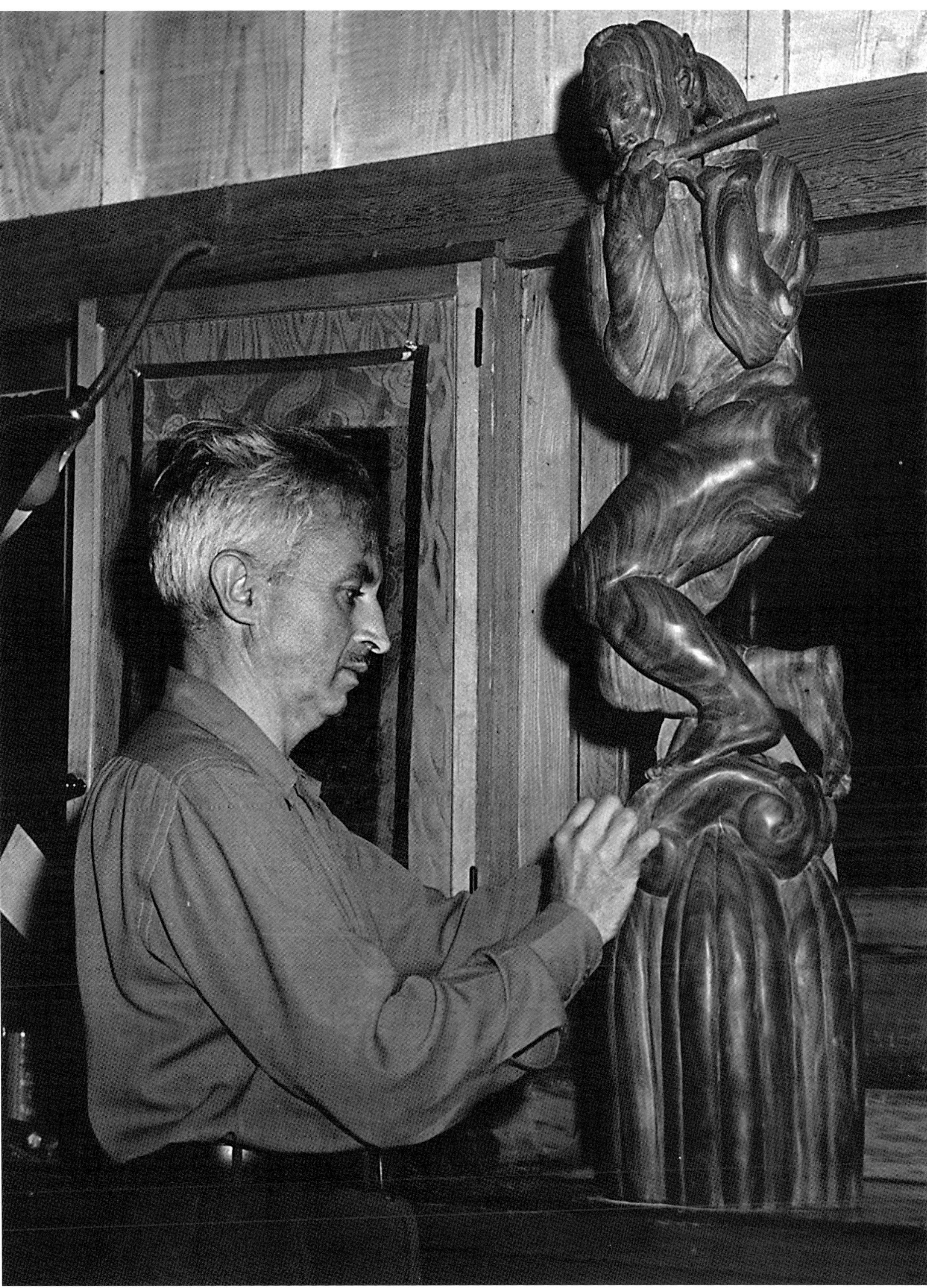

Guardian of the Waters was begun in 1937. Miss H. A. Kutzschbach, an artist's model living in San Diego, was hired to pose for the three-foot nude study that later was draped. Miss Kutzschbach recalled that she was requested by the *Daughters of the Golden West* to confirm she was not "an Indian." "Hord had made an exact replica of my face and hands. I am not an Indian, but of German descent from New York and to make it more ridiculous I said I had never even seen an Indian."

The 32-ton granite stone for *Guardian of the Waters* was quarried near Lakeside. Hord, Dana and George Baker reduced it by taking off 100 pound slabs at a time. Hord supervised its carving and designed the fountain, with the exception of the top tile border designed by George Baker. During the polishing stage, as many as ten people worked on the sculpture simultaneously. Dana remembered: "Clyde Kelly, George Baker, Ernie Hamilton and a few blacksmiths used nine-point air hammers and a bush hammer and a ripper. Only old-fashioned tempered steel tools were used."

Dana also recounted an incident with the ripper: "George Baker was working on the hand of the figure around the pot. Rippers are used back and forth, they have about six rows of teeth on them, but George was going too deep and the finger popped off, and it's a big finger, she's twelve-feet tall. Donal just shook his head, because on Monday we had a delegation coming from Washington D.C. to look at her, we worked all weekend. We had to remove some of the jar to create a new finger and eight hundred pounds off her hip so that it would sit right. Then we had to remove the same amount off of the other hip, it became more static, it had more swing before that." Its adorning swordfish and dolphin relief was carved in plaster, then cast in stone.

In 1939, *Guardian of the Waters* was moved into its place overlooking the San Diego harbor. Leroy Robbins photographed and filmed the procedure. The motion picture is now a part of the San Diego Historical Society archive collection.

During the completion of *Guardian of the Waters*, Hord worked on smaller pieces. He began with a variety of new materials and for the second time with obsidian, which yielded *La Cubana.* This piece debuted at the 1939 New York World's Fair and later was featured on the cover of the December, 1948 *Lapidary Journal.*

The editor remarked on Hord's first work in obsidian entitled *Tlaloc*, "Unusual and rare...the first piece of sculpture in volcanic glass in 4,000 years."

Hord also worked in marble and in 1938 began *Mexican Mother and Child.* President Franklin Delano Roosevelt acquired the piece and insisted that it be placed on his desk at Hyde Park.

Hord married his second wife, Florence Silberhorn Norse, in 1939. She was also a collector of Asian art and a friend to his first wife, Dorr Bothwell. Their twenty-six year marriage lasted until Hord's death in 1966, whereafter, she remained with Dana for many years.

Mexican rosewood, Hord's favorite material, was difficult to find during World War II. As was often the case though with his creativity, the obstacle opened a new opportunity for him. Hord began using lignum vitae, a strong wood with cross-grains used for shipbuilding. It is a relative of the iron tree and one of the hardest woods. It has a green appearance when first carved, unlike Mexican rosewood which appears red when first worked. After aging though, lignum vitae reddens and is difficult to distinguish from Mexican rosewood.

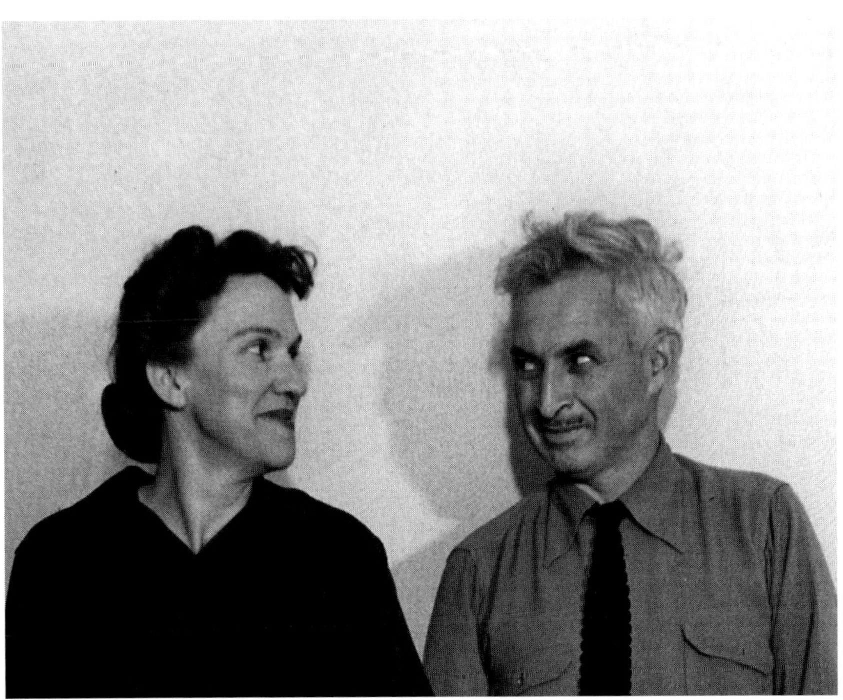

Florence and Donal Hord exchanging a glance

The *Sun* trilogy, begun in 1942, was a collection of forty-two inch to forty-seven inch figures made of lignum vitae. Each piece had at least two titles. *Vernal Sun* or *Morning Sun* is a male nude figure representing the sun walking through a rainbow and rain clouds. *Midday Sun* or *Noon Sun* is a male figure sitting on top of a ram's horns. And *Descending Sun* or *Evening Sun* is a male figure descending into the ocean with arms outstretched to the setting sun.

While Hord was working on the last sculpture in the trilogy, he had a heart attack. Doctors told him he would never sculpt again. However, Hord recovered sufficiently to finish *Descending Sun* and many other pieces. In fact, it was the beginning of a period for national recognition.

In 1942, he was elected an Associate of the National Sculpture Society, after his exhibition of *Aztec, La Cubana, Mexican Mother and Child*, *Mexican Beggar Woman*, and *Veiled Figure,* at the Museum of Modern Art in New York. Hord's stature in the art world grew with this recognition as well as from honors by the National Academy of Design.

In 1945 and 1947, he received Guggenheim Fellowships. In 1948, he received for *El Colorado* an Award of Merit Medal from the Academy of Arts and Letters. In 1950, he was named a life member of the National Institute of Arts and Letters along with Andrew Wyeth, Oscar Hammerstein, and eight other distinguished artists.

Later Works 1945 - 1966

As Hord reached maturity in his style, his subjects became less literal, more abstract and symbolic. Titles such as *Descending Sun*, *Desert Night, the Wind*, and *Summer Rain* were indicative of his attempts to interpret nature's forms, moods and forces through idealized figures, often with strong ethnic features.

In 1948, in his spirit of working with challenging materials, Hord completed the jade *Thunder.* At that time, the largest known full-round jade sculpture, it measured twenty-inches and weighed 120 pounds.

Thunder was sculpted from a 460-pound boulder that required fifteen months to finish. Professional interest in this accomplishment was high and *Thunder* graced the cover of the *Lapidary Journal* and other publications.

Amateur Gem Cutter reported, "The piece is undoubtedly one of the masterpieces of America and certainly the most ambitious project ever attempted in jade by an American." He would later surpass himself in 1950 with the jade sculpture *Yang Kwei Fei*, measuring twenty one-inches and weighing 124-pounds.

Spring Stirring, now at the University of California at San Diego Scripps Institution of Oceanography, was created in 1947 - 1948 under Hord's second Guggenheim Fellowship. This diorite figure measuring forty six-inches high and weighing 2,200-pounds, was Hord's fourth monumental work in black diorite. It was shown in the Third International Exhibition of Sculpture at the Philadelphia Museum of Art in 1949. It was donated to the University of California at San Diego in 1964 by Ida and Cecil Green.

The final major sculpture Hord was to complete, also in black diorite, was entitled *Morning*. The six-foot three-inch, 3,000-pound sculpture depicted a young man awakening at dawn, seated on a base that represents the jaws of the earth where sprouting corn, the sun and the moon are symbolized. Dana polished the piece in three different finishes to create a triple color effect. *Morning* was acquired by the Port of San Diego and is located in Marina Park.

In 1956, Hord was commissioned to sculpt *Angel of Peace* in honor of soldiers killed at the Battle of the Bulge. The site was to be in the American cemetery, Henri-Chappelle, Belgium. Dana recalls in oral history transcripts, "General North didn't believe it would stand up, he said it was the windiest spot in Europe."

Hord and Dana went to Florence, Italy to complete the full-sized plaster before shipping it to Milan for bronze casting. Soon after, they returned home and Hord never saw the final twelve-foot bronze *Angel of Peace* installed.

In 1964, he completed the *Swedish Swimming Federation Trophy*. Then, just one year later while working on *Daybreak*, he suffered his second heart attack.

[Next two pages] Hord completed work on *Morning* in 1955. It was his last diorite sculpture.

A year later in Italy, he was making final touches on the plaster mold for *Angel of Peace*.

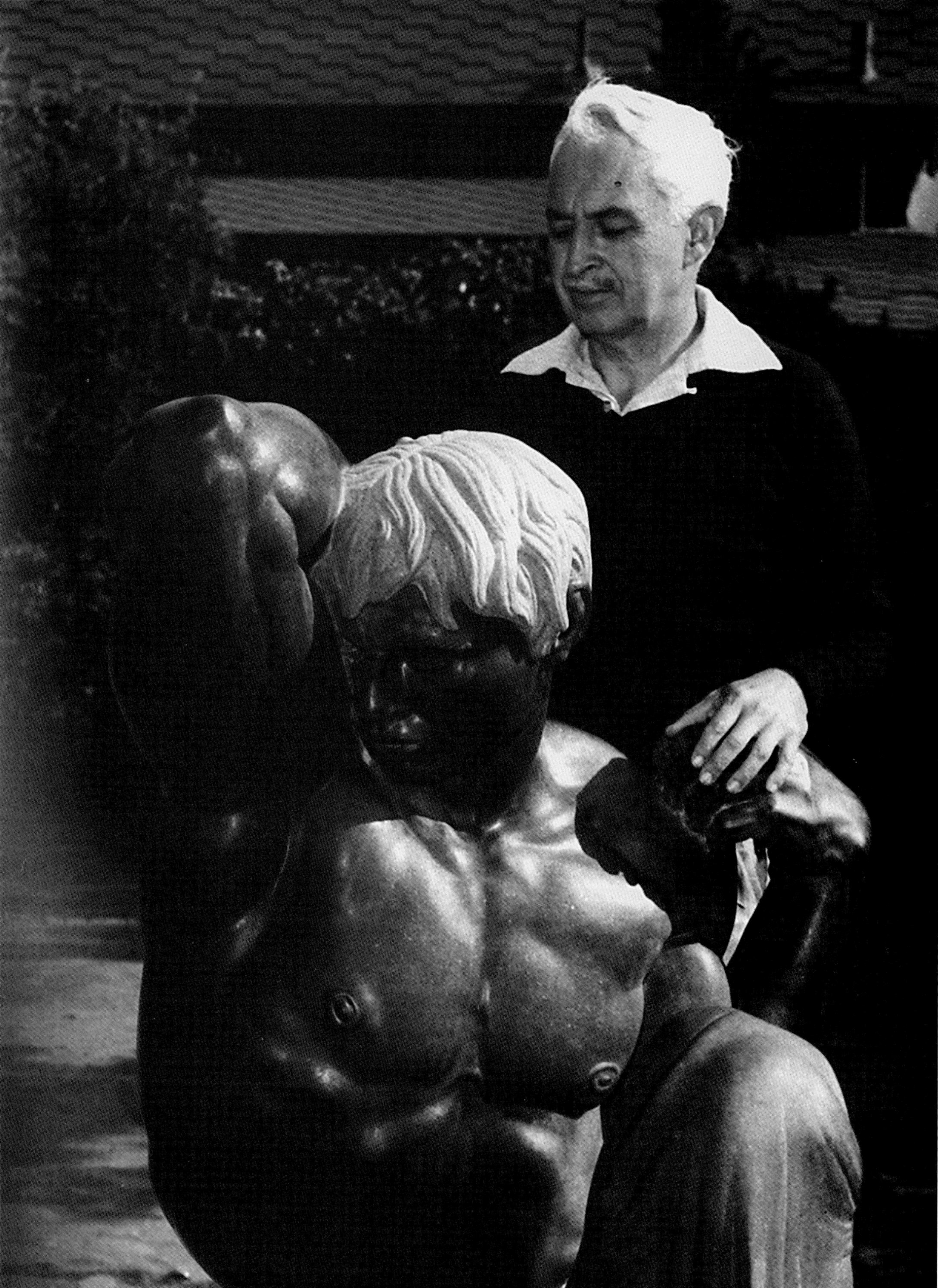

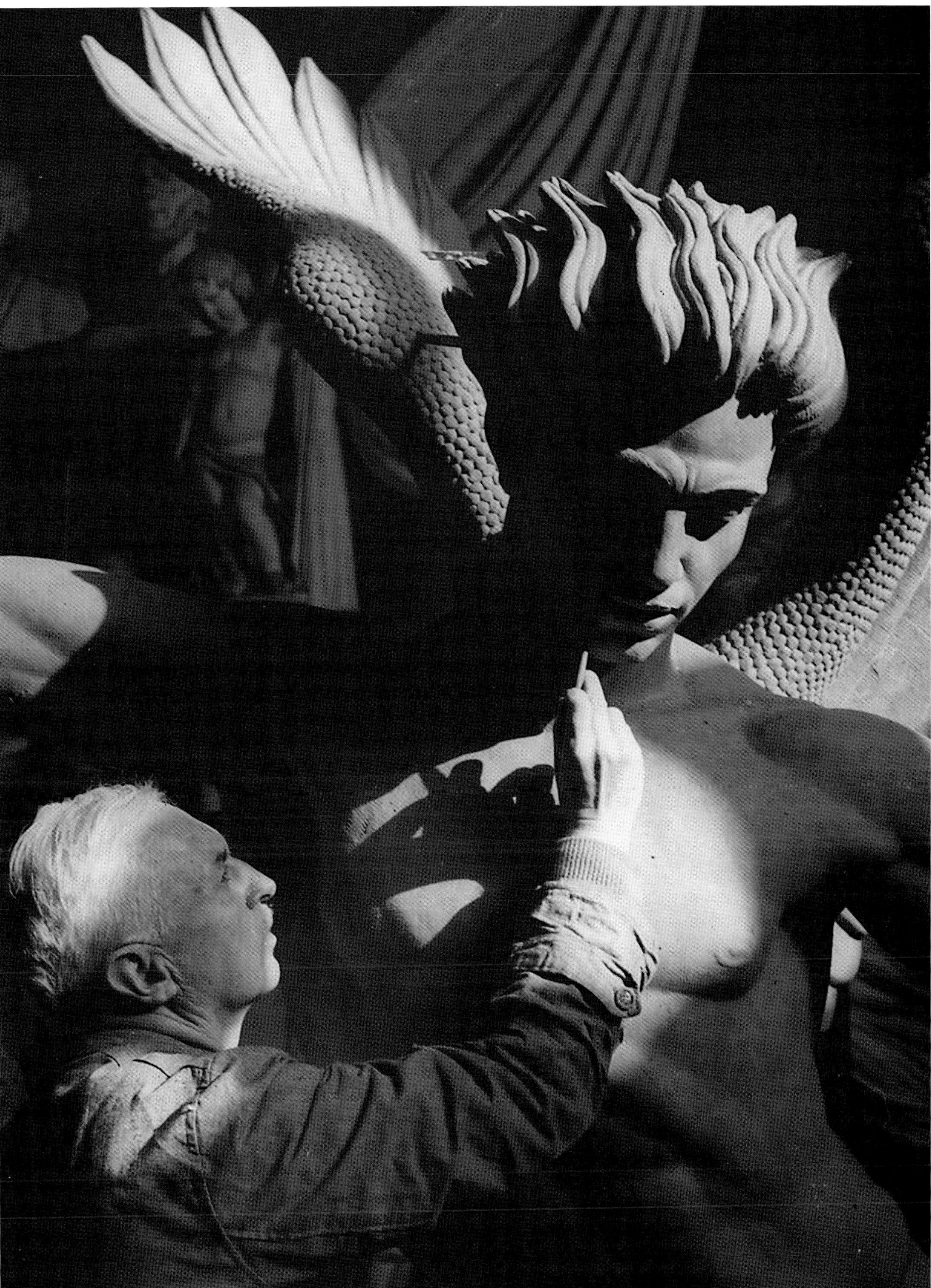

Summer Rain

The following June, after finishing a plaster cast for a larger version of *Summer Rain*, Hord again felt chest pains which proved to be his third and this time fatal heart attack. Surviving eighteen days at Mercy Hospital before his death on June 29, 1966, he gave Dana final instructions for *Summer Rain:*

Well I think we might just as well have that piece cast in bronze...I think it's good enough to cast now.

After his passing, Dana supervised casting of the six-foot sculpture.

Like so many others, Donal Hord originally came to San Diego for health reasons. Here he was nurtured, inspired, and helped to fulfill his dreams. He, in turn, left San Diego and the world a legacy of beauty that will be an inspiration and source of wonder for centuries.

[Next page] The desert's peace continued to soothe the Hord throughout his life.

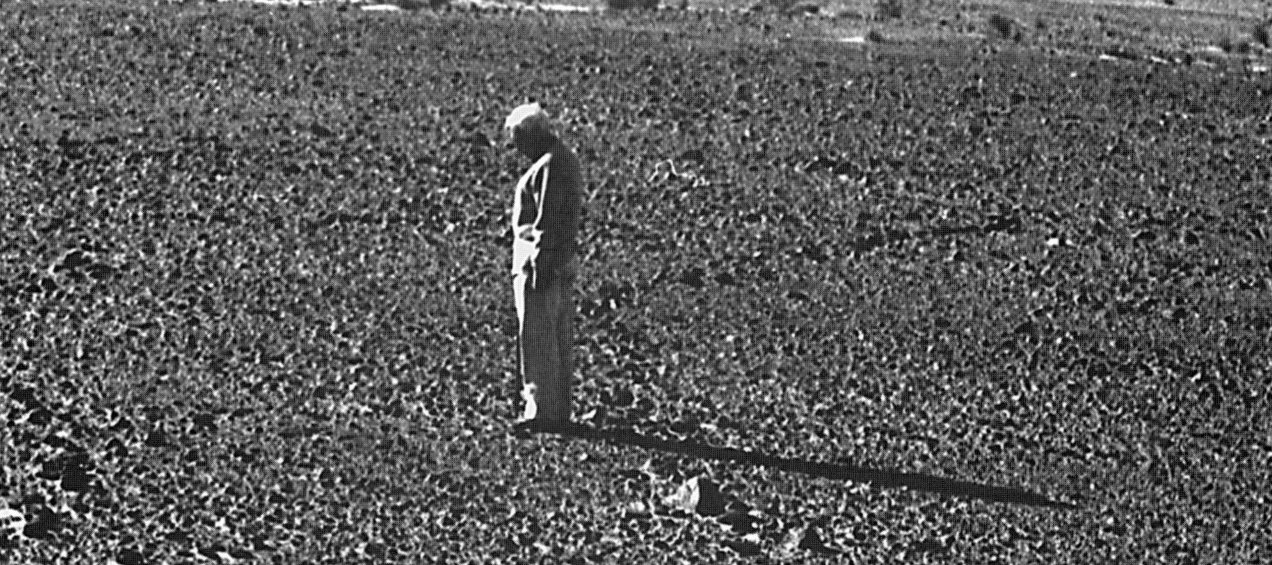

Donal Hord

San Diego Historical Society

Exhibition Plates

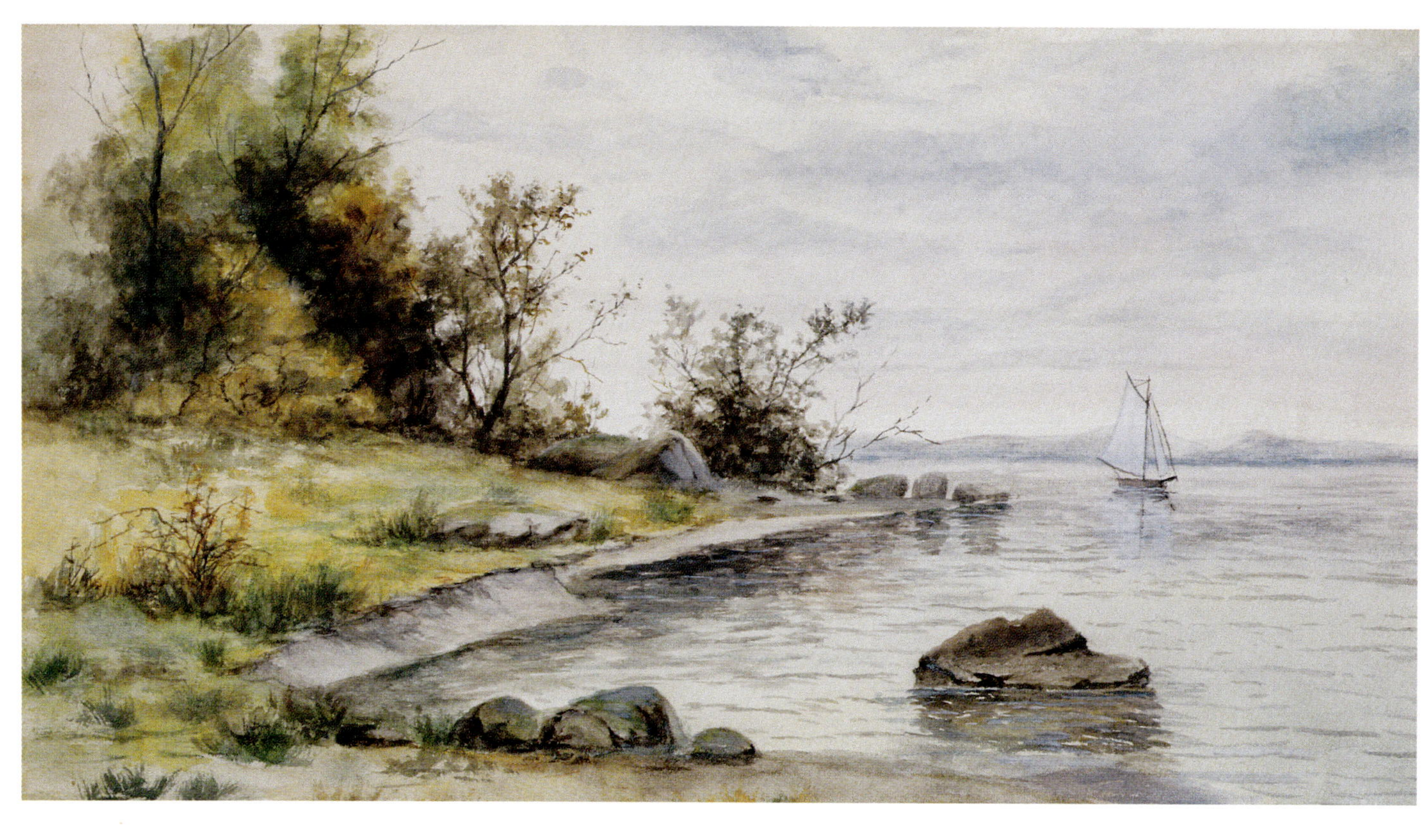

Landscape
1915
Watercolor
4 x 8 inches
San Diego Historical Society

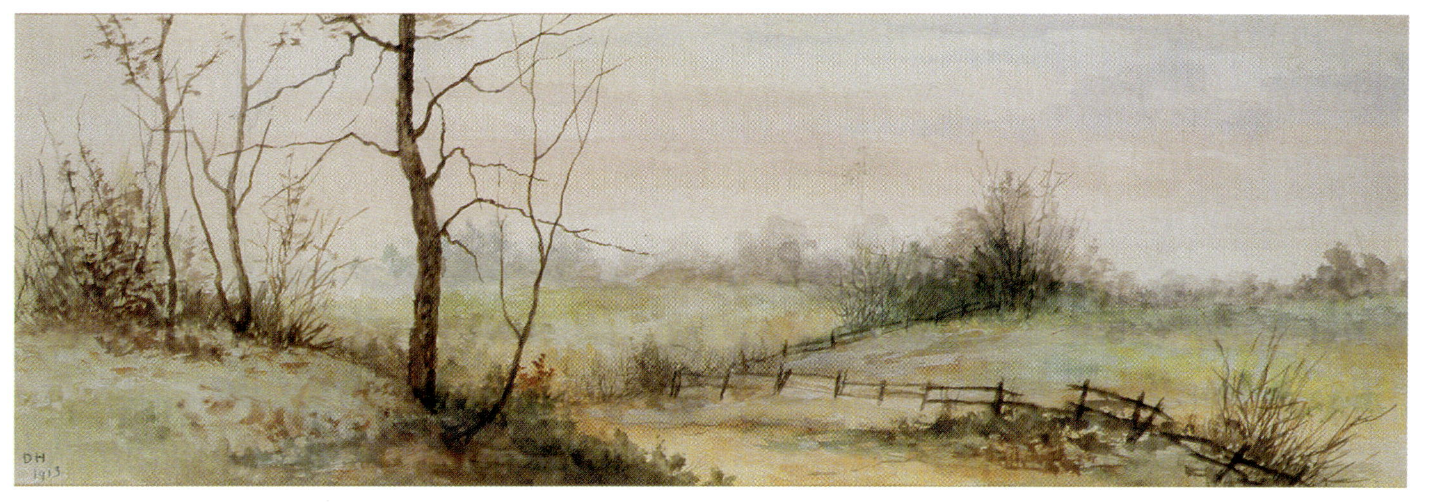

Landscape
1914
Watercolor
4 x 8 inches
Anonymous loan

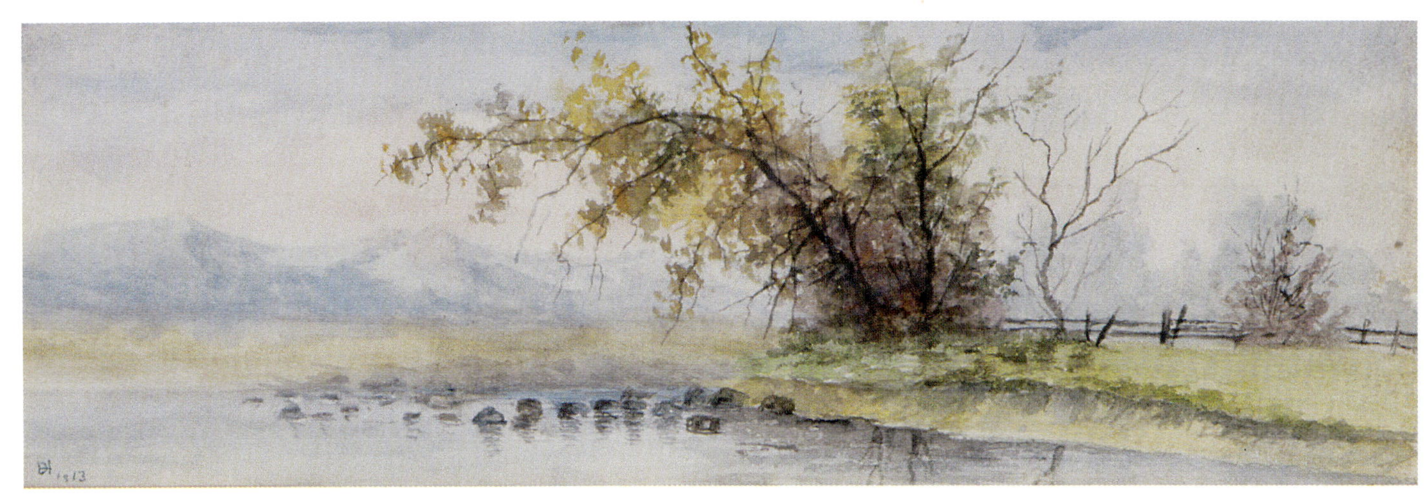

Landscape
1914
Watercolor
4 x 8 inches
Anonymous loan

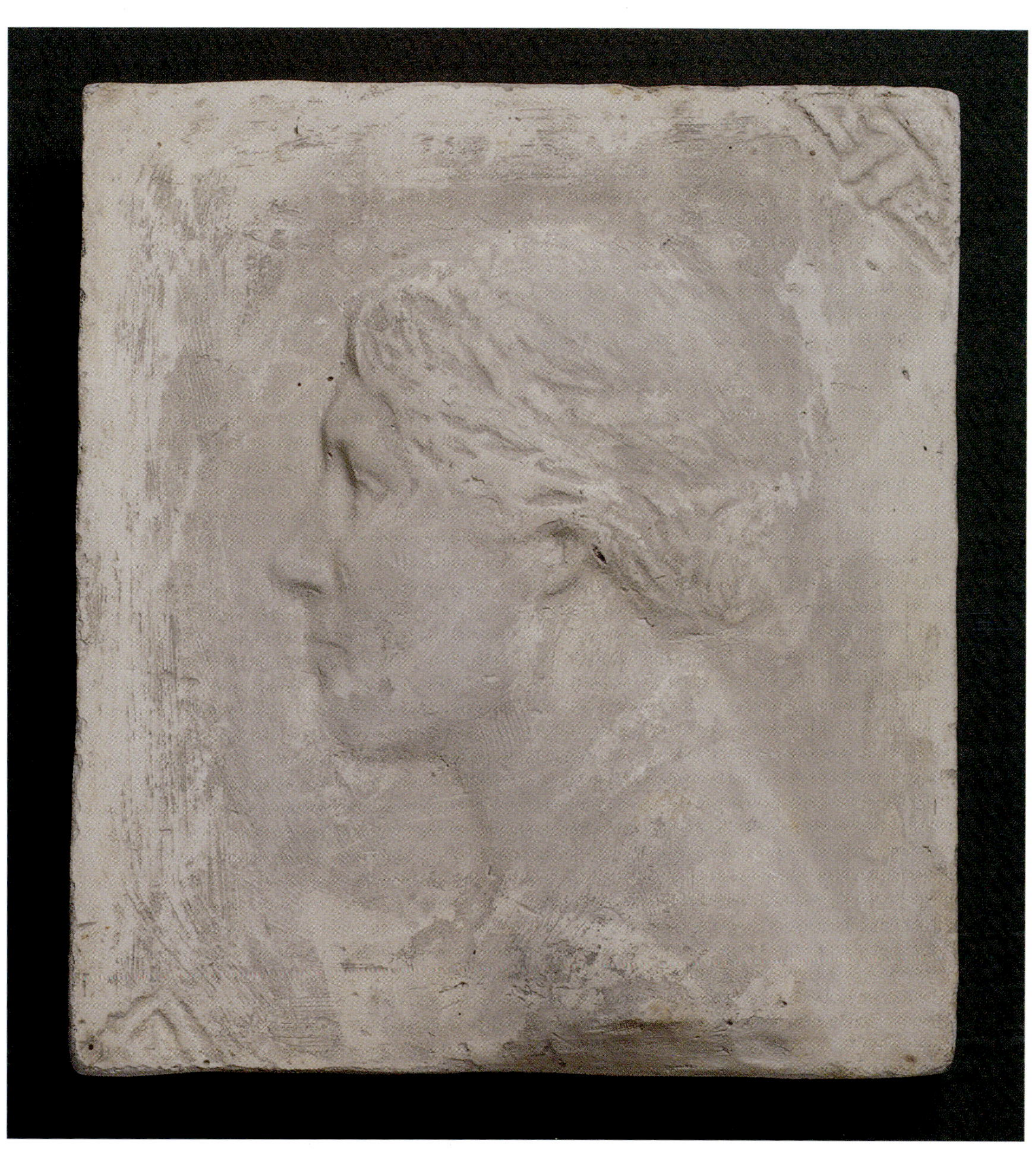

Profile Relief of Woman's Head
1916
Plaster
5 ¾ inches
San Diego Historical Society
Gift of Mavina McFeron

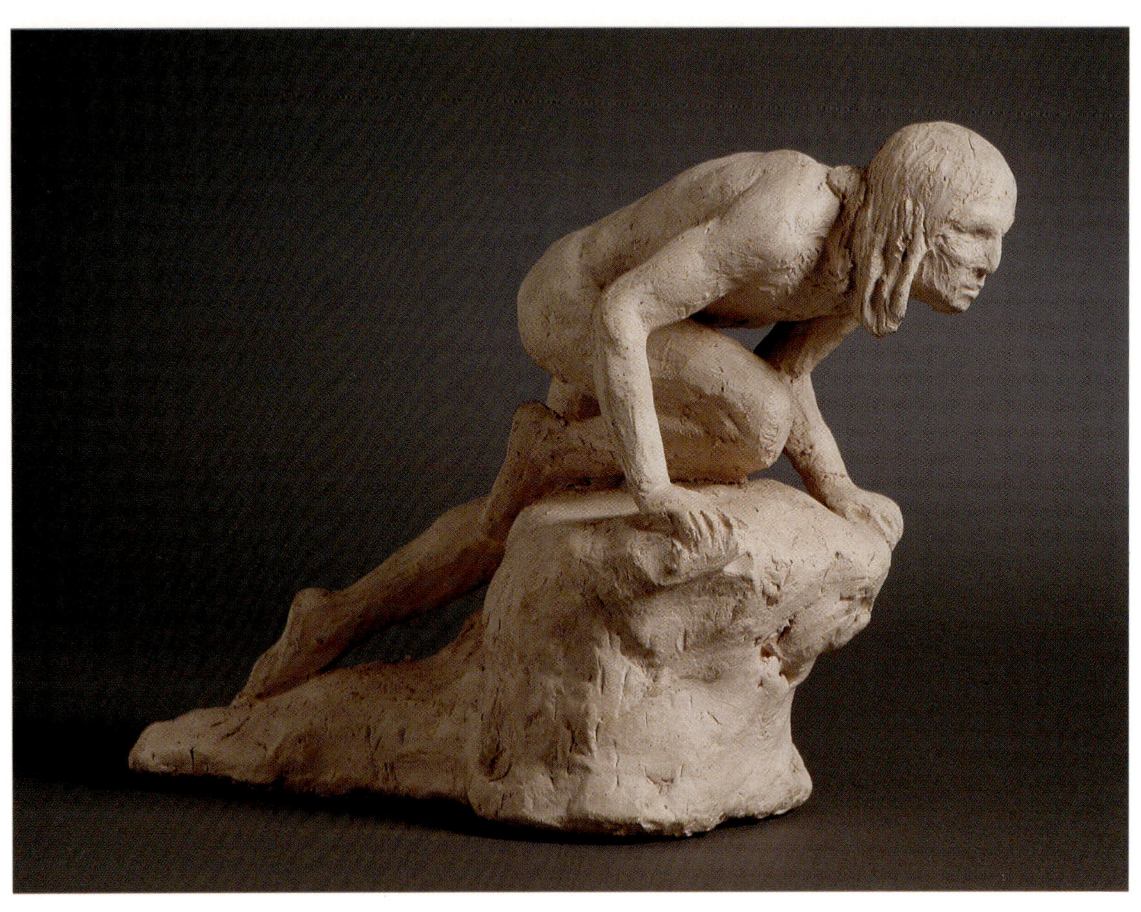

Creeping Indian
1918
Terracotta
4 ¾ inches
Courtesy of San Diego Museum of Art

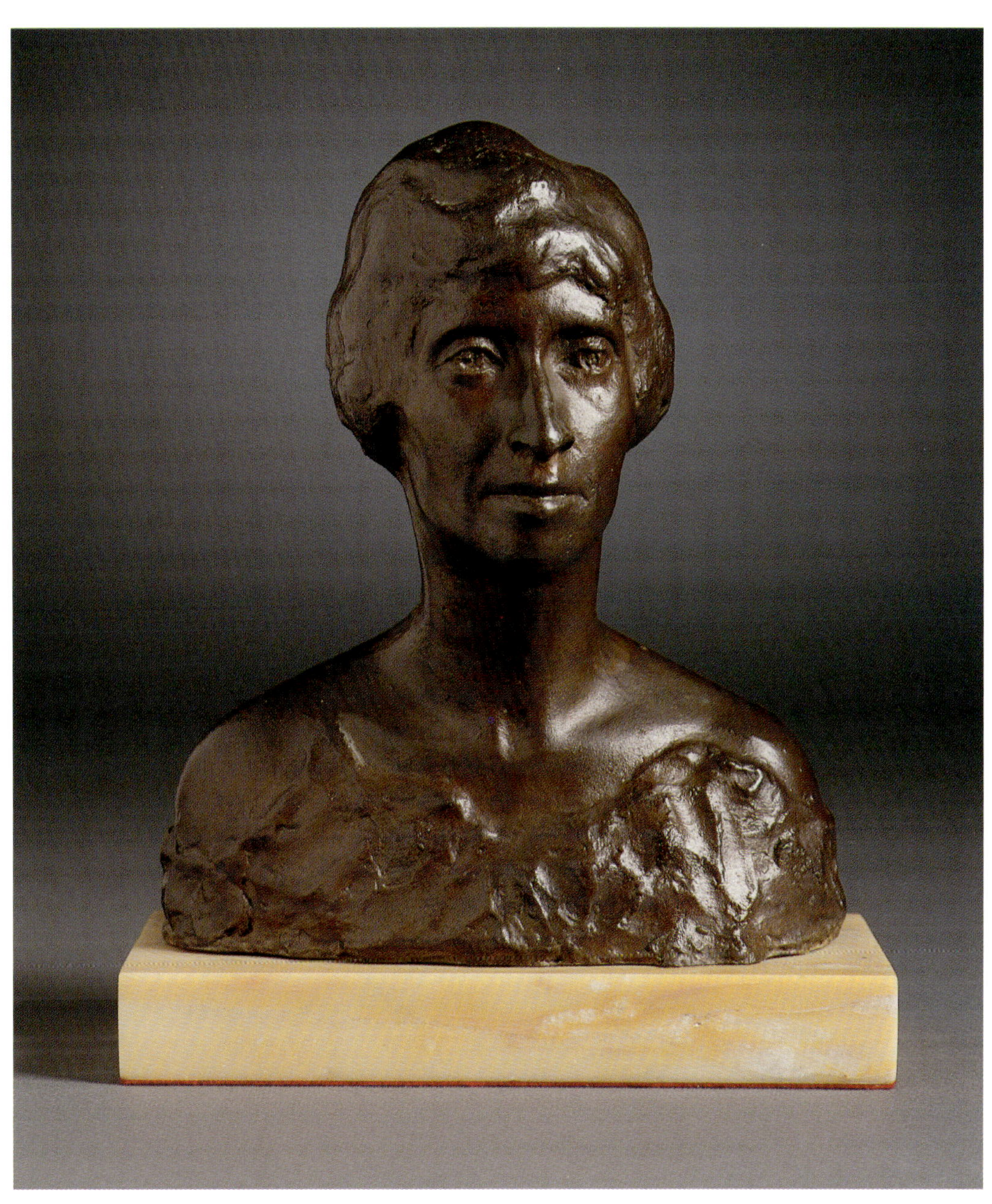

Laura
1919
Bronze
6 ¼ inches
San Diego Historical Society
Gift of Florence Hord and Homer Dana

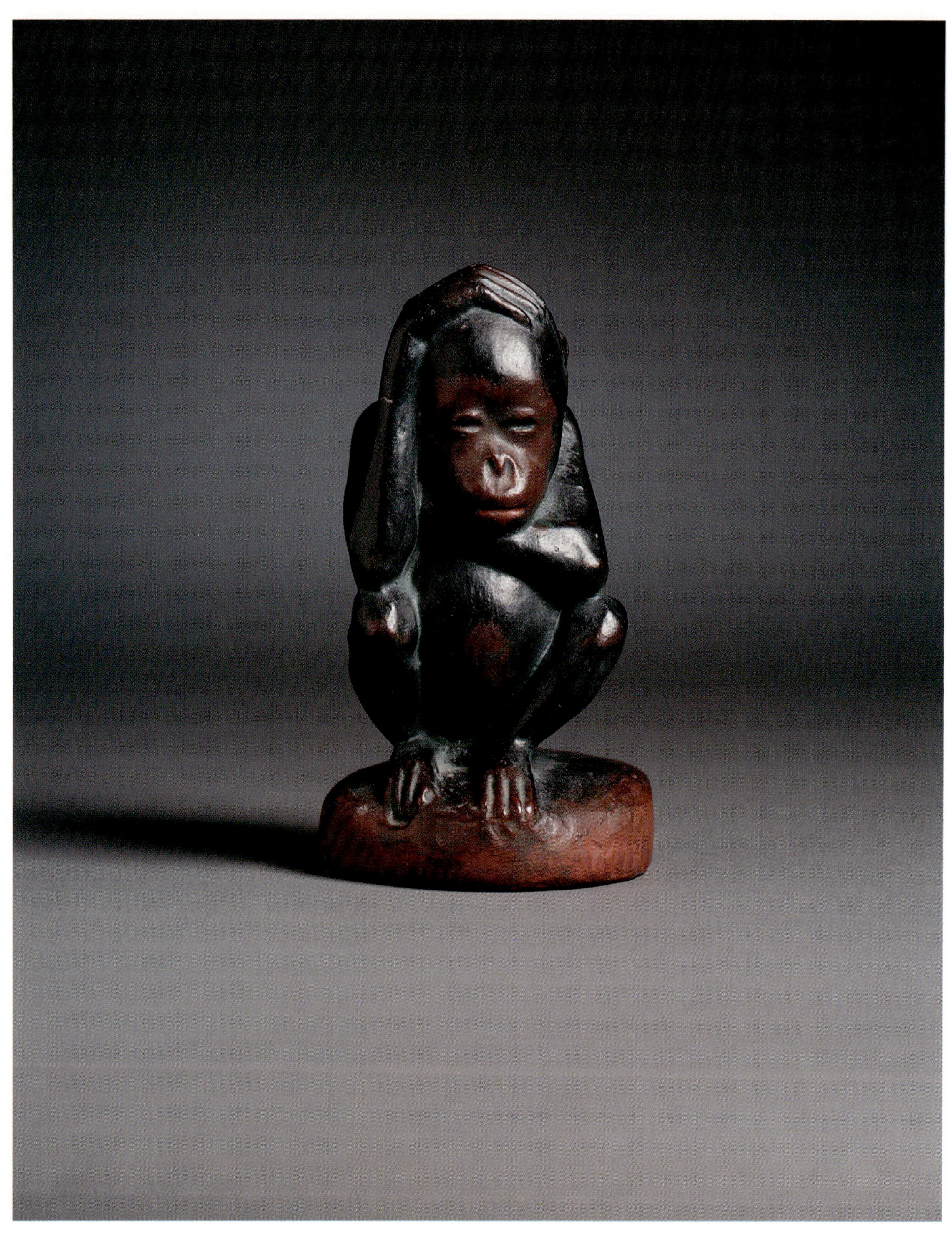

Mike
1922
Plaster
5 ¼ X 3 ¼ inches
San Diego Historical Society
Gift of Mavina McFeron

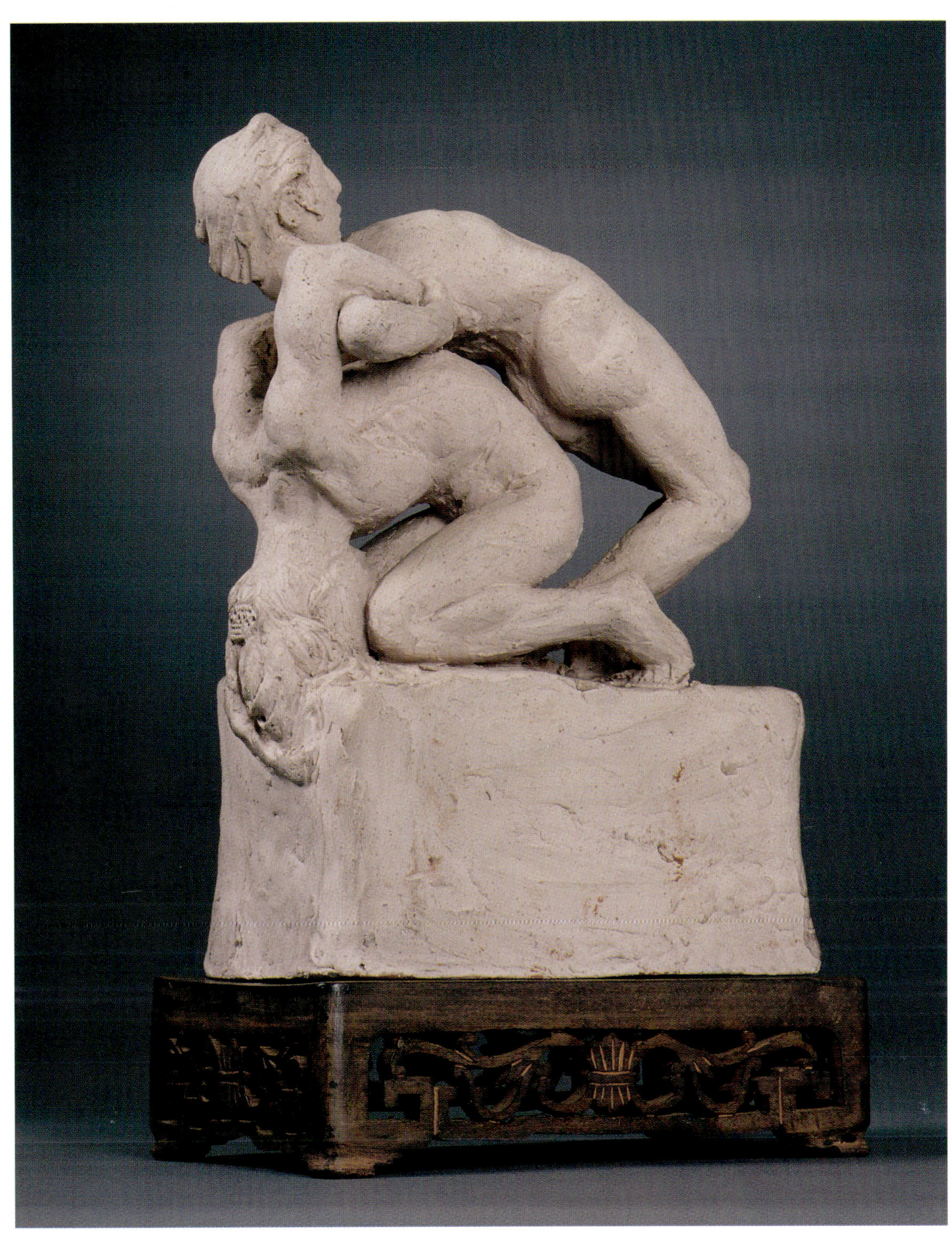

Wrestlers
1922
Terracotta
8 ¼ x 5 ½ x 3 ¼ inches
Courtesy of San Diego Central Library

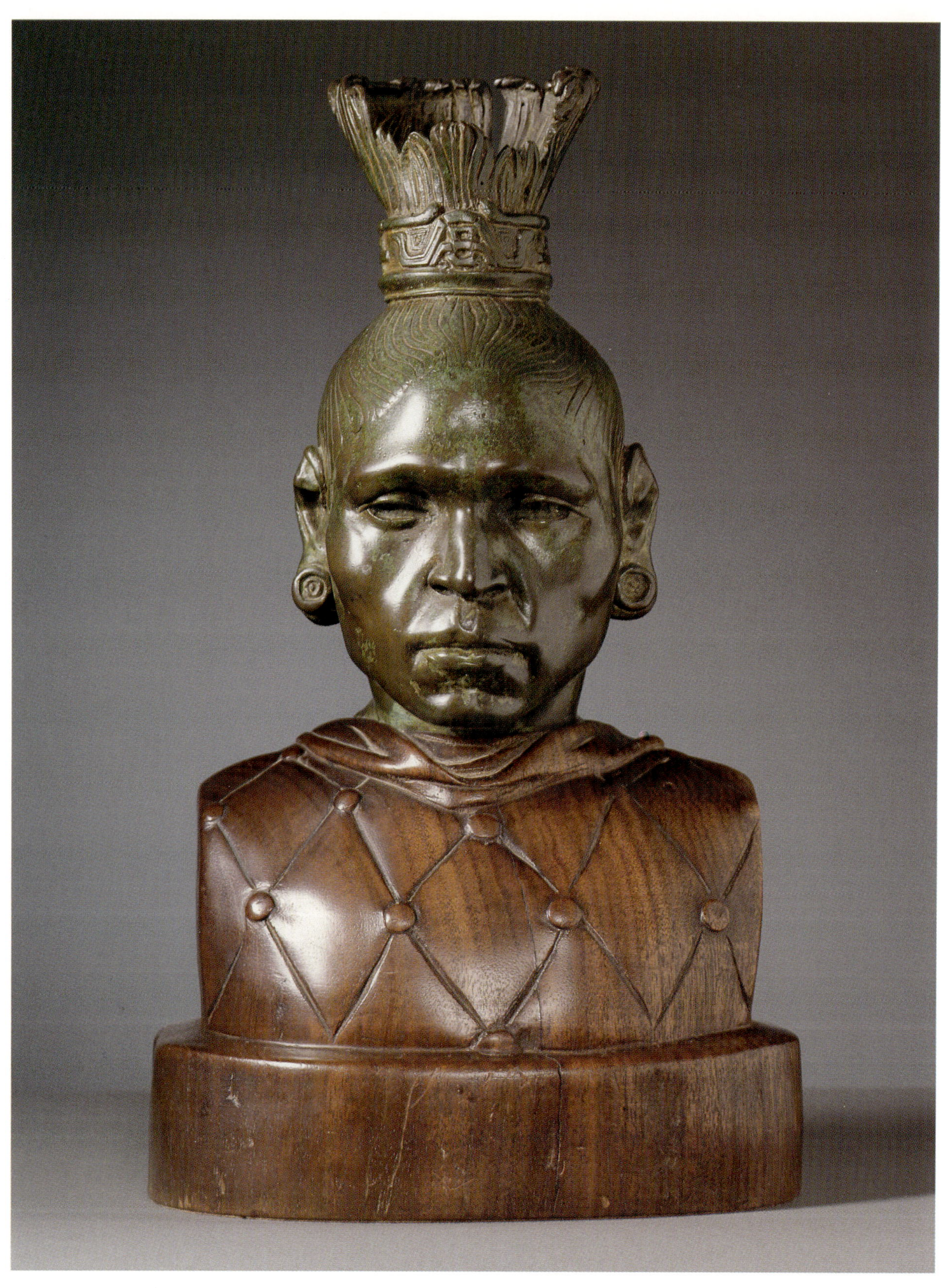

El Cacique
1926
Bronze and Mahogany
14 ¼ inches
Anonymous loan

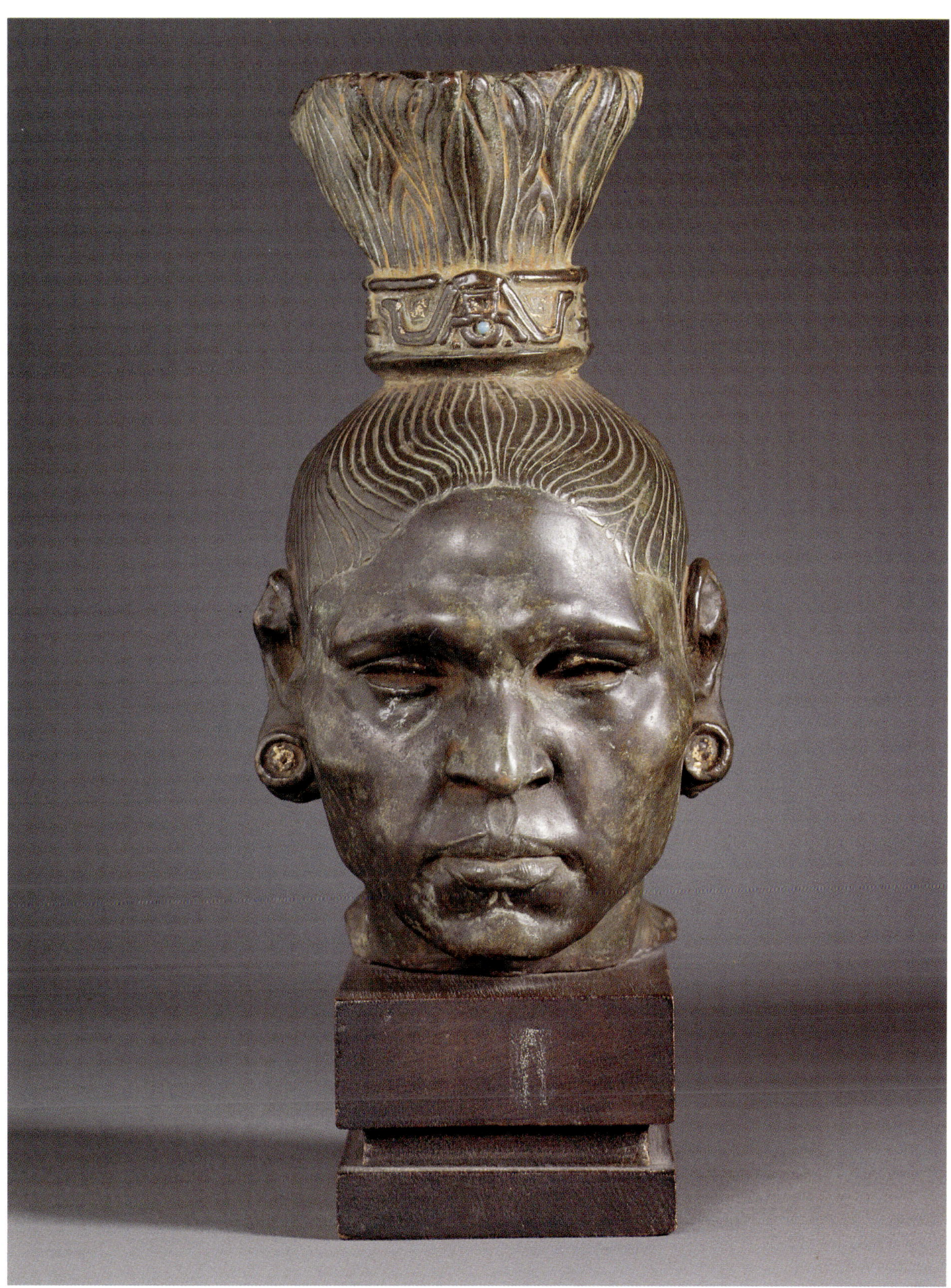

El Cacique
1926
Bronze
8 ⅝ inches
Courtesy of San Diego Museum of Art

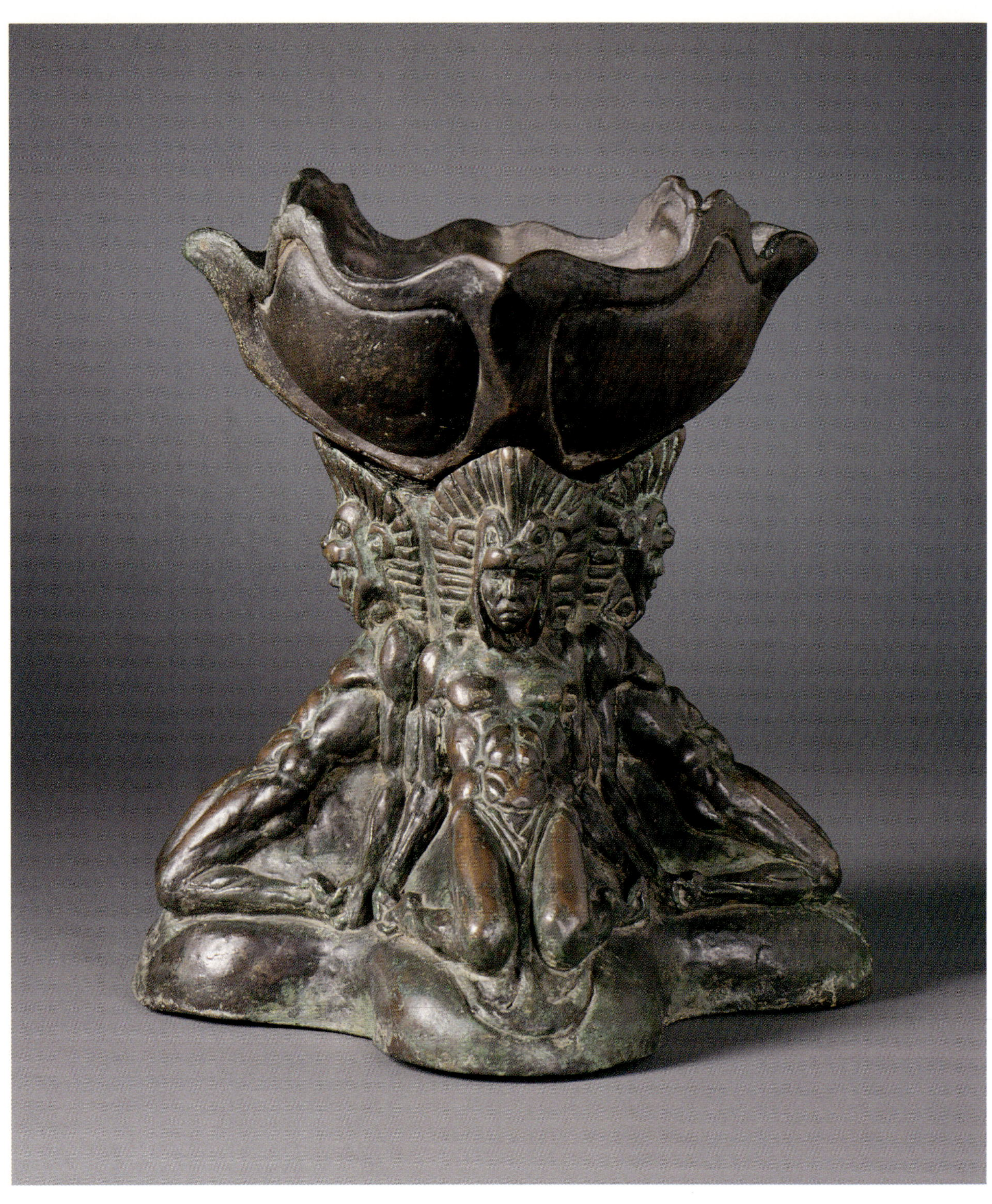

Stand and Bowl
1926-27
Bronze
10 x 7 inches
San Diego Historical Society
Gift of Bruce A. Kamerling

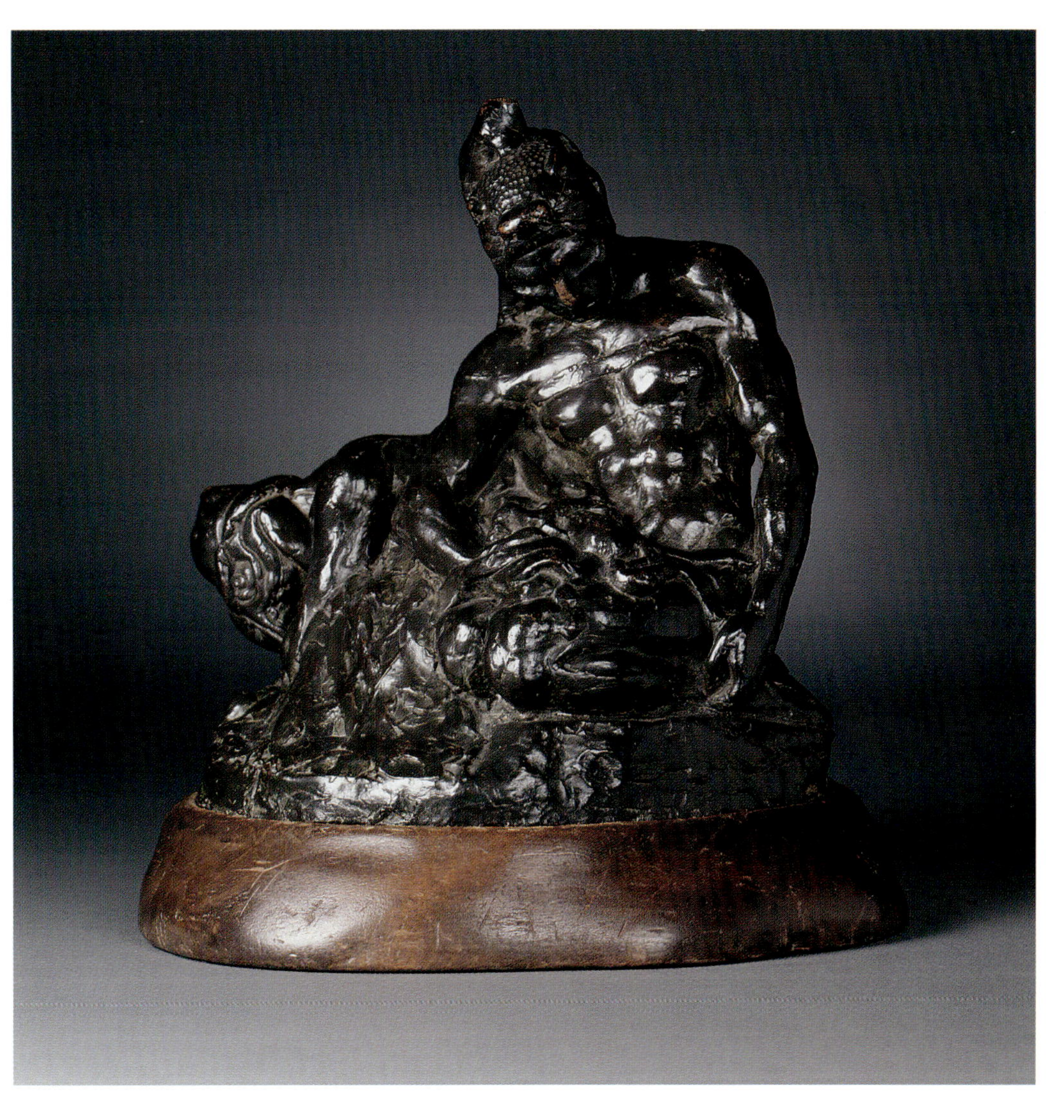

Dying Warriors
1927
Bronze
9 ½ inches
Courtesy of Gary Breitweiser Studio 2
Santa Barbara, California

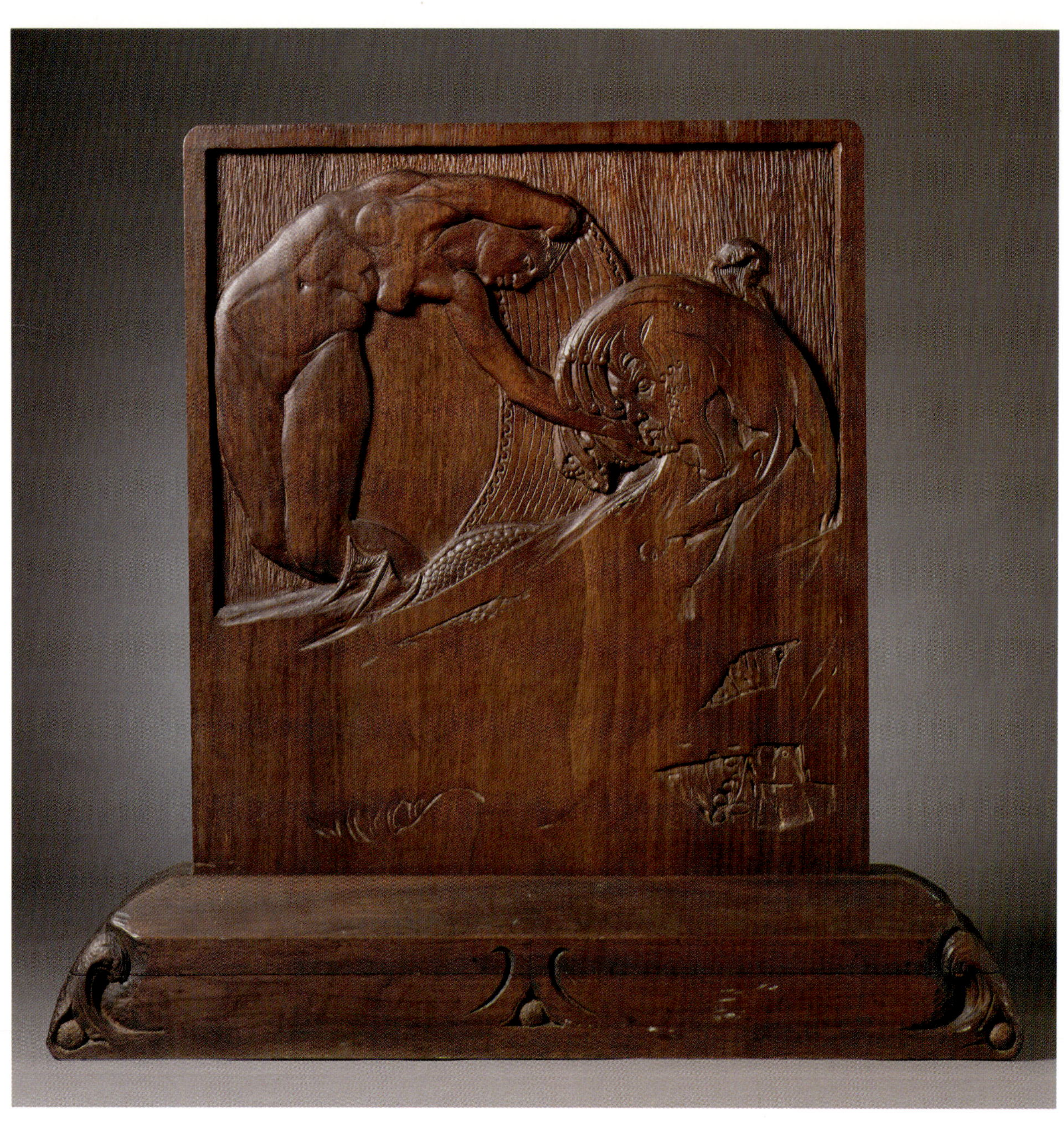

Moon and Sea
1928
Tabasco Mahogany Relief
30 x 31 ½ inches
Courtesy of San Diego Museum of Art

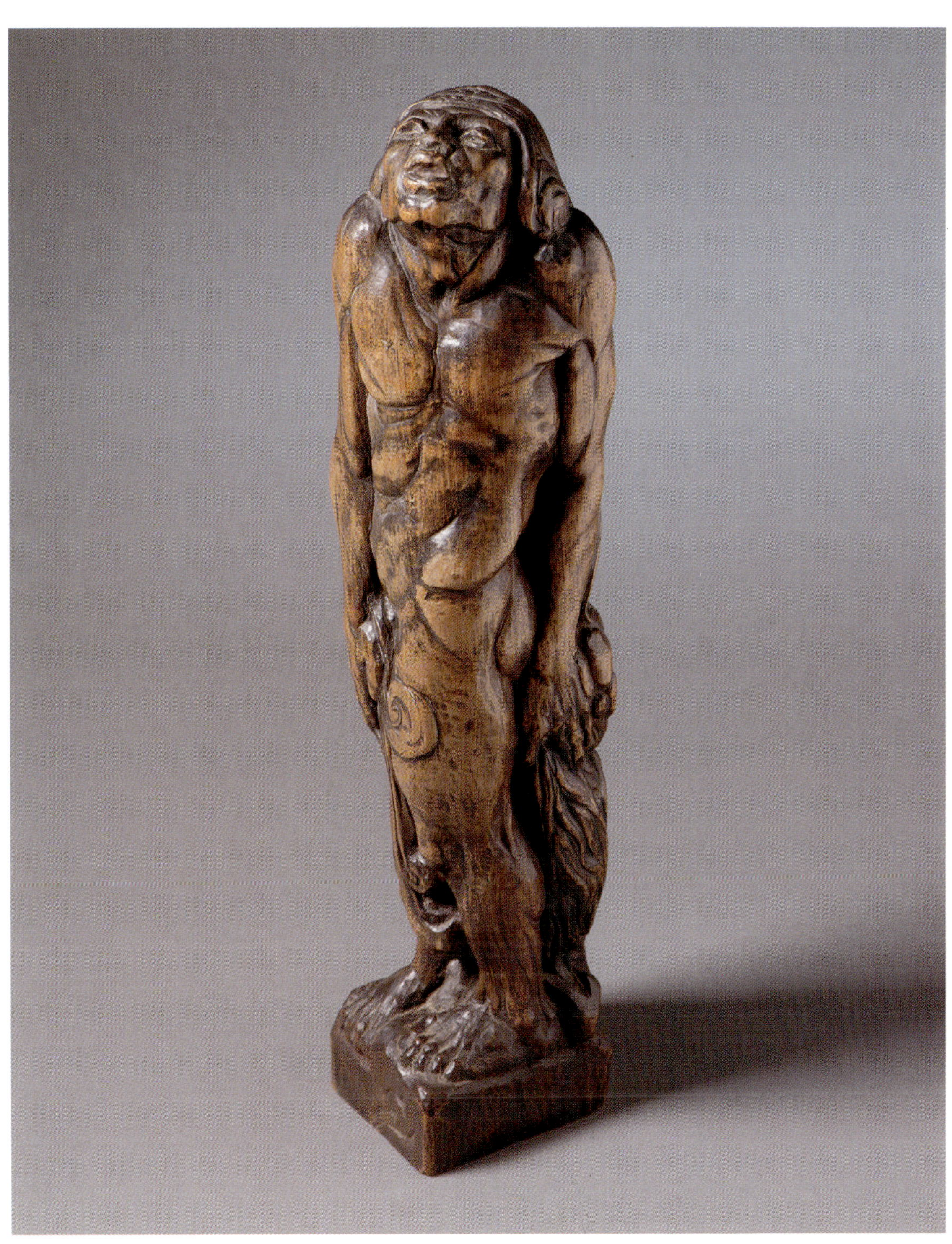

Tezcatlipoca or Smoking Mirror Dance
1928
12 inches
Tropical Hardwood
Anonymous loan

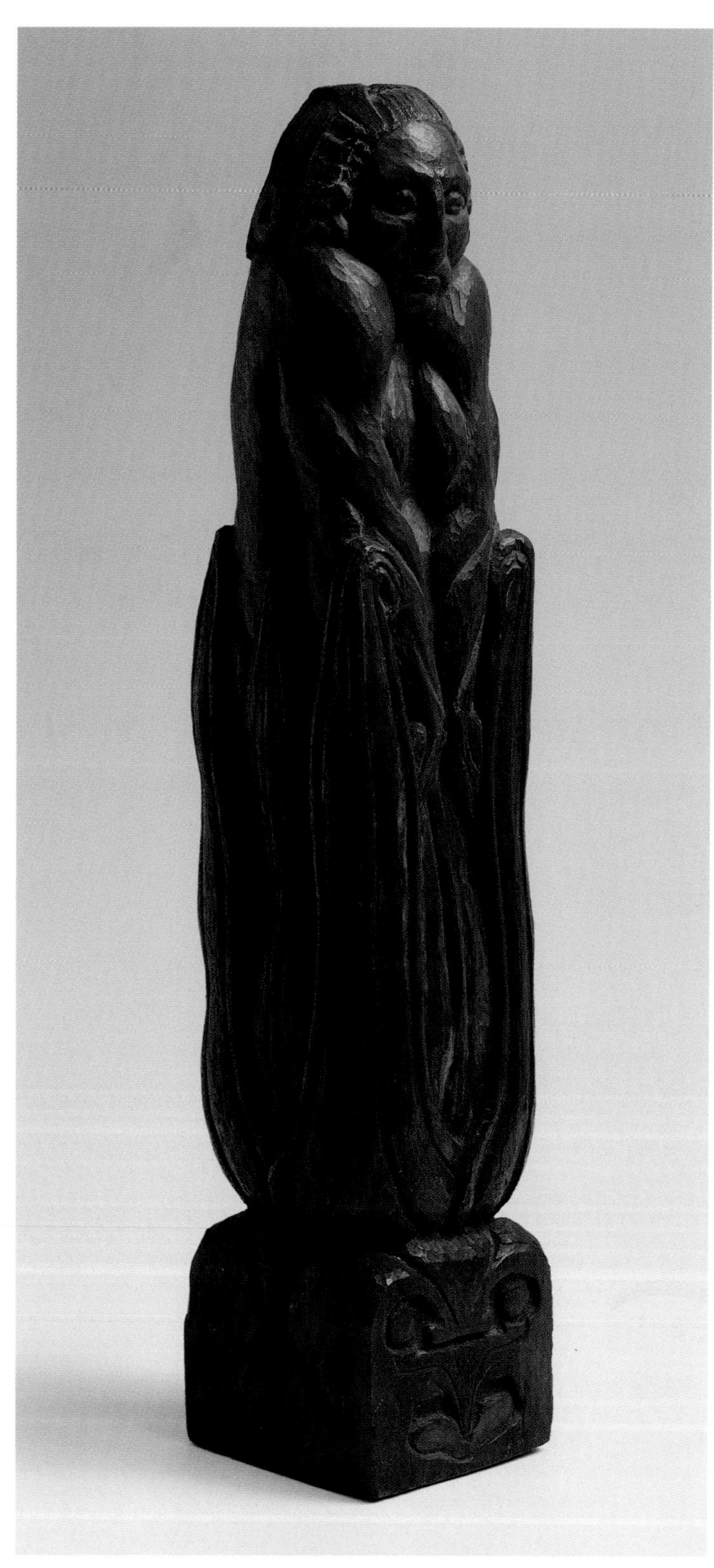

Ome-Tochtli or *El dios del Maguey*
1928
12 inches
Tropical Hardwood
Courtesy of Steve Turner Gallery
Los Angeles, California

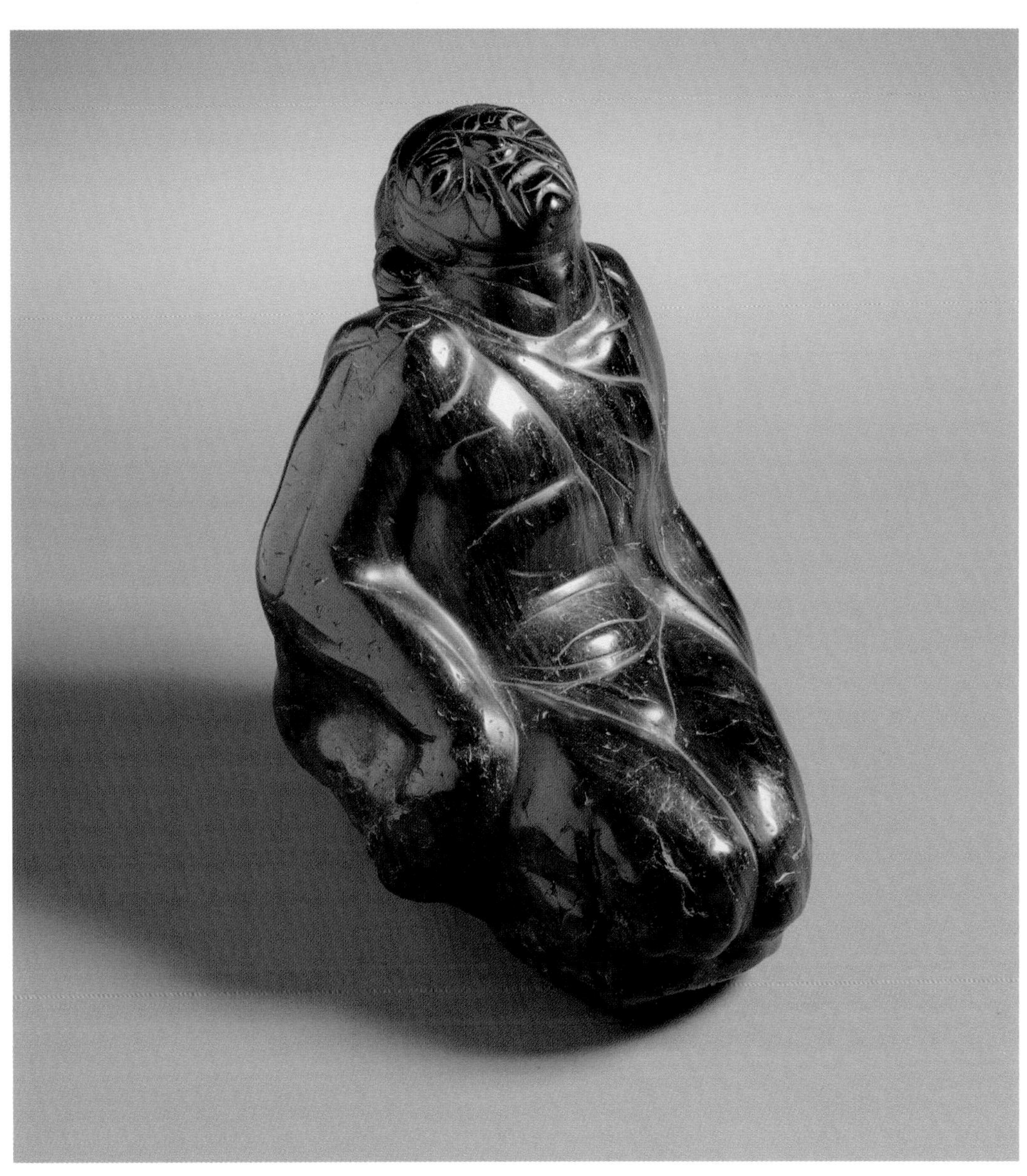

Tlaloc or Thirst
1928-29
Obsidian
12 inches
San Diego Historical Society
Gift of Margaret Wood Bancroft

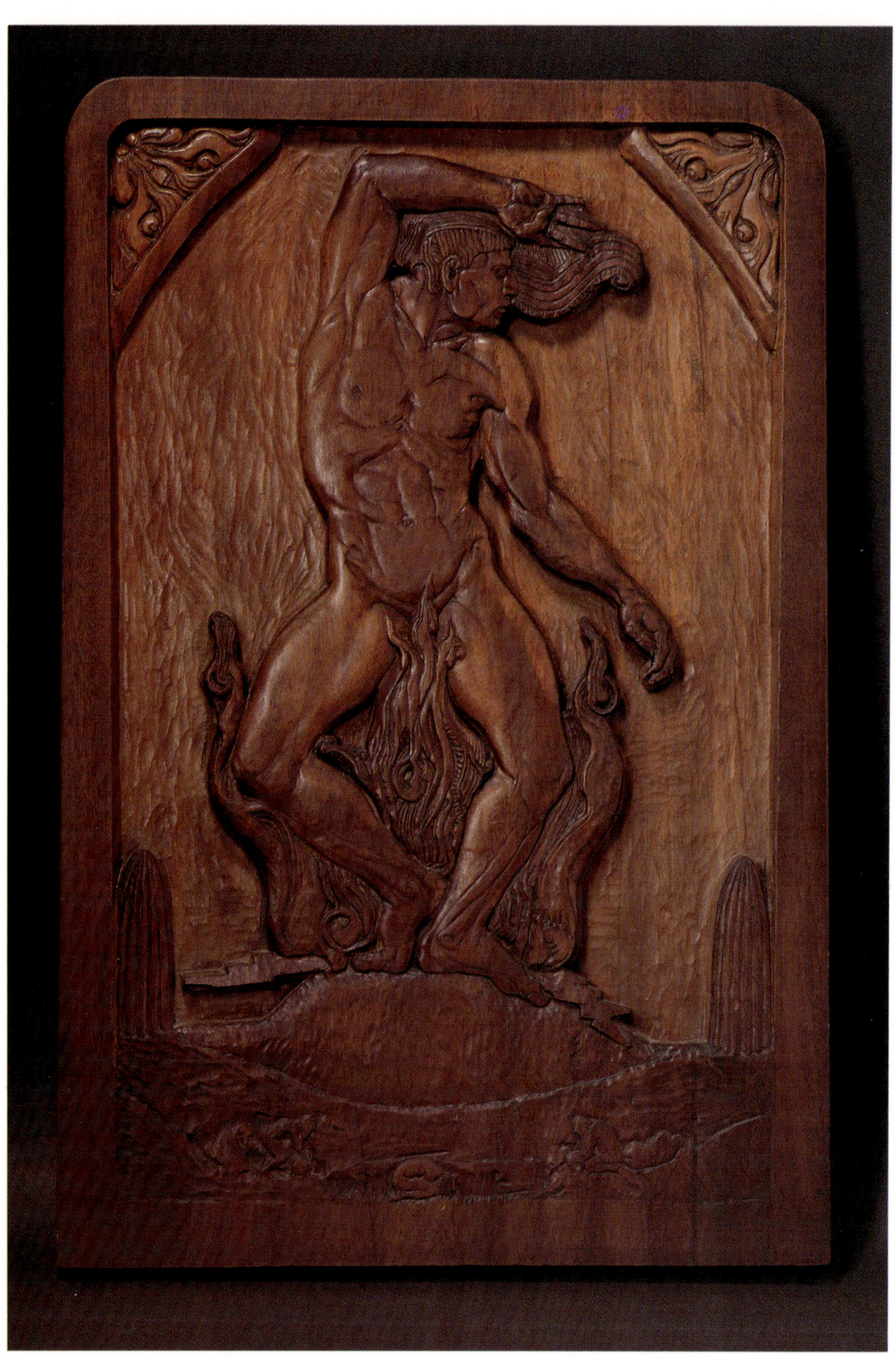

Desert Sun
1929
Tabasco Mahogany Relief
35 x 23 inches
San Diego Historical Society
Bequest of Florence Hord

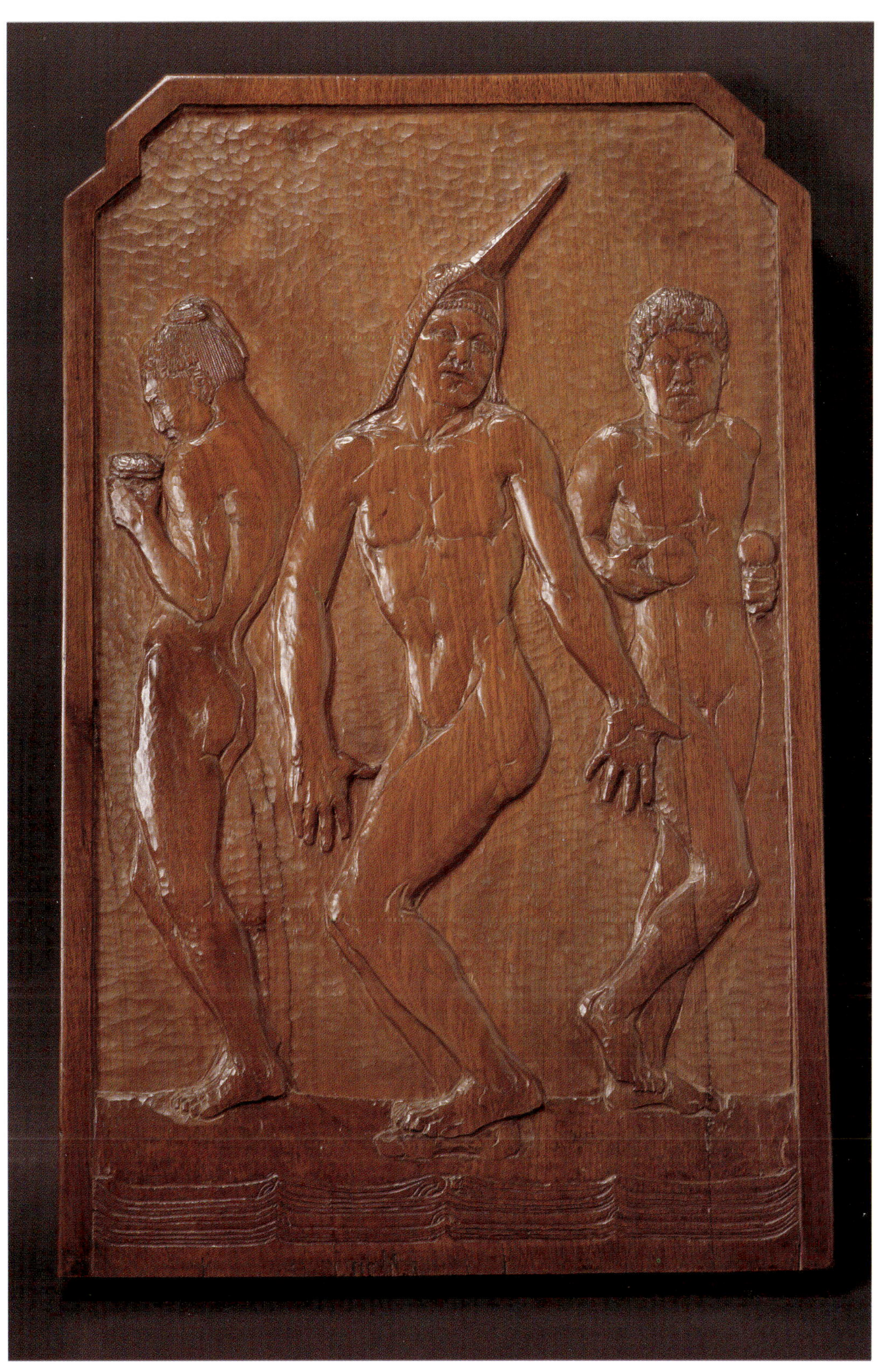

Swordfish Dancers
1930
36 x 23 inches
Tabasco Mahogany Relief
Courtesy of Gil and Lynne Harrington Collection

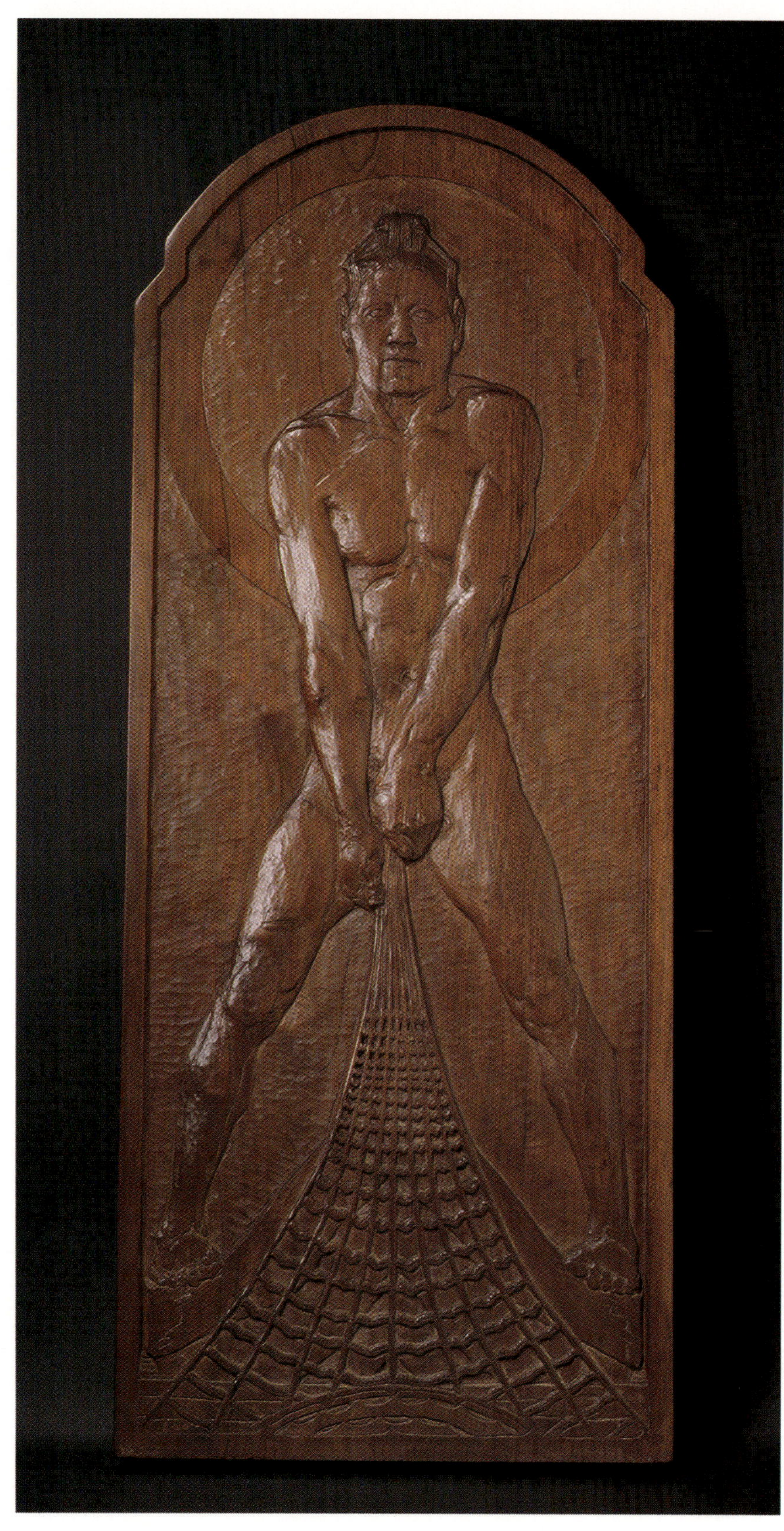

Chumash Fisherman
1930
57 x 24 inches
Tabasco Mahogany Relief
Anonymous loan

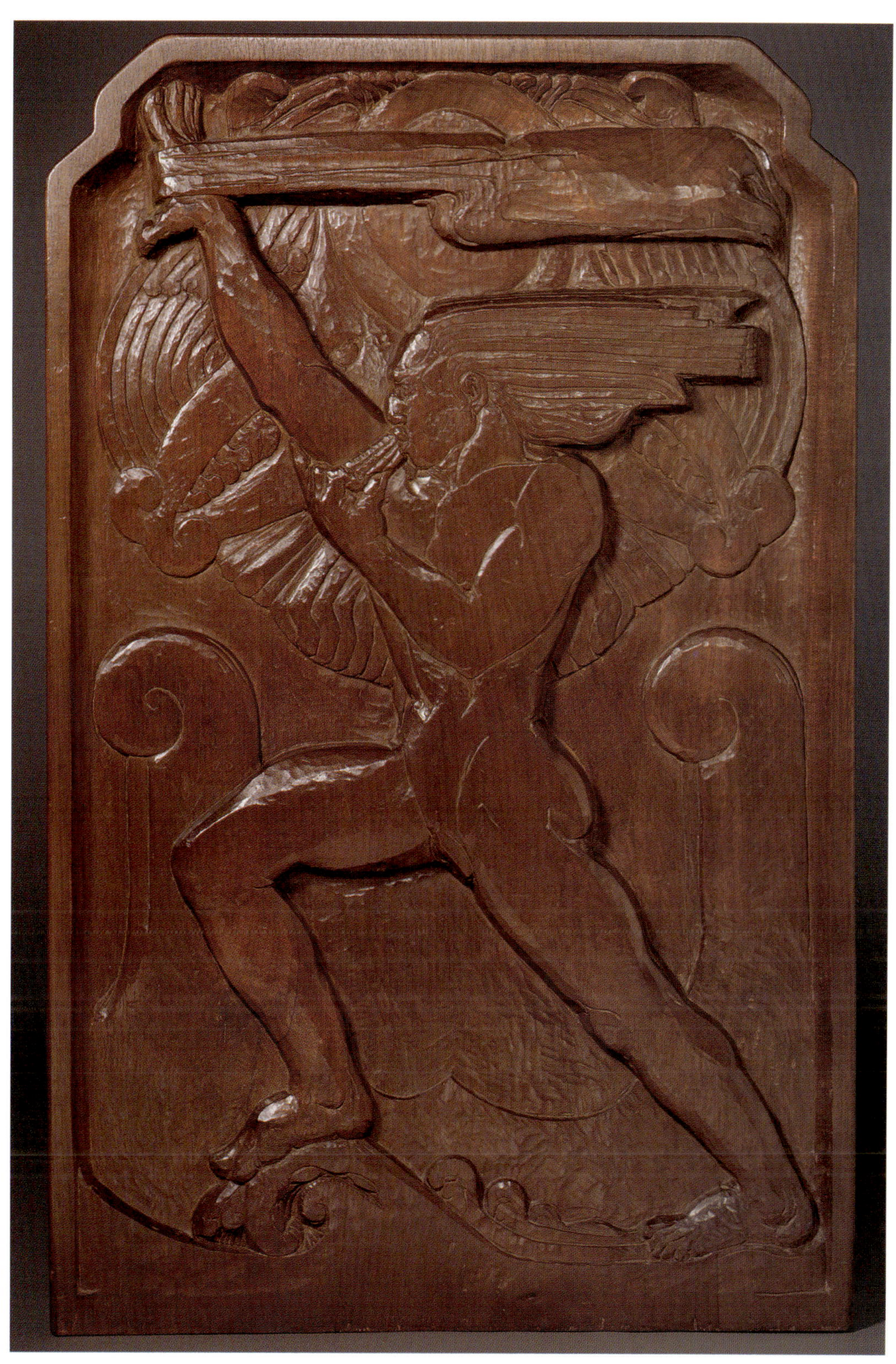

Channel Wind
1930
Tabasco Mahogany Relief
36 x 23 ½ inches
Anonymous loan

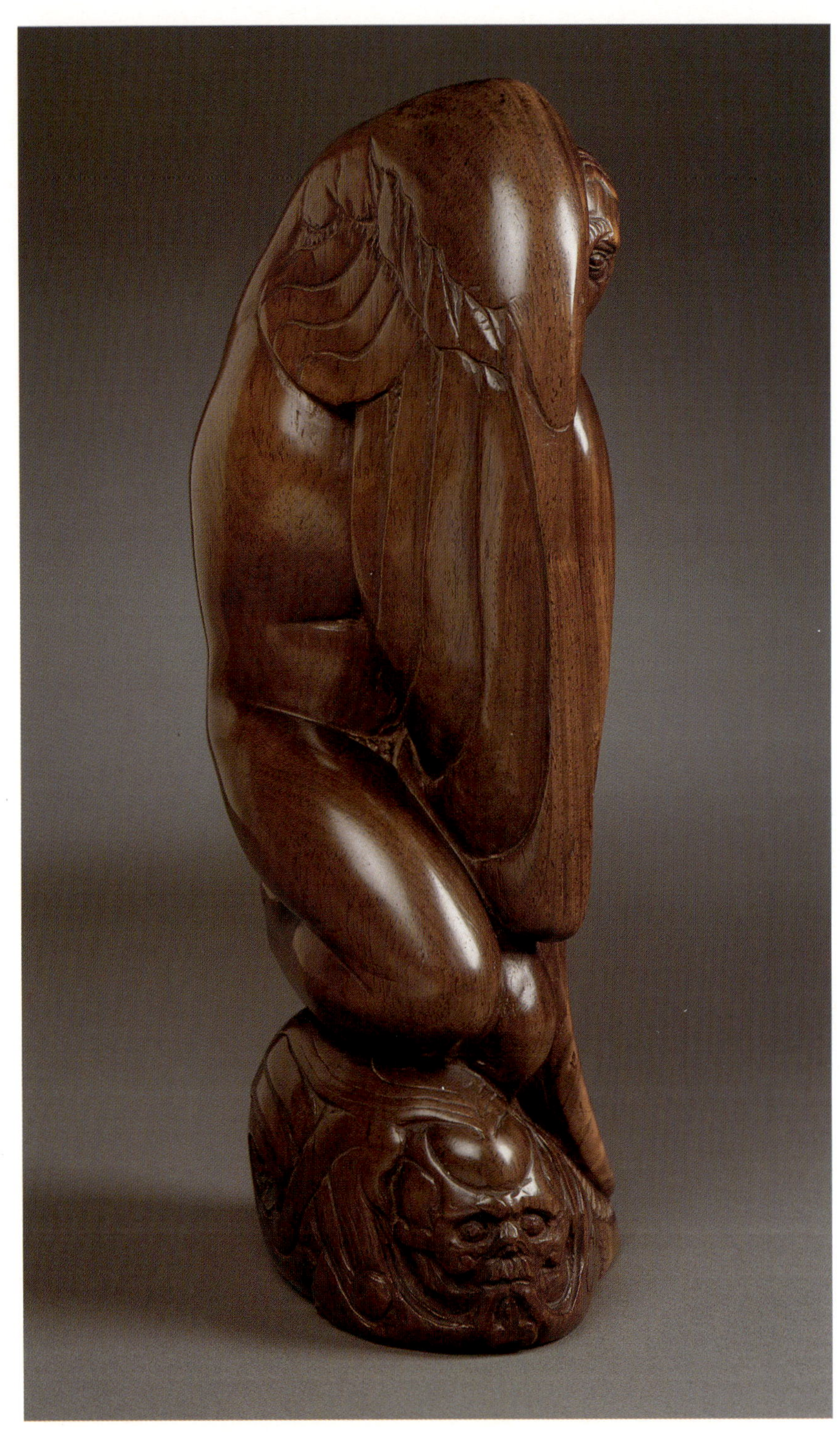

Hurakan
1930
Mexican Rosewood
12 ¼ inches
San Diego Historical Society
Gift of Bruce A. Kamerling

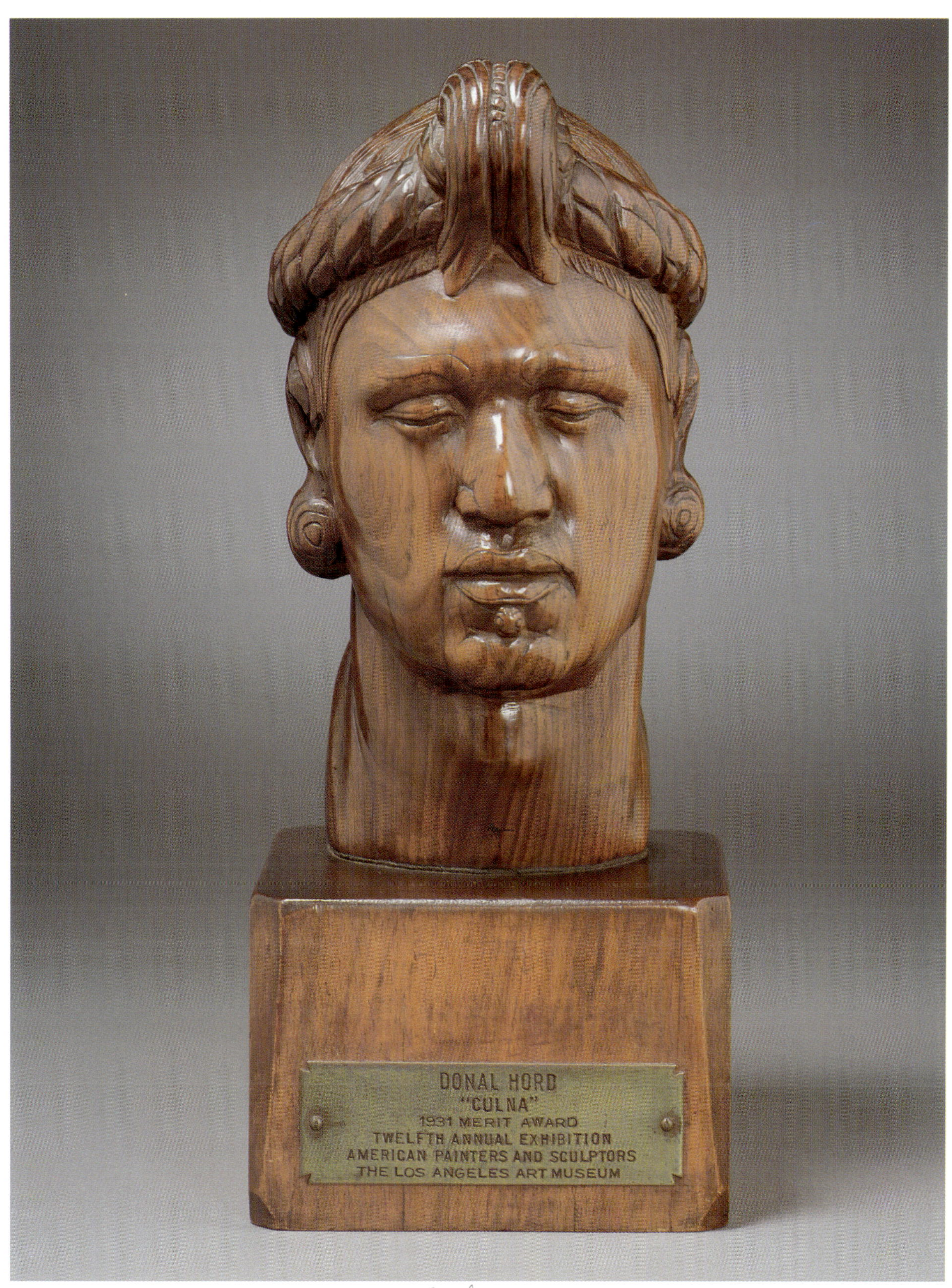

~~Culna~~
1930
Mexican Rosewood with Mahogany Base
13 ¾ inches
San Diego Historical Society
Gift of Mrs. John C. Rhodes

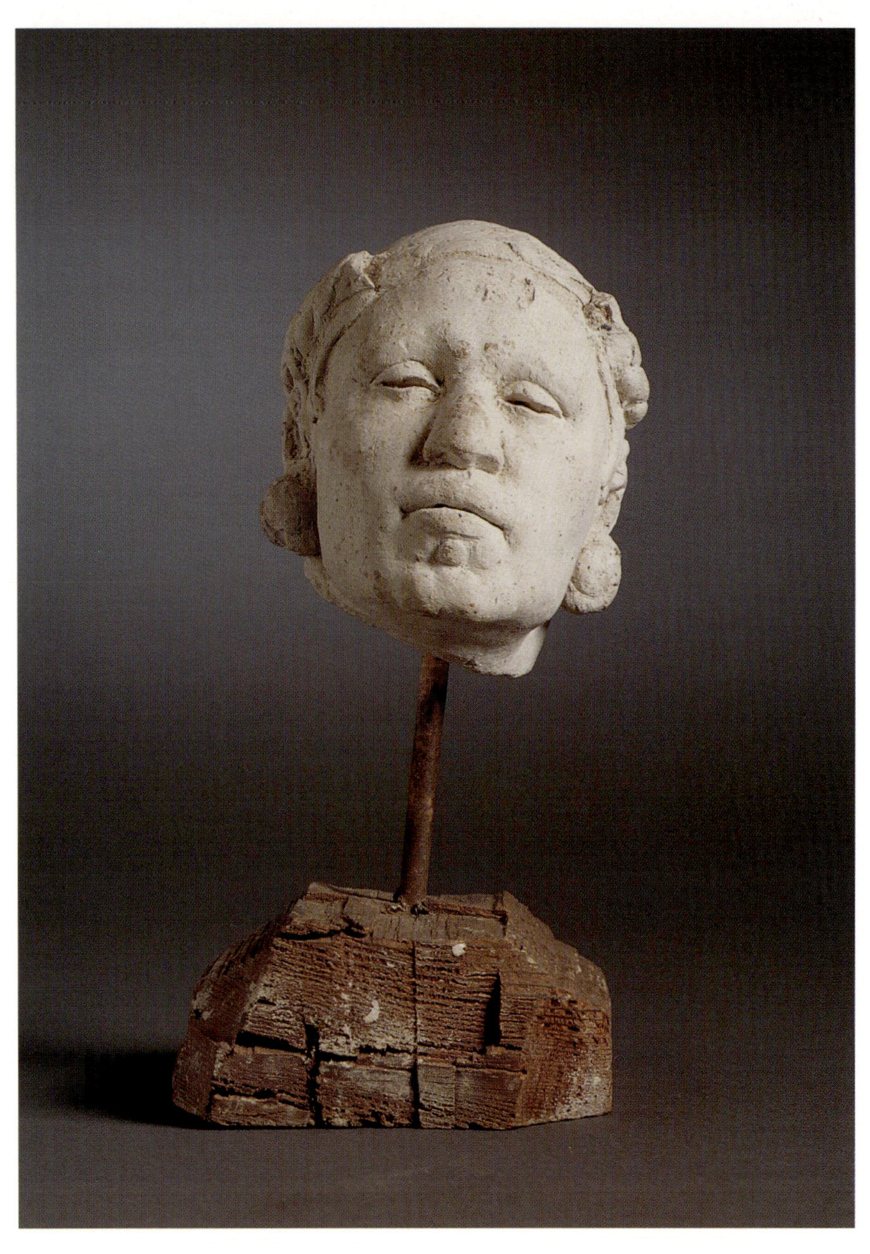

Study for Culna
1930
3 inches
Clay Head Mounted on Wooden Block
Courtesy San Diego Museum of Art

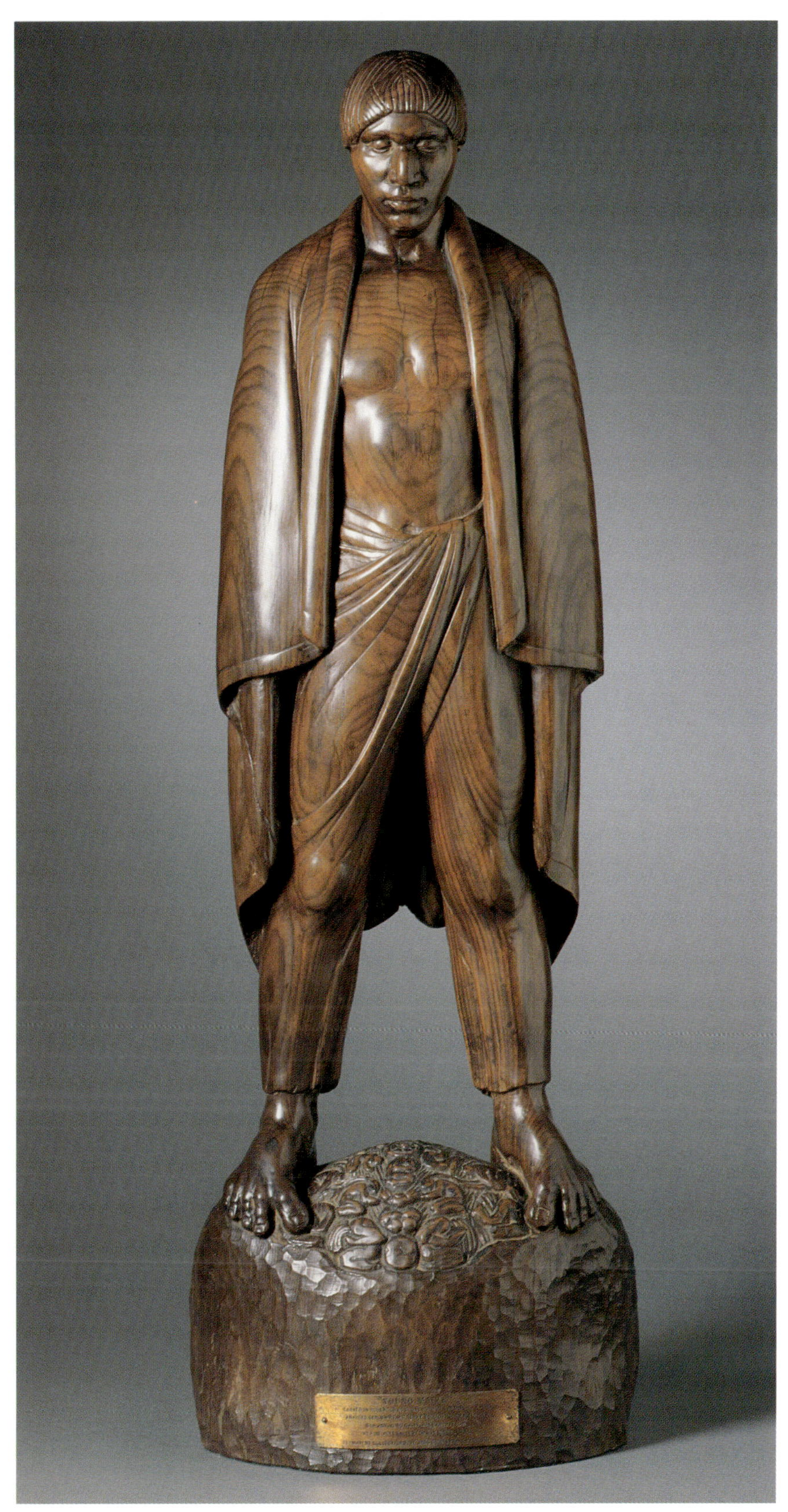

Young Maize
1931
Mexican Rosewood
30 inches
Courtesy of San Diego Museum of Art

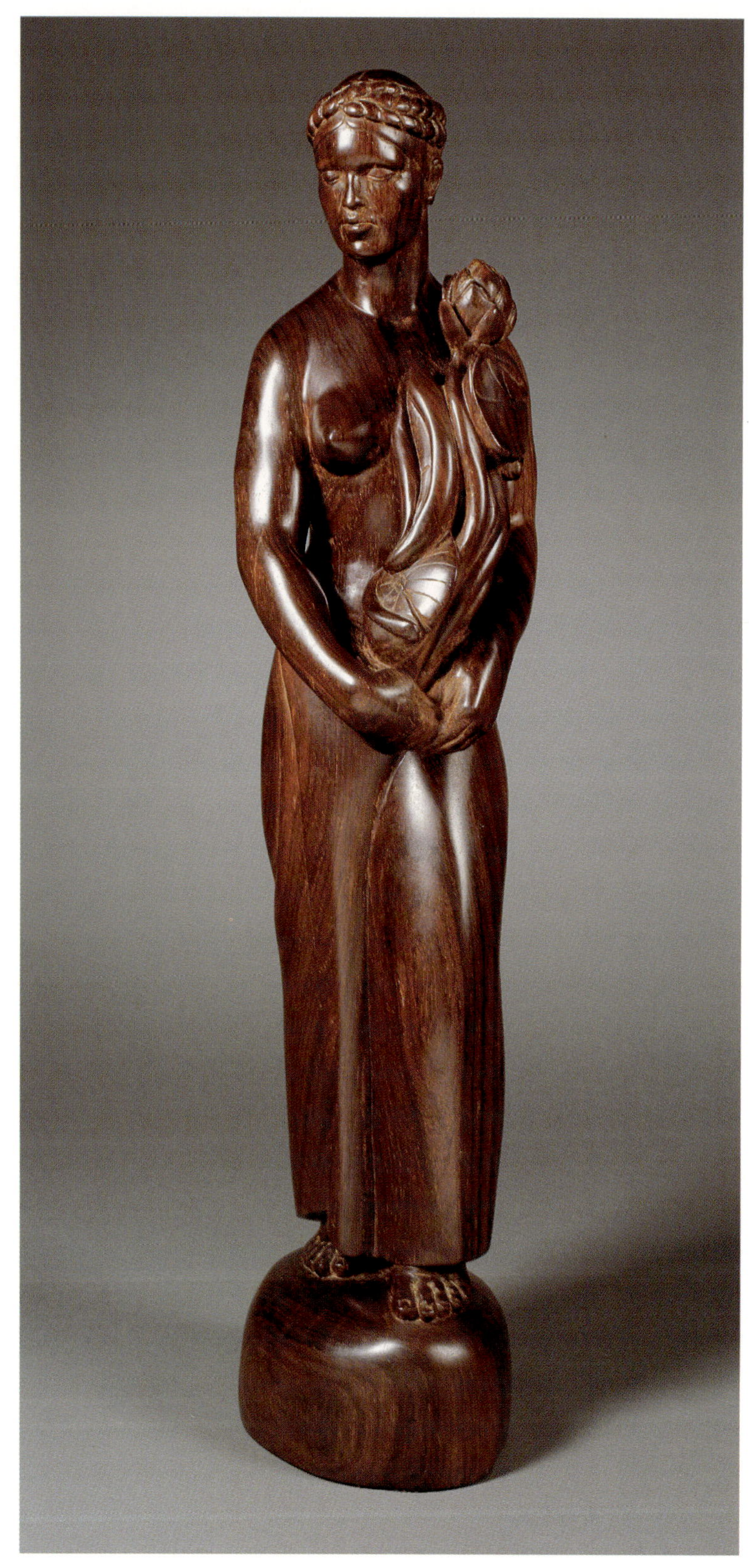

Dream of Summer
1931
Rosewood
21 inches
Anonymous loan

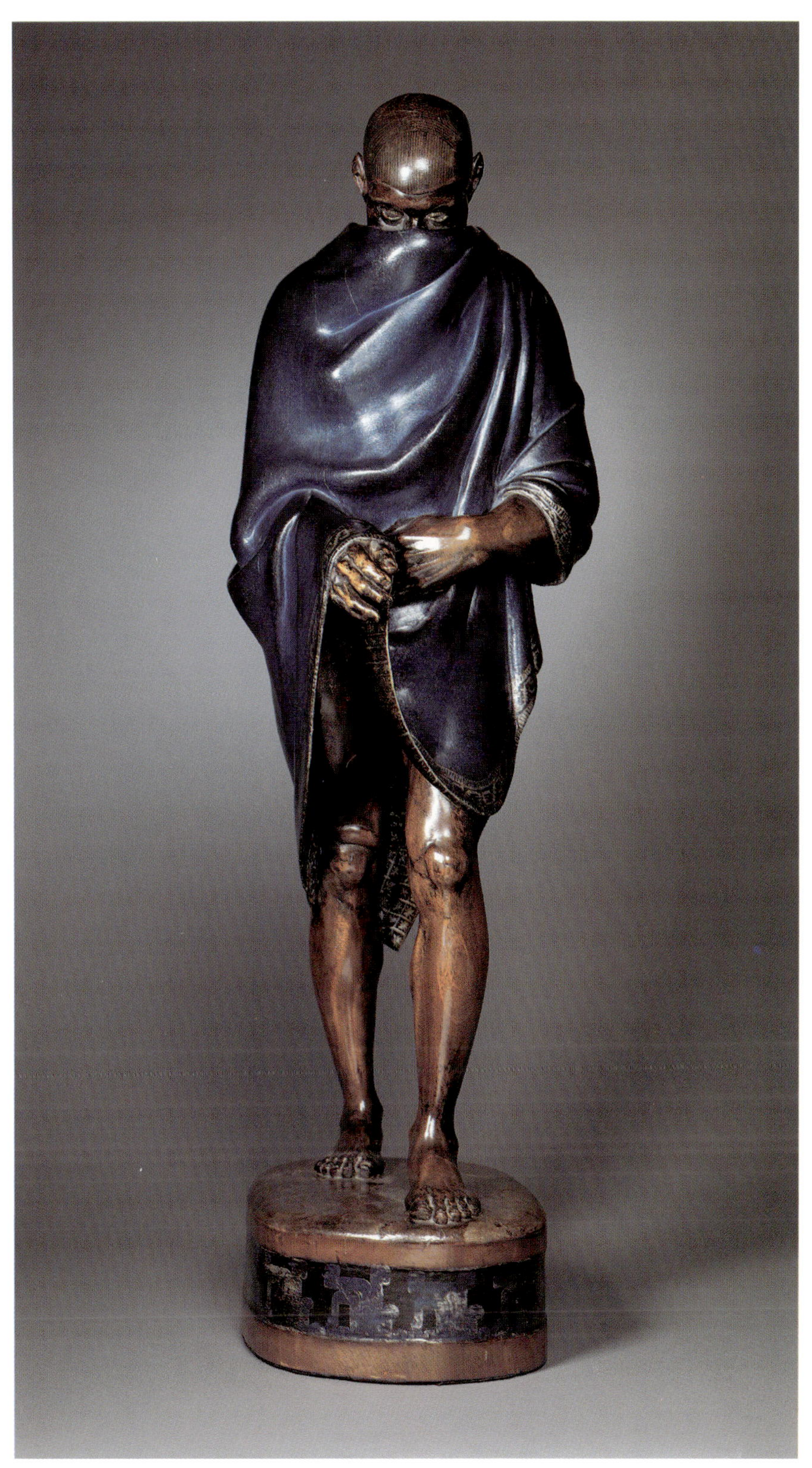

Desert Night
1932
Philippine Mahogany with Polychrome Details
36 inches
Courtesy of Gary Breitweiser Studio 2
Santa Barbara, California

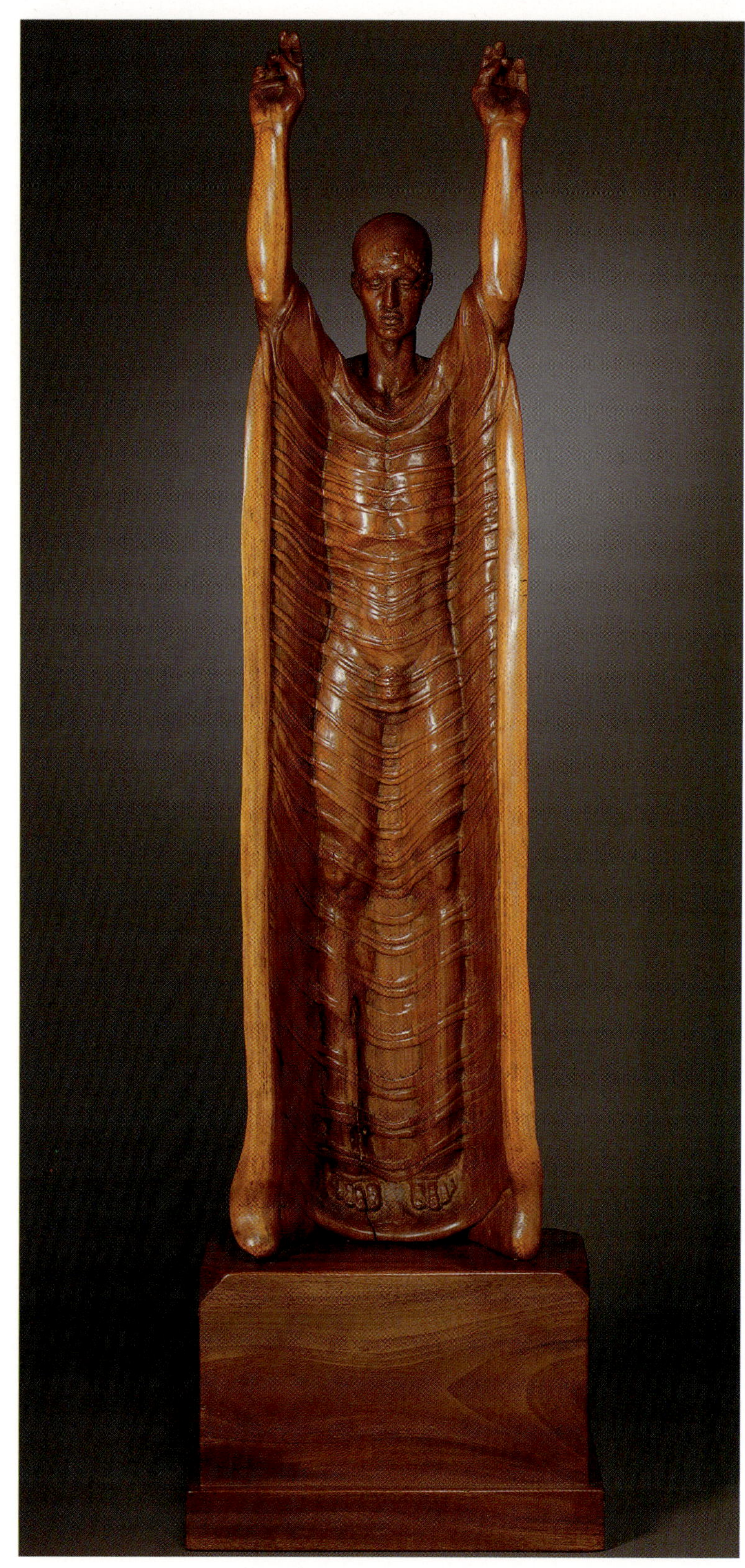

Desert Sunrise
1932
Tropical Hardwood
40 inches
Courtesy of Edward-Dean Museum of Decorative Arts
Cherry Valley, California

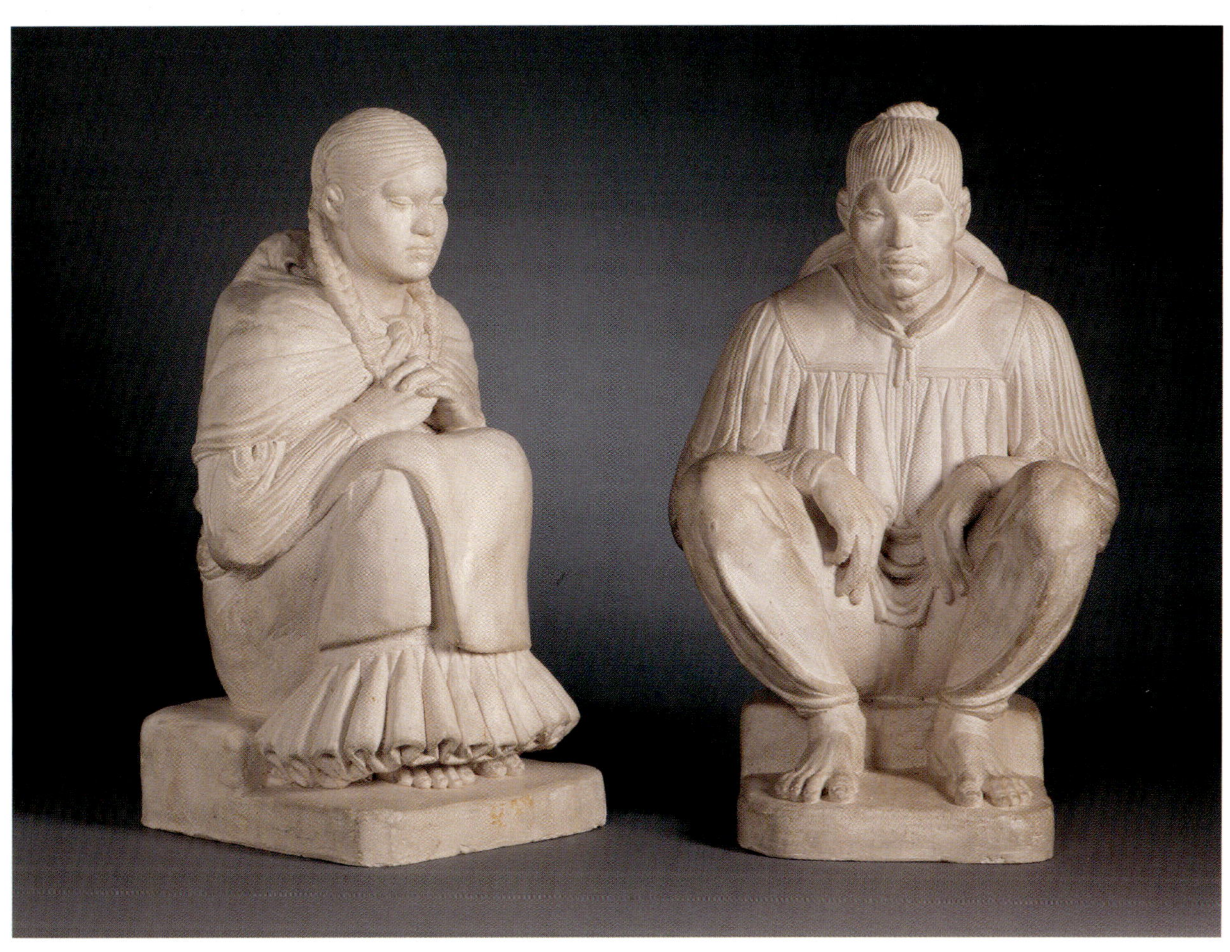

Family on the Curb
1932 - 1933 (Female)
Terracotta
15 ¼ x 8 ¼ inches
Courtesy of San Diego Museum of Art

Family on the Curb
1932 - 1933 (Male)
Terracotta
15 ¼ x 8 ¼ inches
Anonymous loan

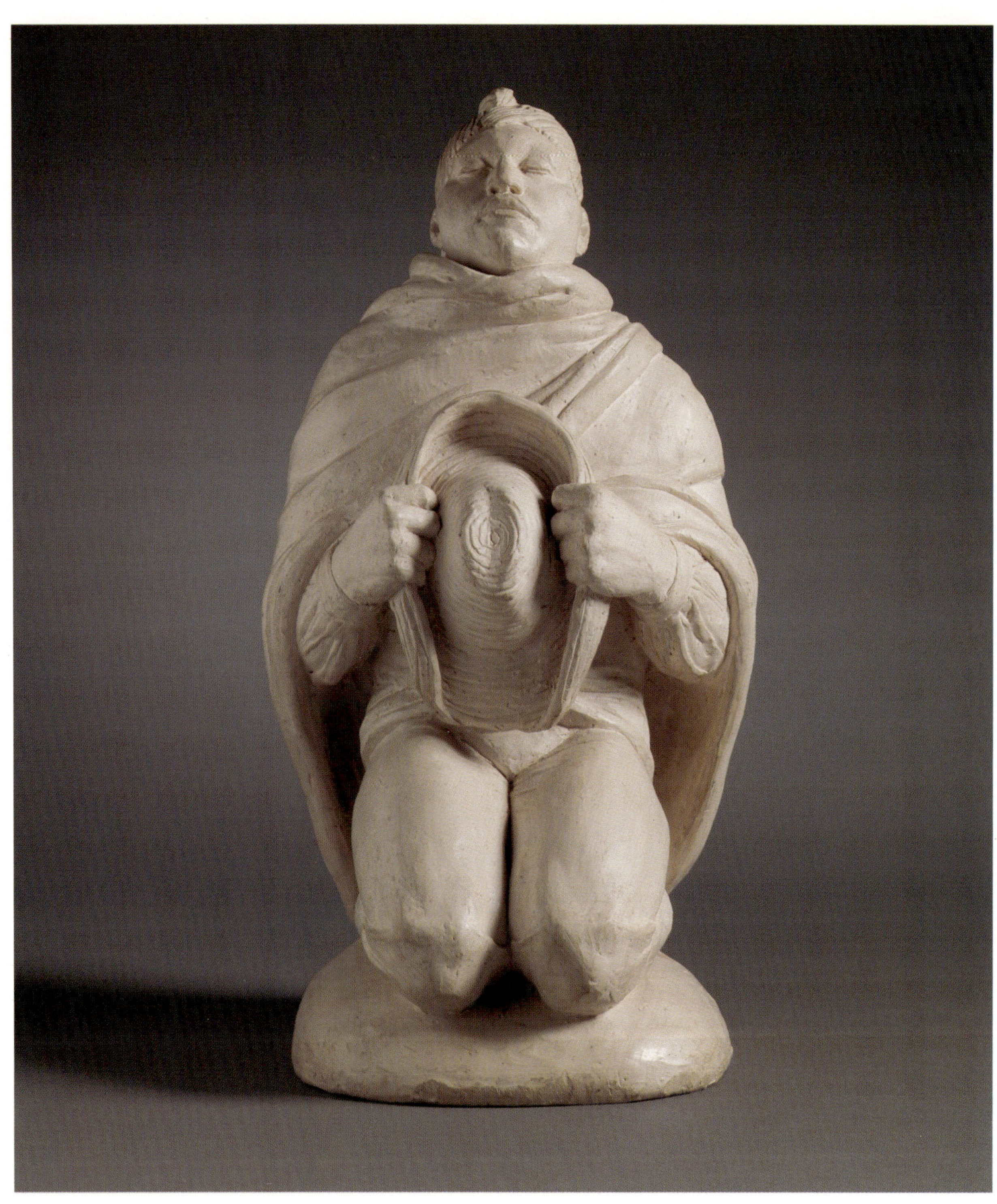

Peon Praying
1932 - 1933
Terracotta with Wax Polish Finish
12 ¾ inches
Courtesy of San Diego Museum of Art

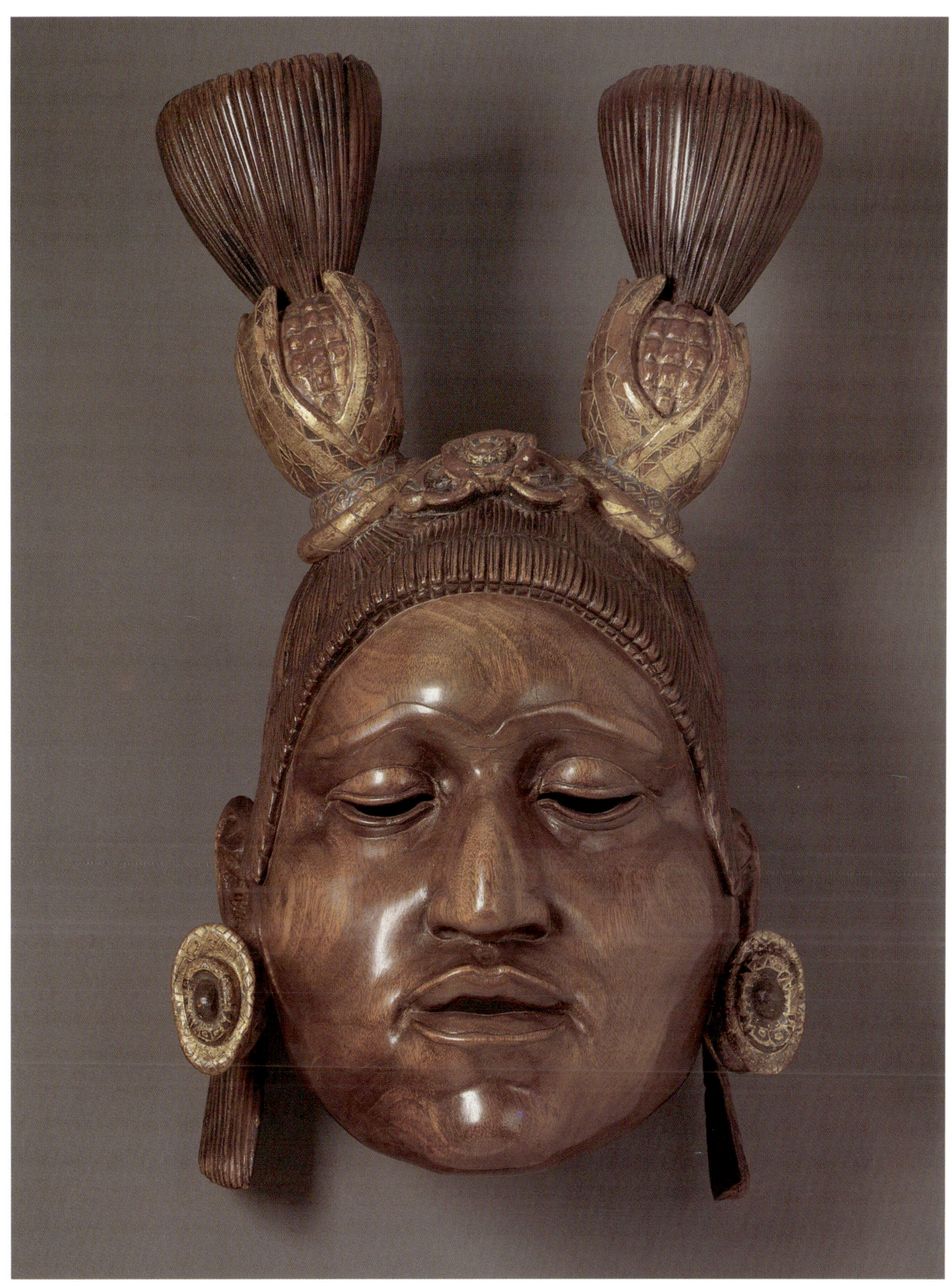

Aztec Bride
1933
Polychrome Mahogany
21 x 11 ½ x 9 ½ inches
San Diego Historical Society
Bequest of Florence Hord

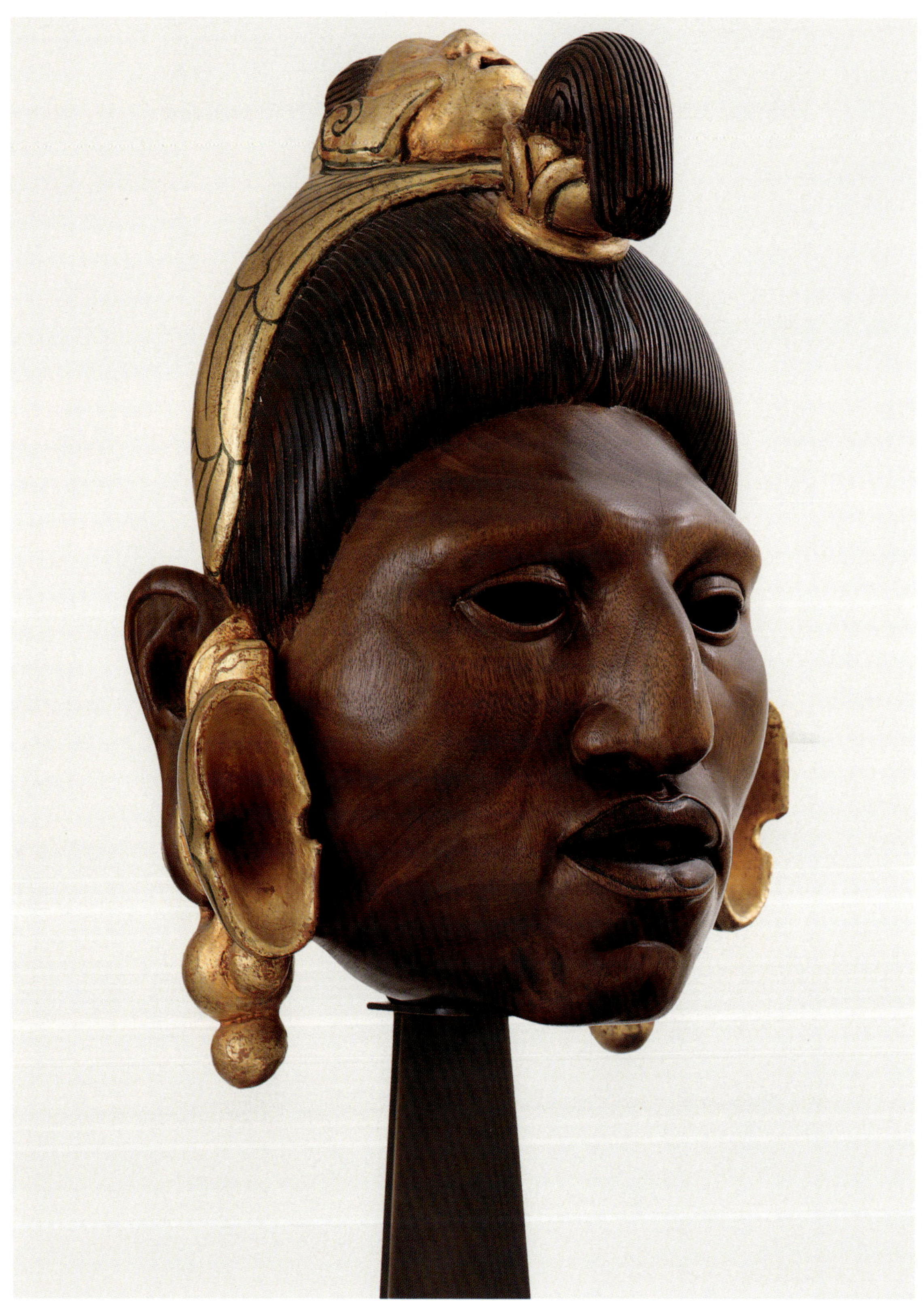

Mayan Mask
1933
Polychrome Mahogany
14 ¾ inches
Courtesy of Steve Turner Gallery
Los Angeles, California

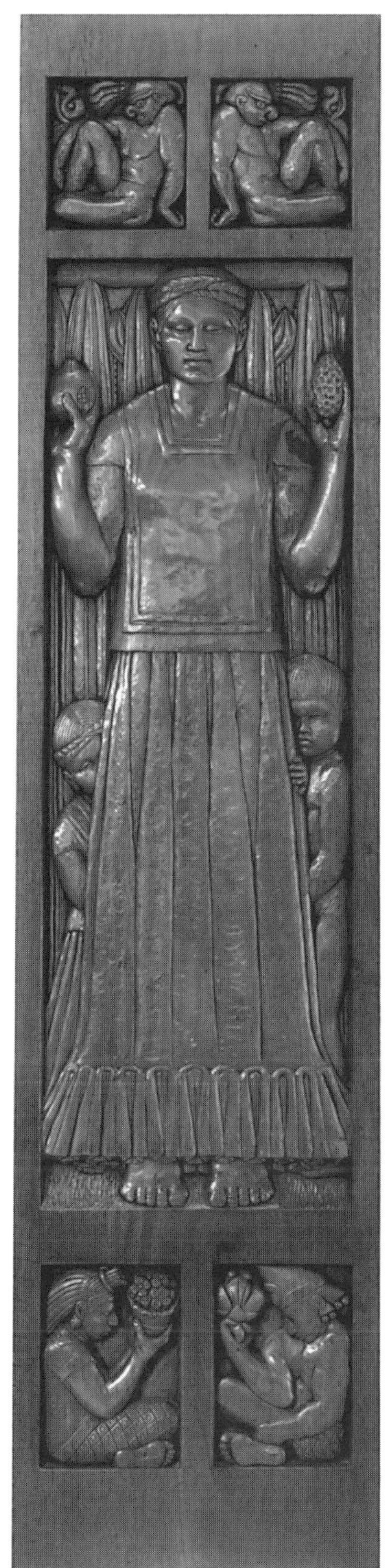
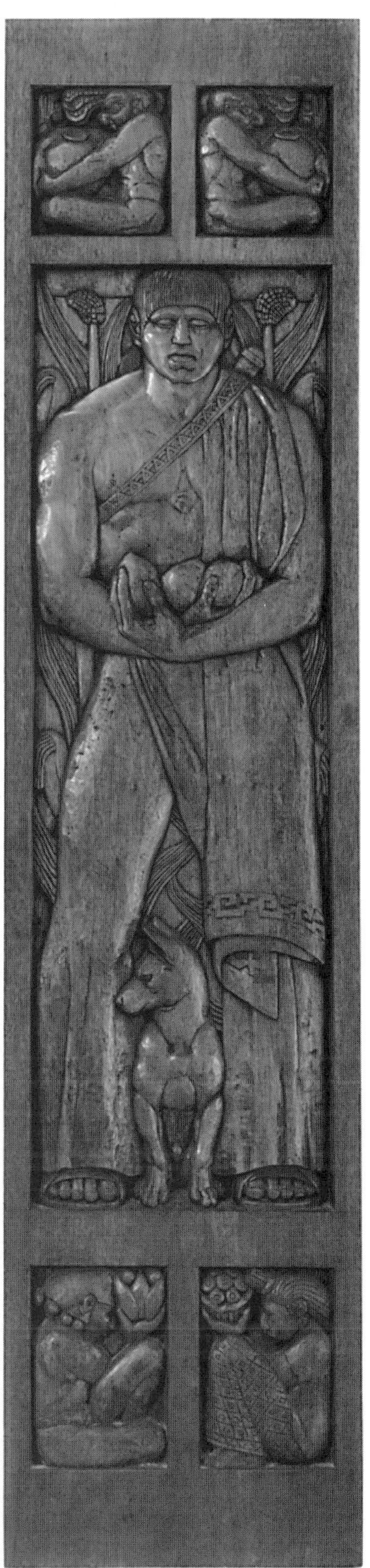

Indigenas
1933
Mahogany Door Panels
Each 72 x 17 x 2 inches
Courtesy of Tobey C. Moss Gallery
Los Angeles, California

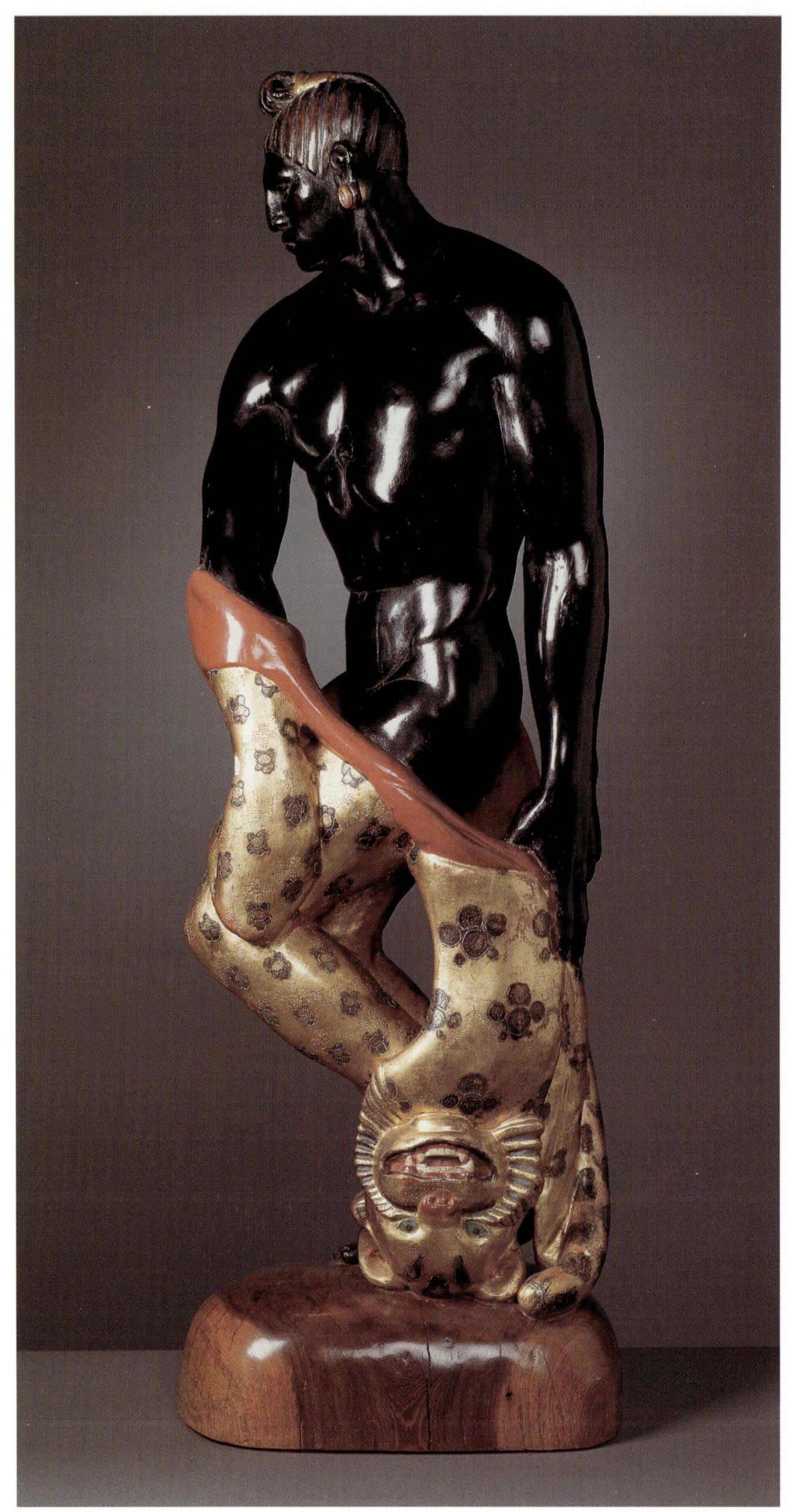

Tropic Cycle
1933
Tropical Mexican Hardwood with Gesso and Lacquer
32 inches
Courtesy of Edward-Dean Museum of Decorative Arts
Cherry Valley, California

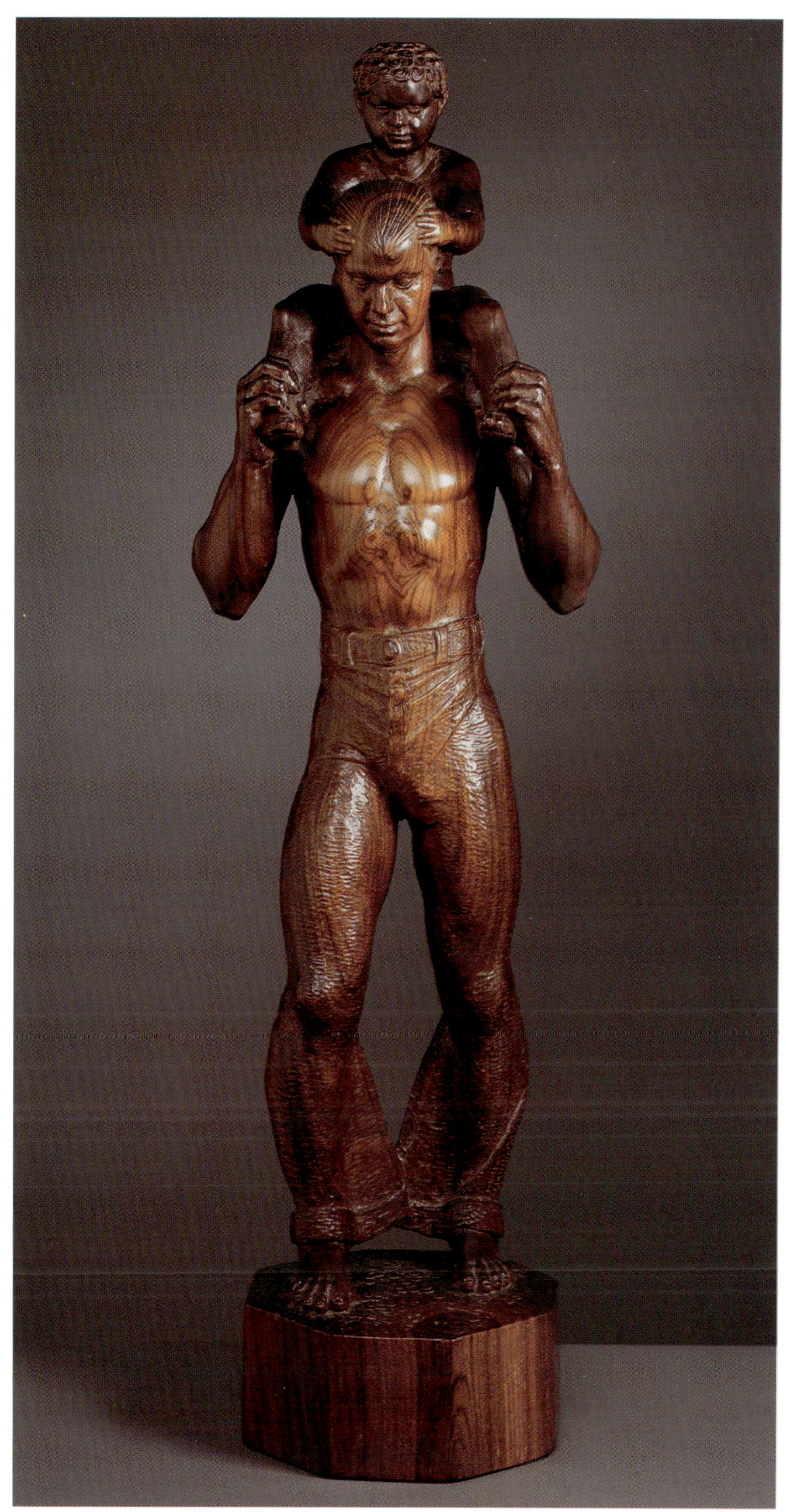

Indian Father and Son or Christopher Group
1935
Mexican Rosewood
27 inches
Courtesy of Edward-Dean Museum of Decorative Arts
Cherry Valley, California

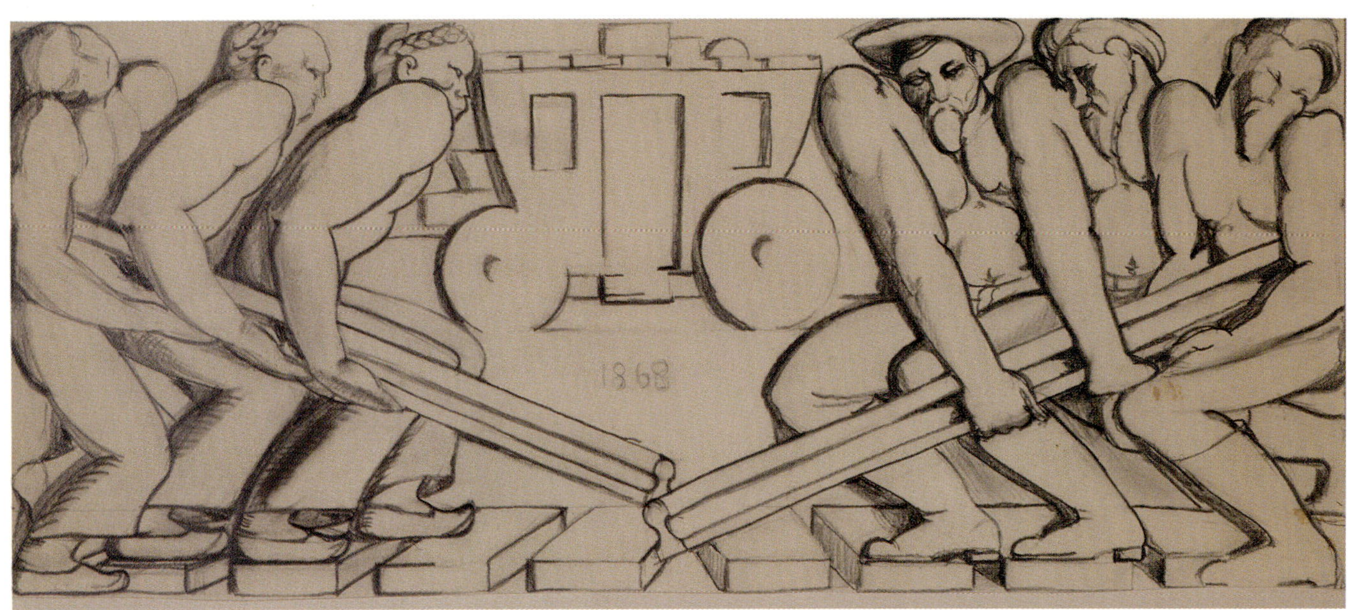

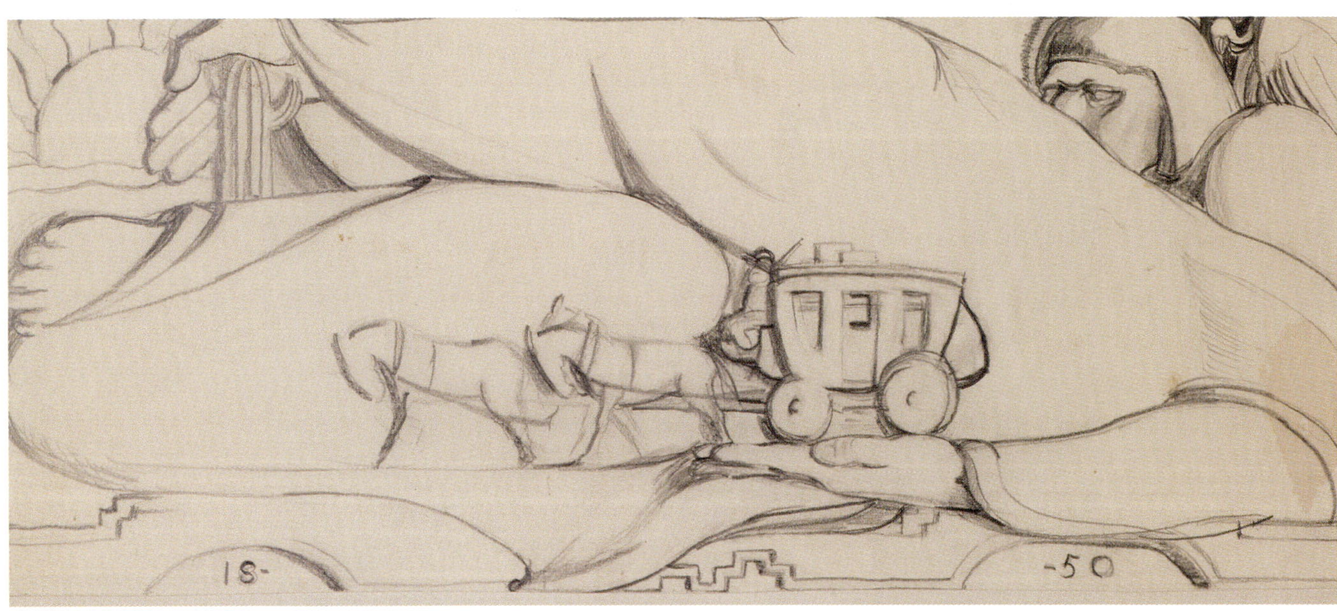

Transportation of the Mail
1936
Five studies: Railroad 1868, Stagecoach 1850, Pony Express 1860, Riverboat, and Airplane 1936
Pencil on Paper
Each 10 x 24 inches
San Diego Historical Society
Gift of Florence Hord and Homer Dana

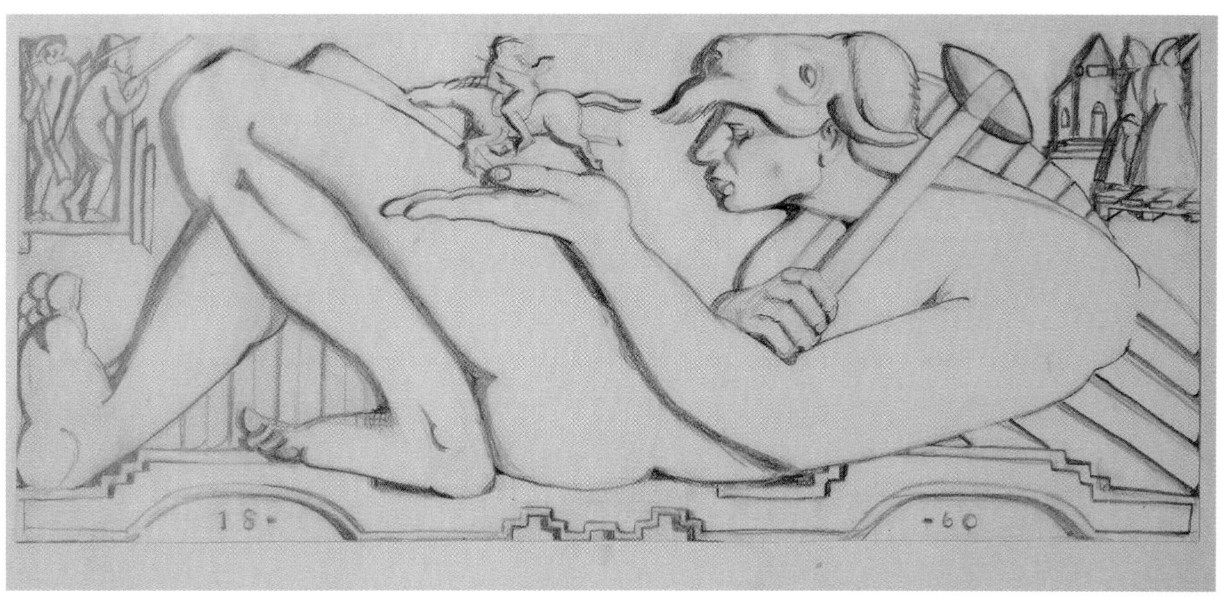
18
60

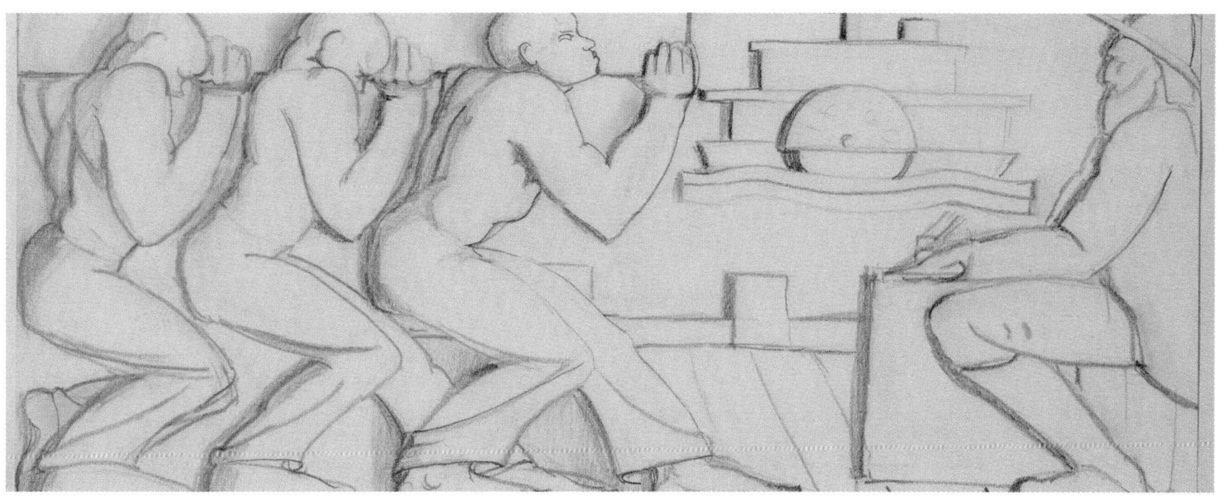

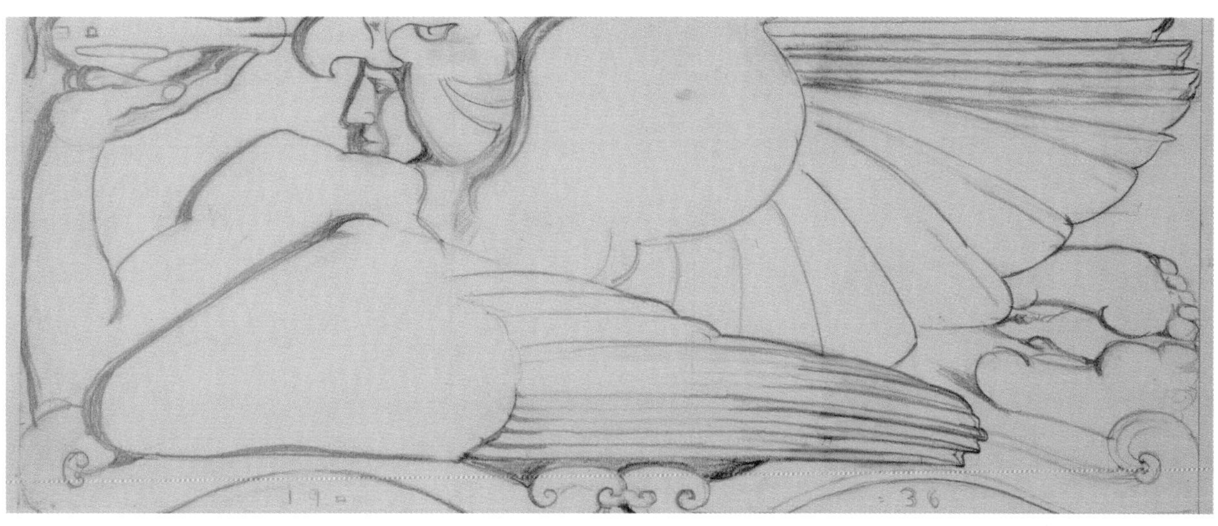
19
36

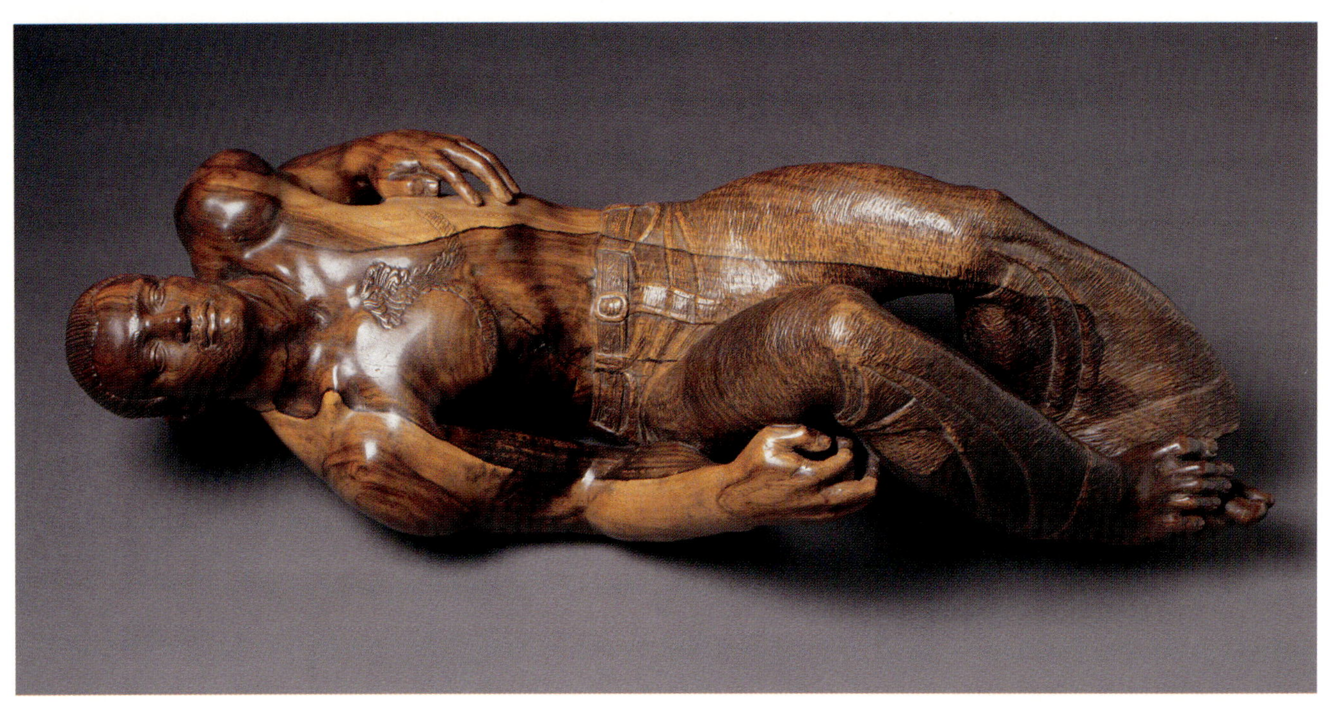

Siesta at Noon
1936
Mexican Rosewood
10 ½ x 25 ½ inches
Courtesy of San Diego Museum of Art

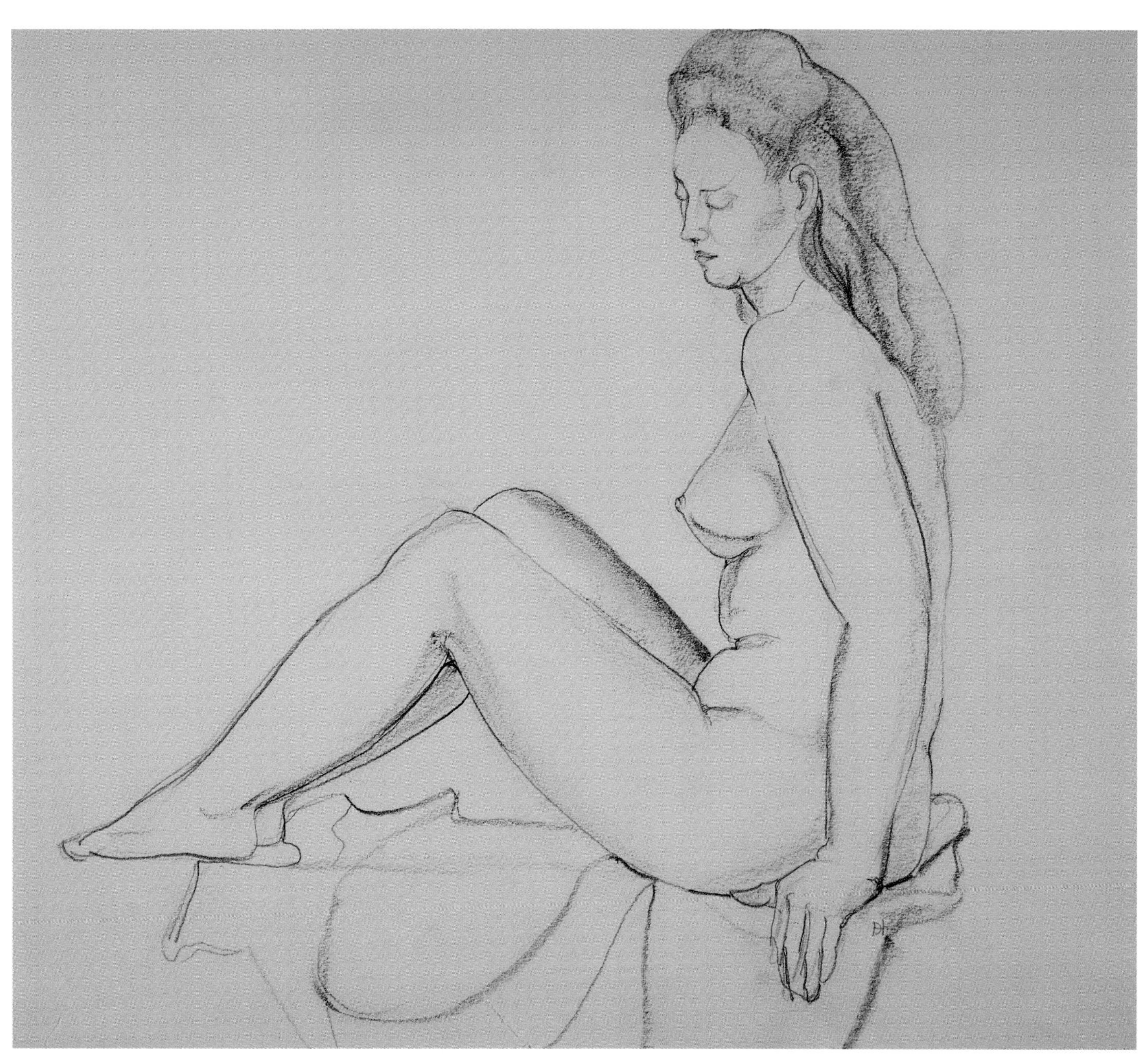

Nude Figure
1936
Pencil on Paper
11 X 14 inches
Courtesy of Bente and Gerald E. Buck
The Buck Collection

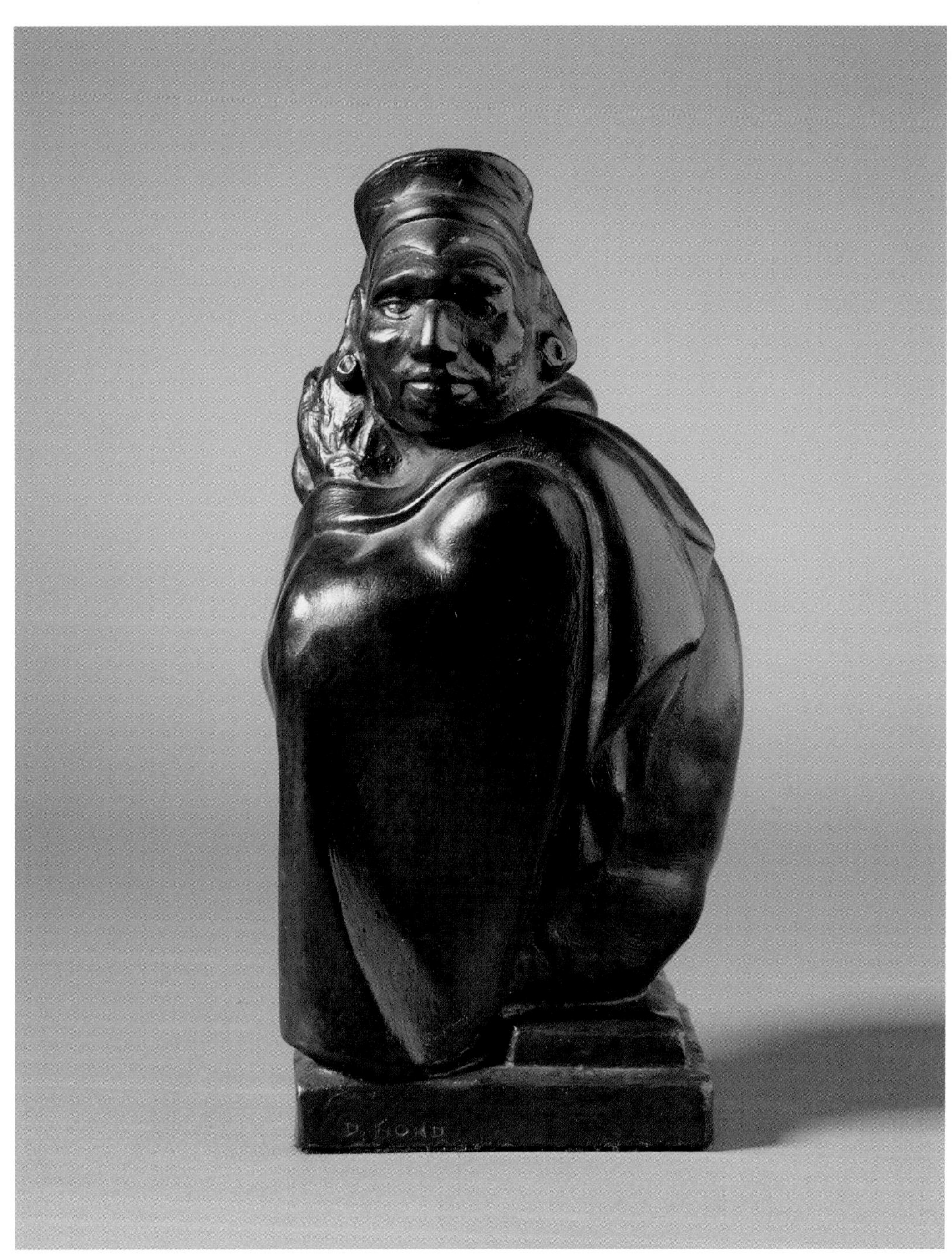

Aztec miniature
date unknown
Bronze
10 inches
Anonymous loan

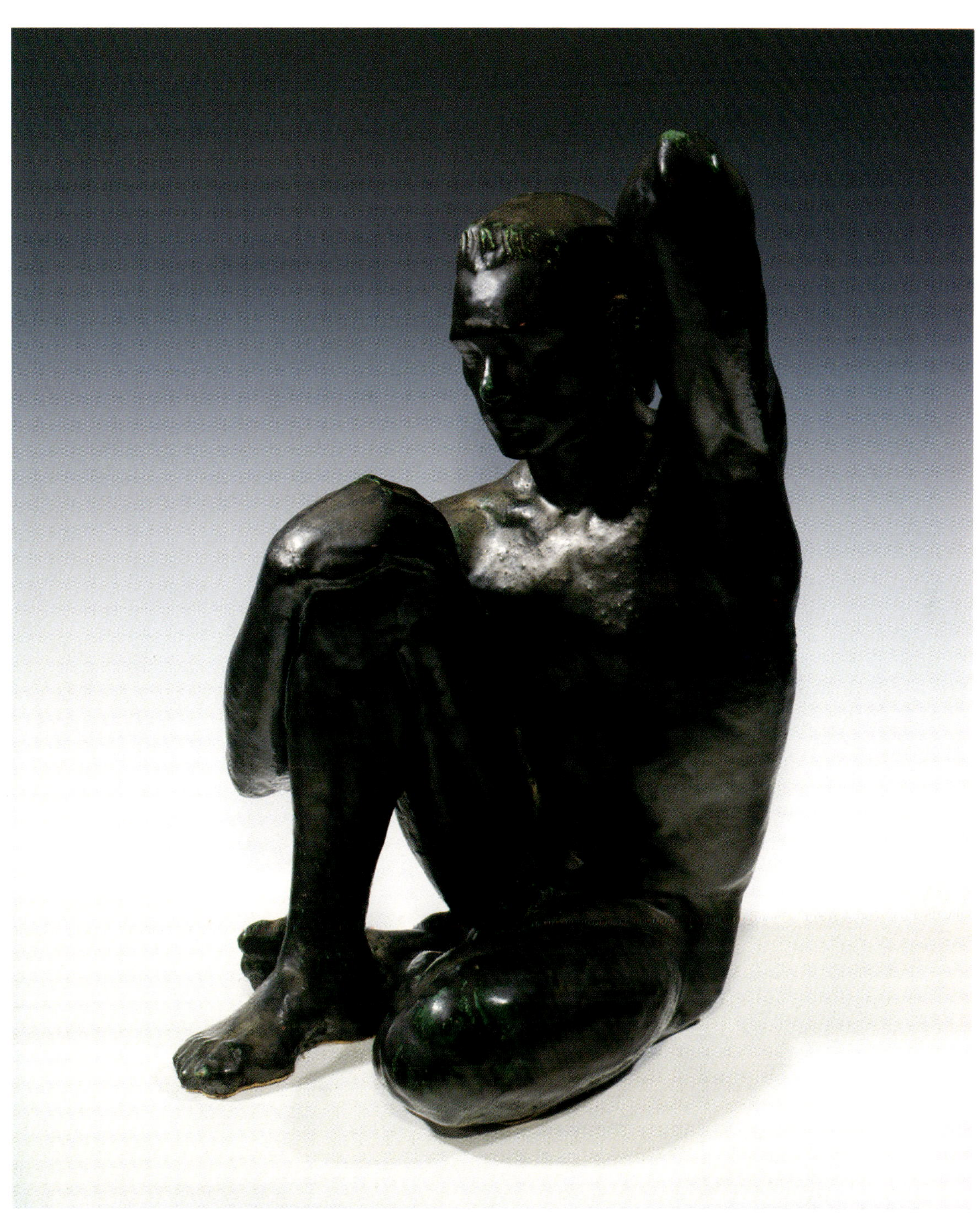

Portrait of Fred Sietz
1937
Glazed Terracotta
17 inches
Courtesy of Bente and Gerald E. Buck
The Buck Collection

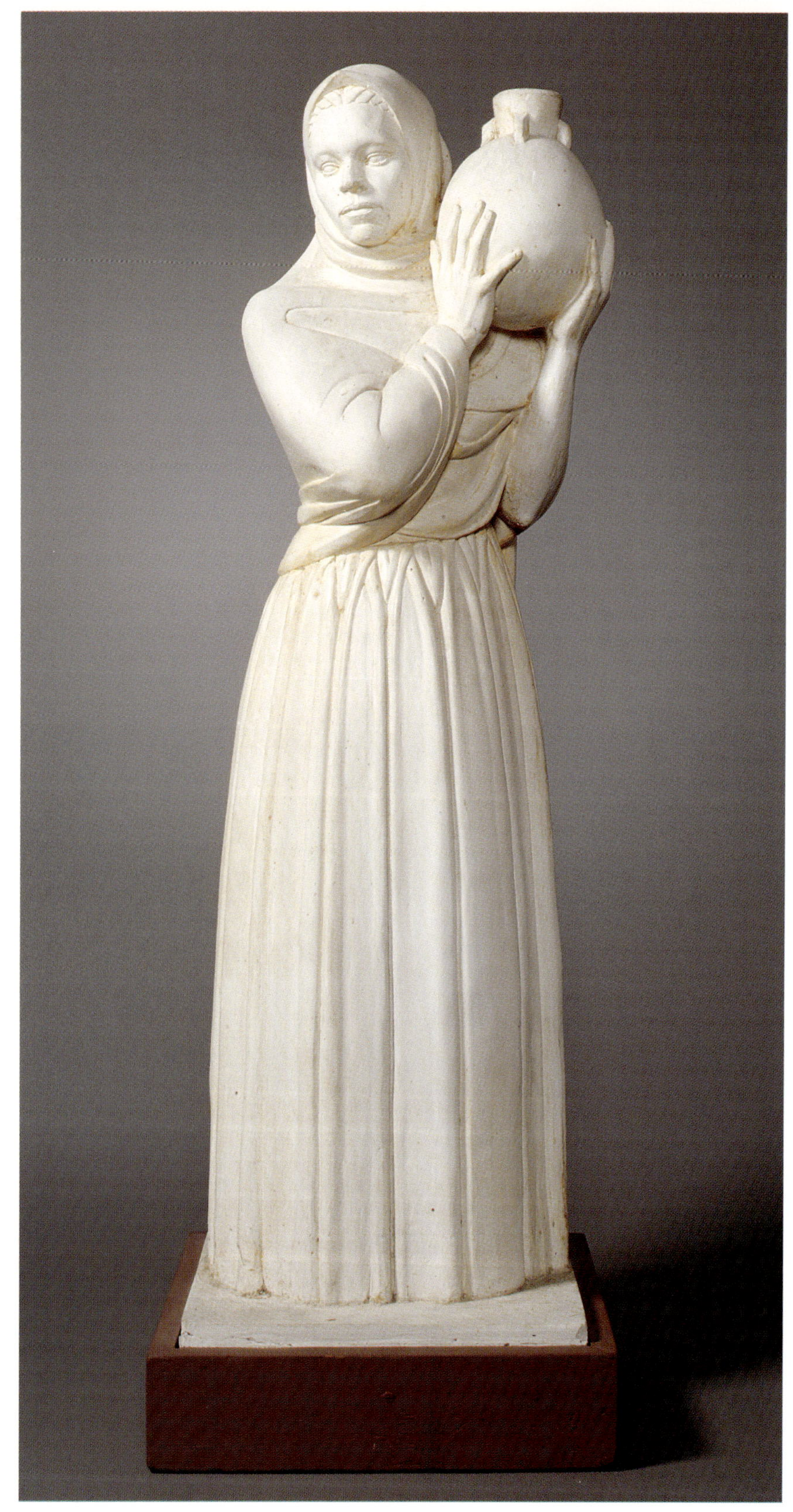

Guardian of the Waters draped maquette
1937
Plaster
39 inches
San Diego Historical Society

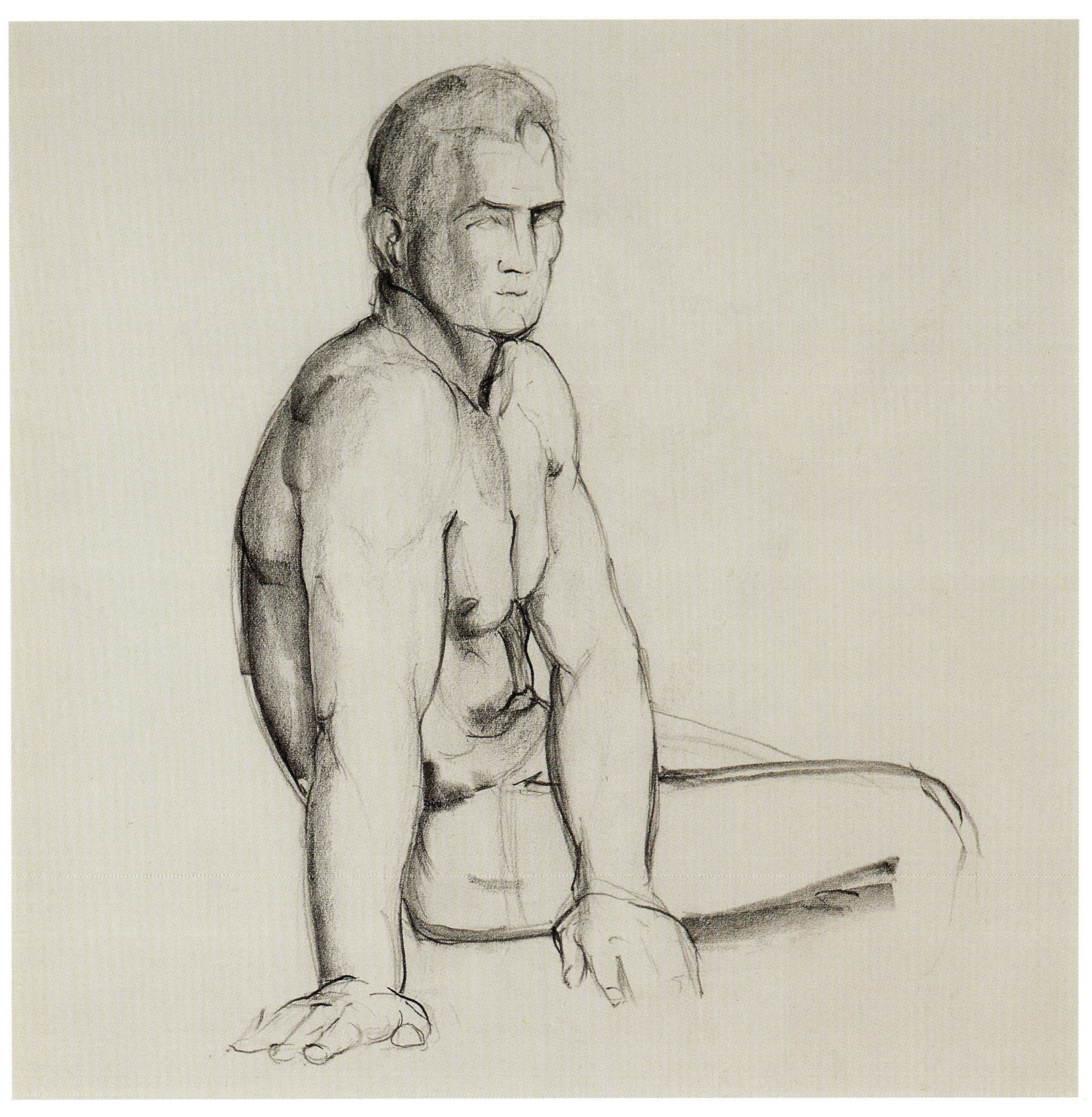

Nude Figure
1937
Pencil on Paper
11 X 14 inches
Courtesy of Bente and Gerald E. Buck
The Buck Collection

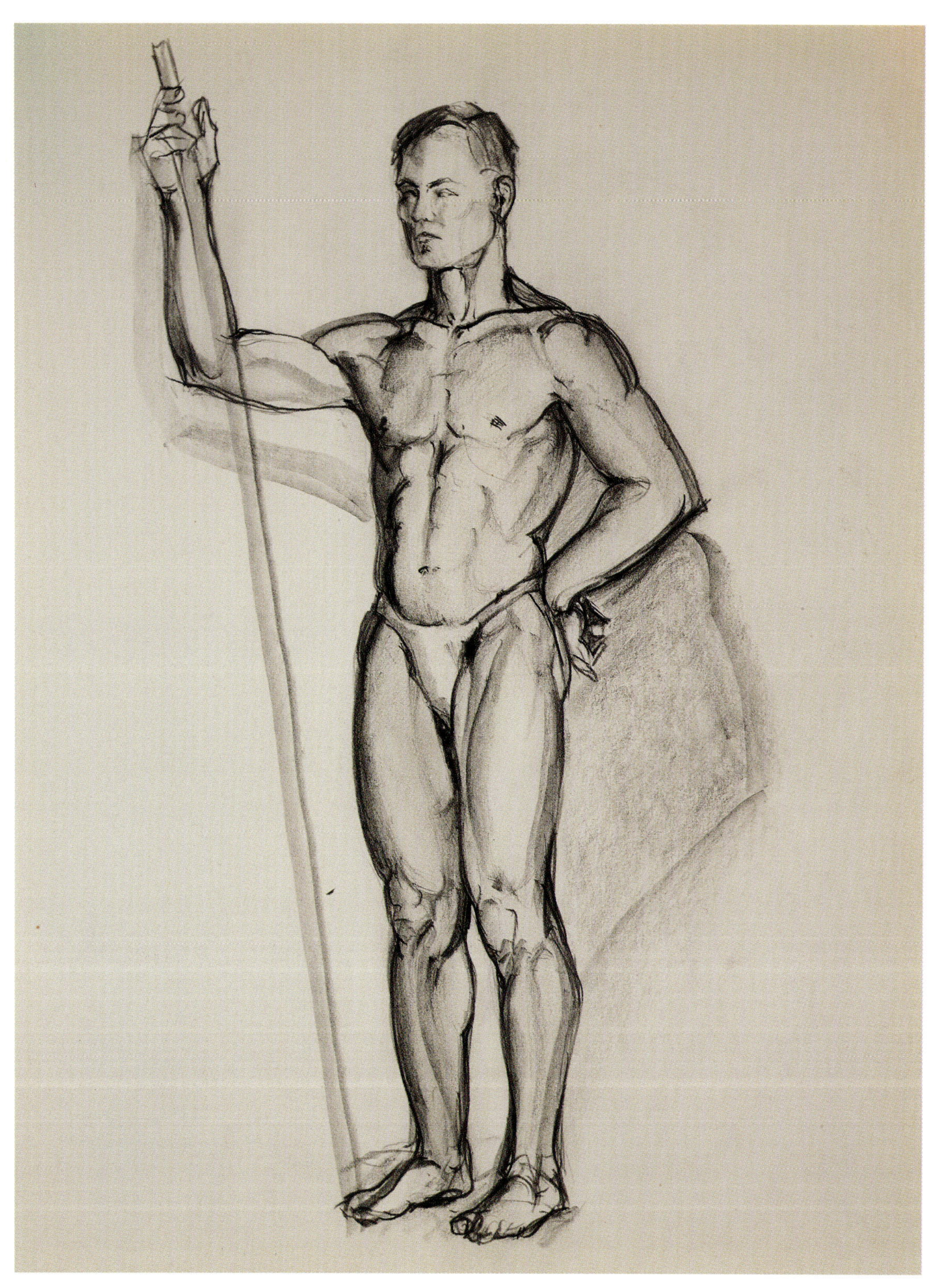

Male Figure
1937
Pencil on Paper
11 X 14 inches
Courtesy of Bente and Gerald E. Buck
The Buck Collection

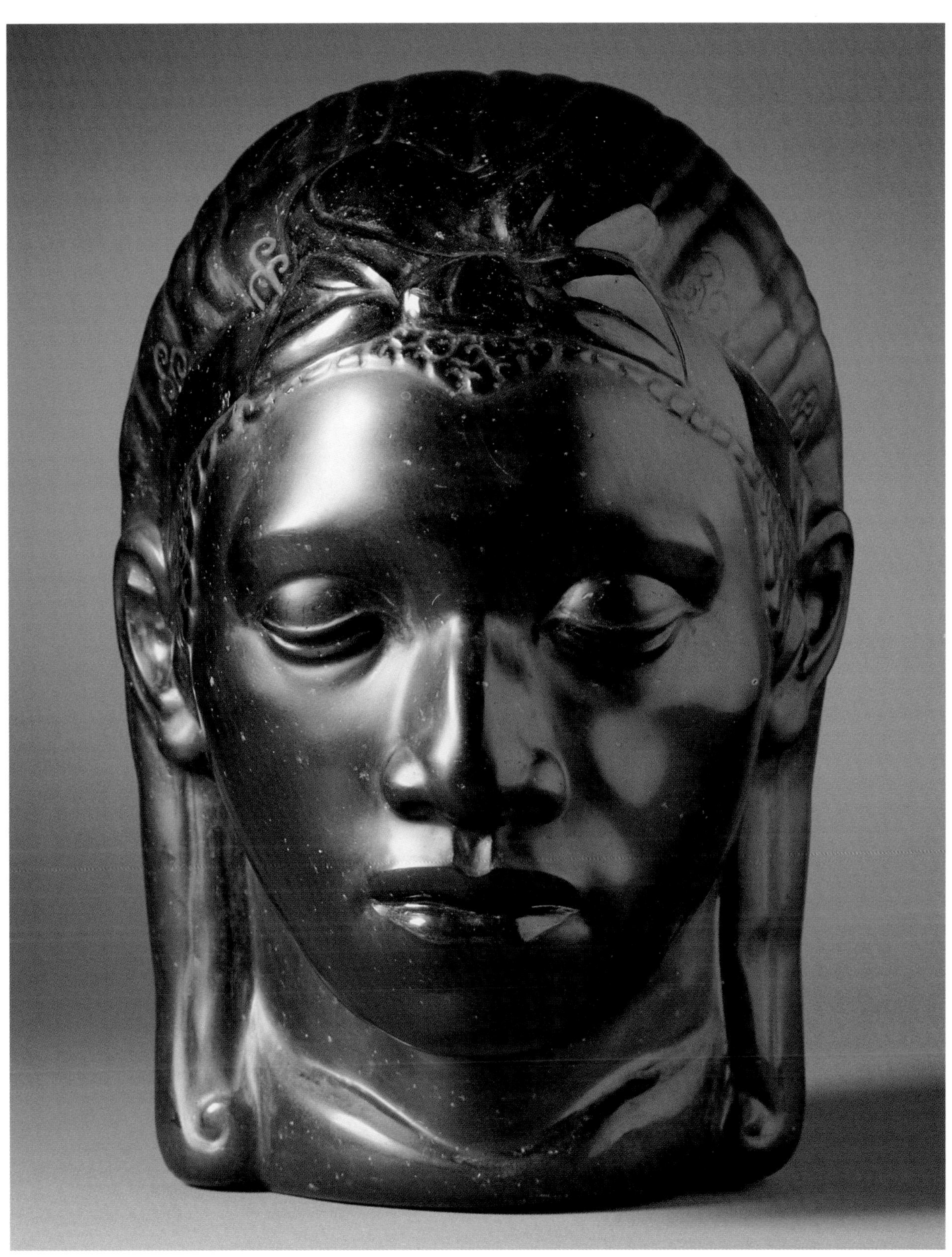

La Cubana
1937 - 1939
Obsidian
11 ¾ inches
Courtesy of San Diego Museum of Art

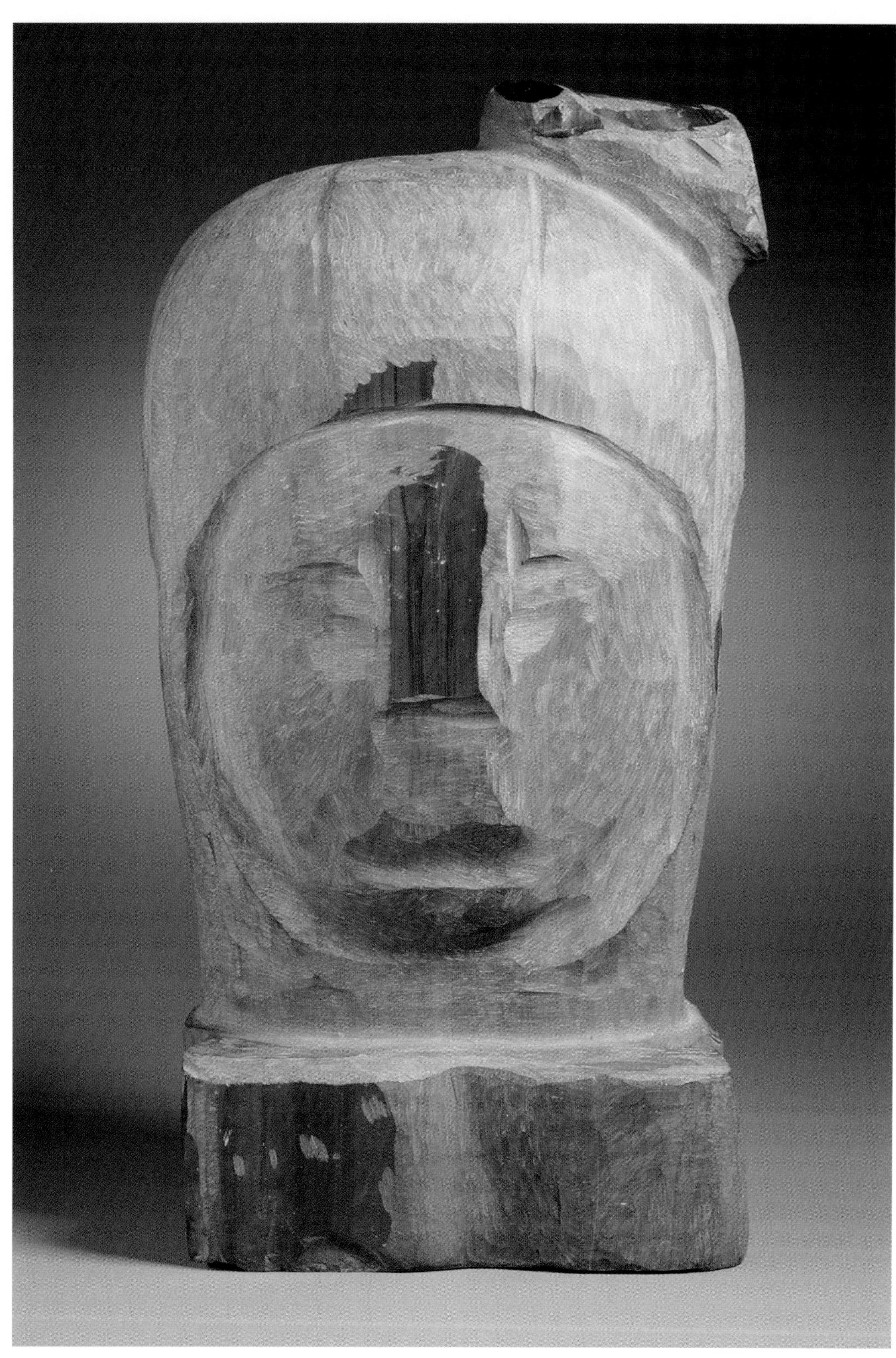

Unfinished Mask
date unknown
Obsidian
12 inches
San Diego Historical Society
Gift of Florence Hord and Homer Dana

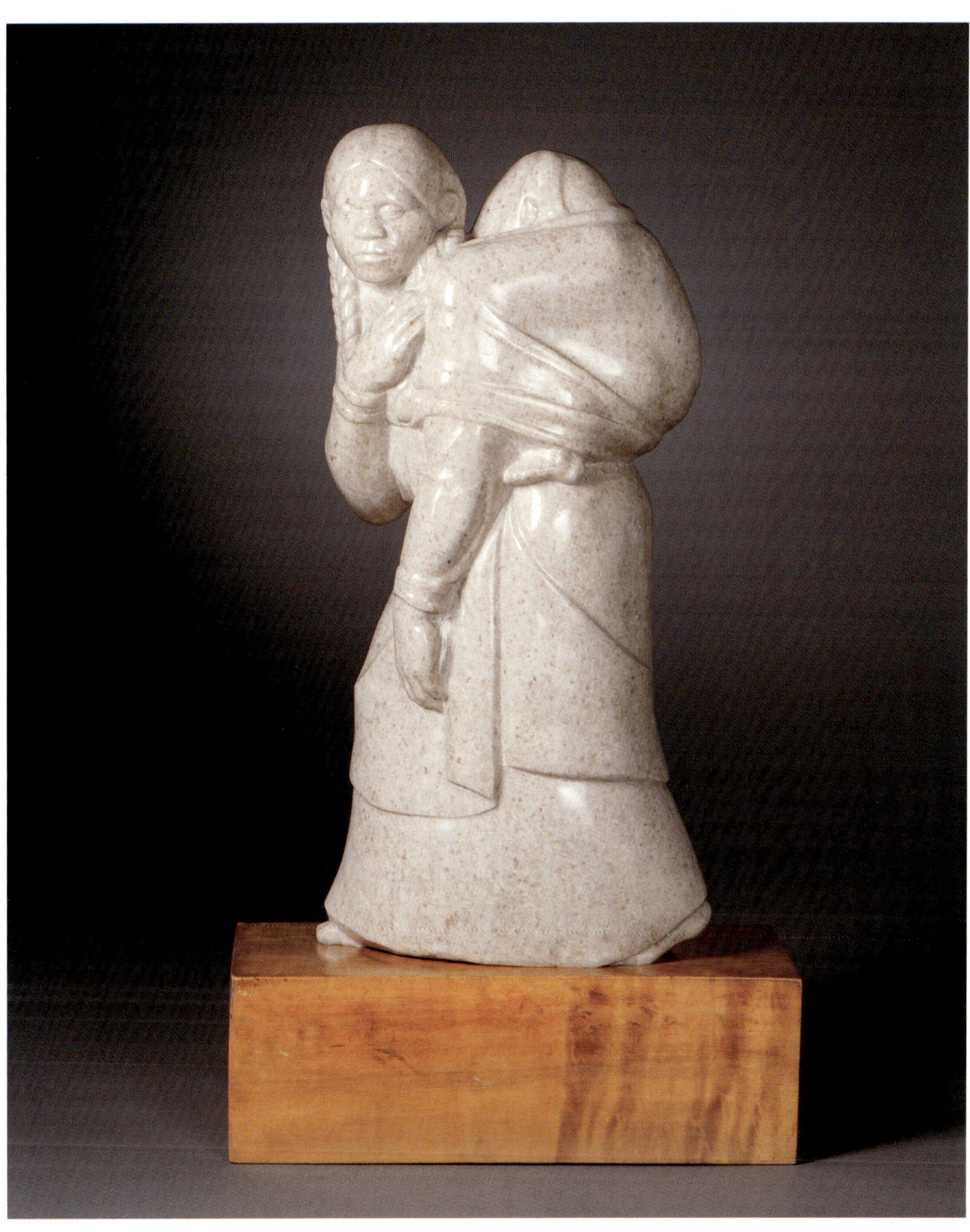

Mexican Mother and Child
1938
Tennessee Pink and Beige Marble
16 ¾ inches
Courtesy of Franklin D. Roosevelt Library
Hyde Park, New York

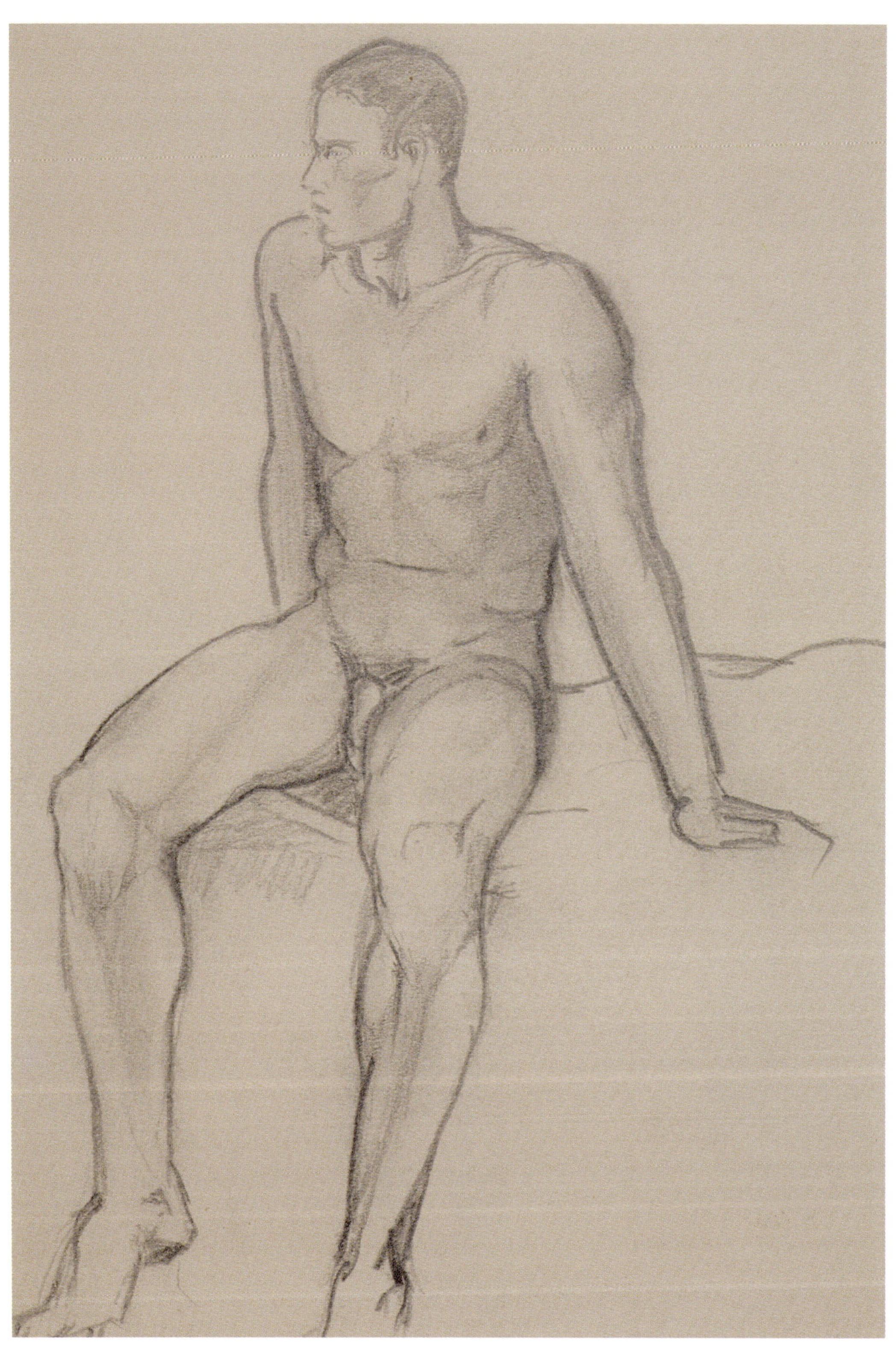

Nude Figure
1939
Pencil on Paper
8 ½ x 11 inches
Anonymous loan

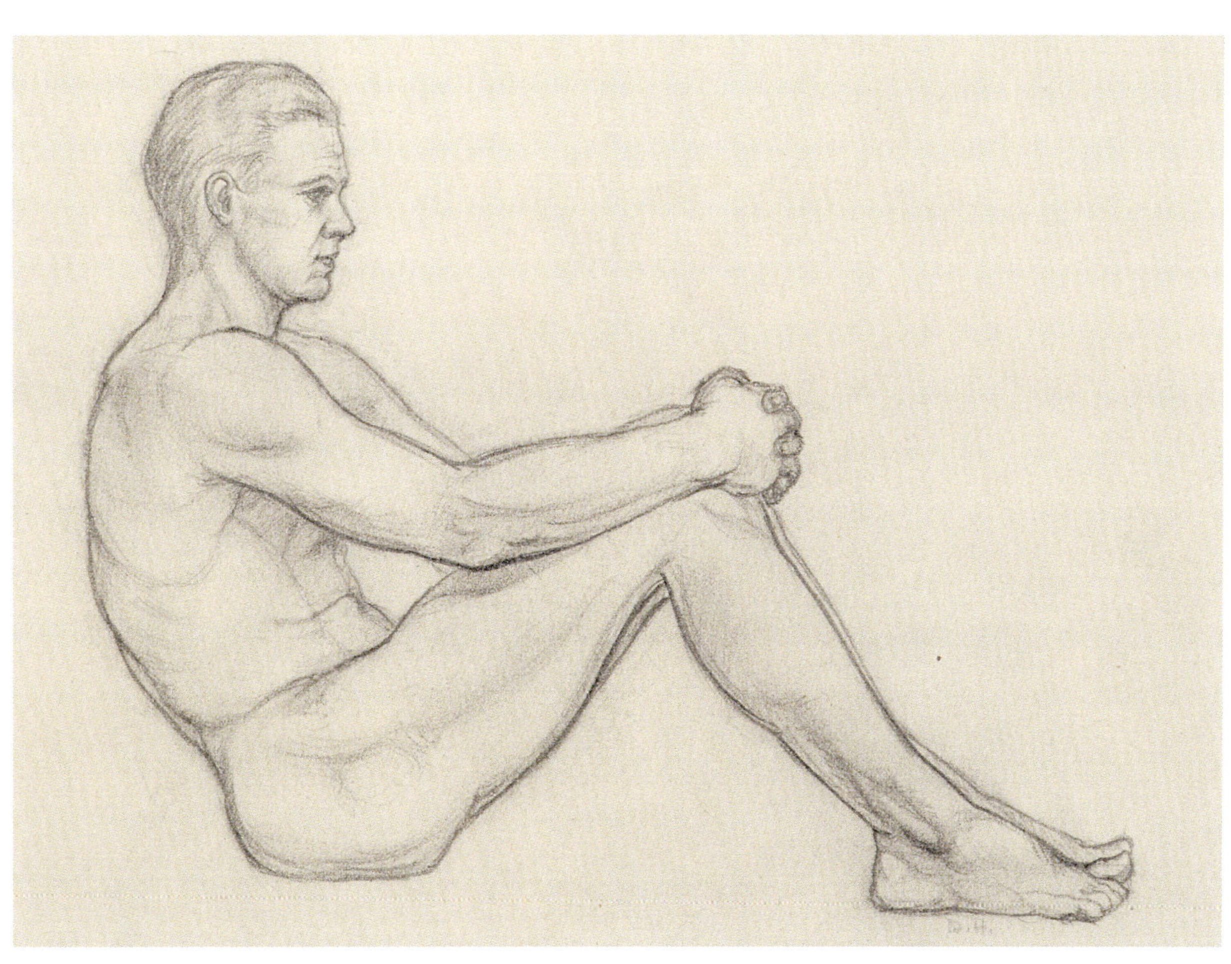

Nude Figure
1939
Pencil on Paper
8 ½ x 11 inches
San Diego Historical Society
Gift of George A. Baker

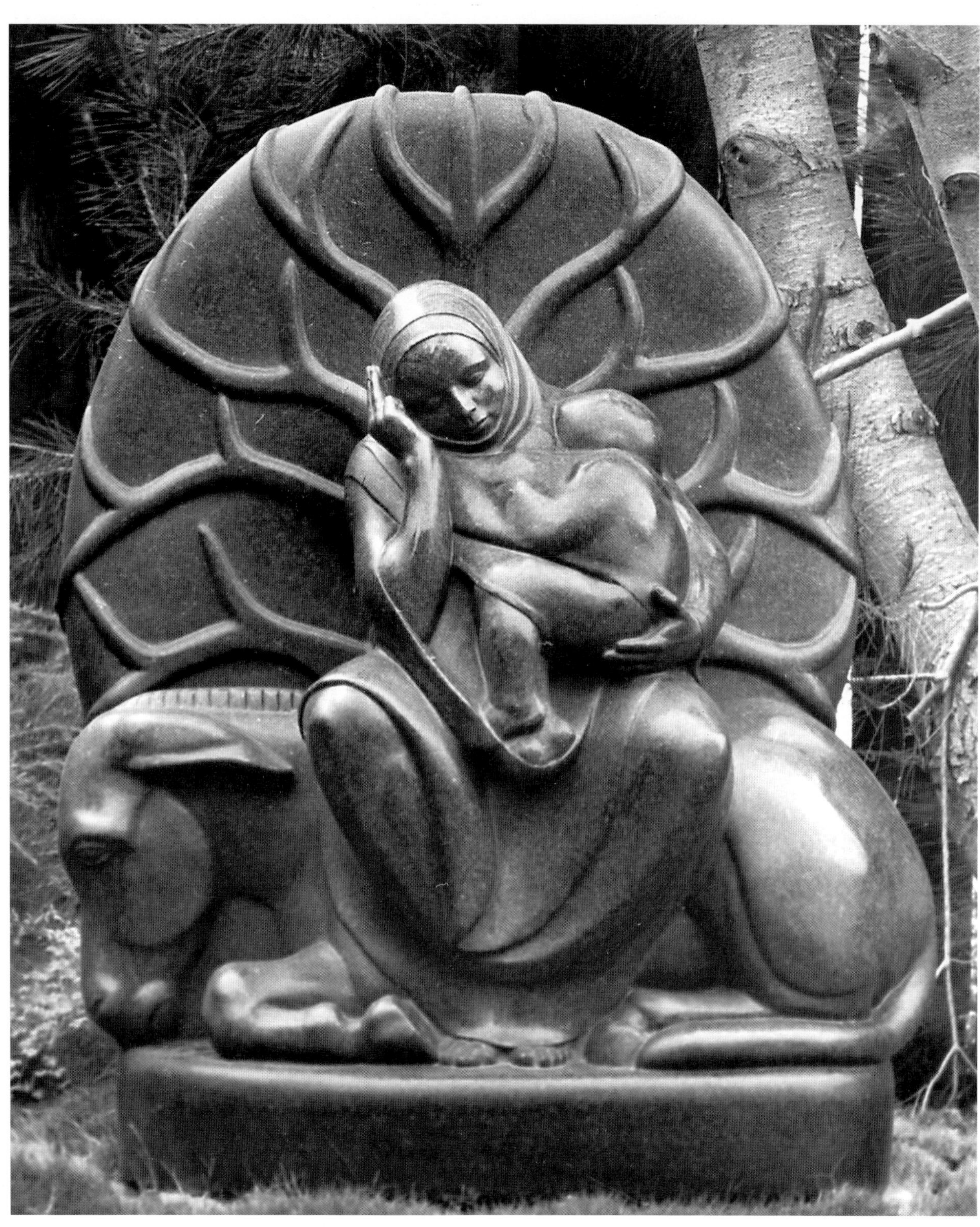

Rest on the Flight into Egypt
1939 - 1941
Black Diorite
30 inches
Courtesy of San Diego Zoological Society

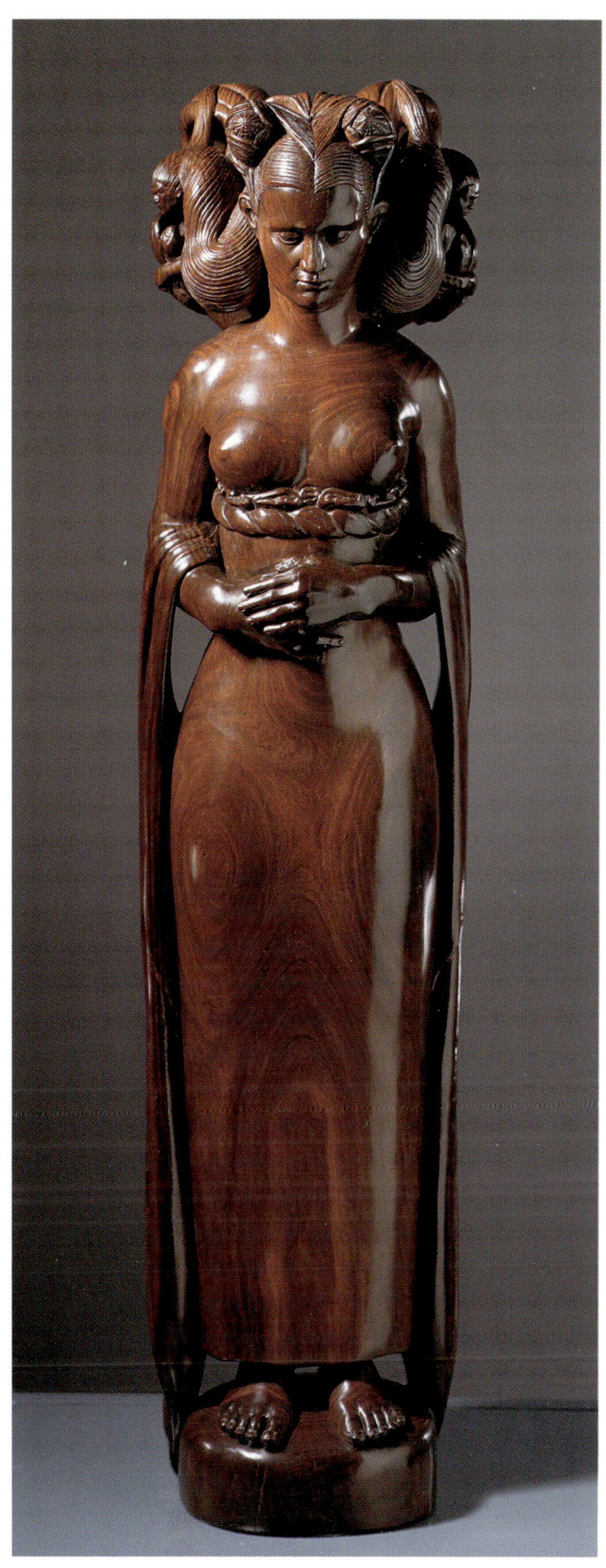

Corn Goddess
1942
Lignum Vitae
40 inches
Courtesy of Los Angeles County Museum of Art
Anonymous Gift

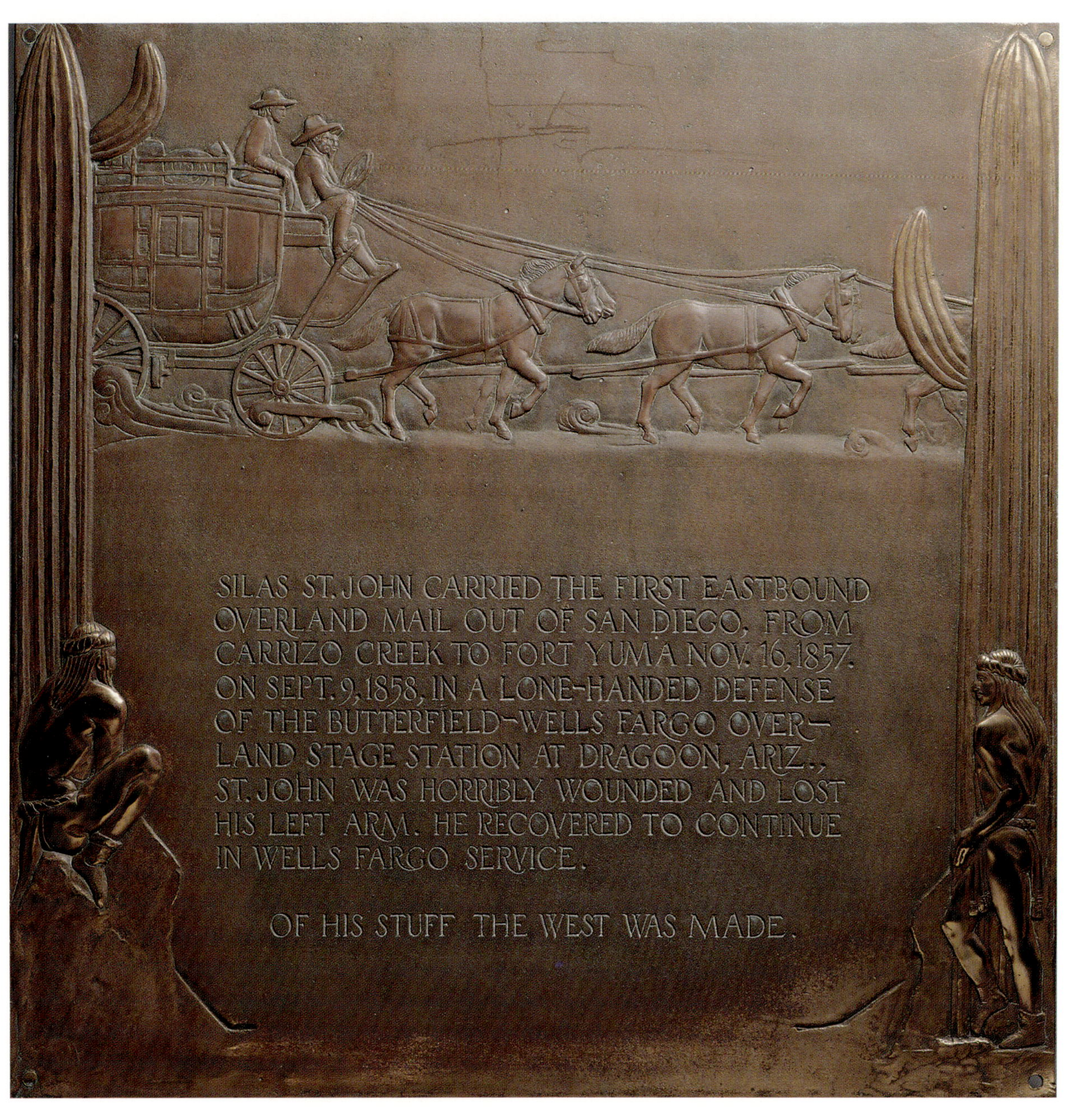

Silas St. John Memorial
1942
Bronze
24 inches
San Diego Historical Society
Gift of Benjamin C. Cheney

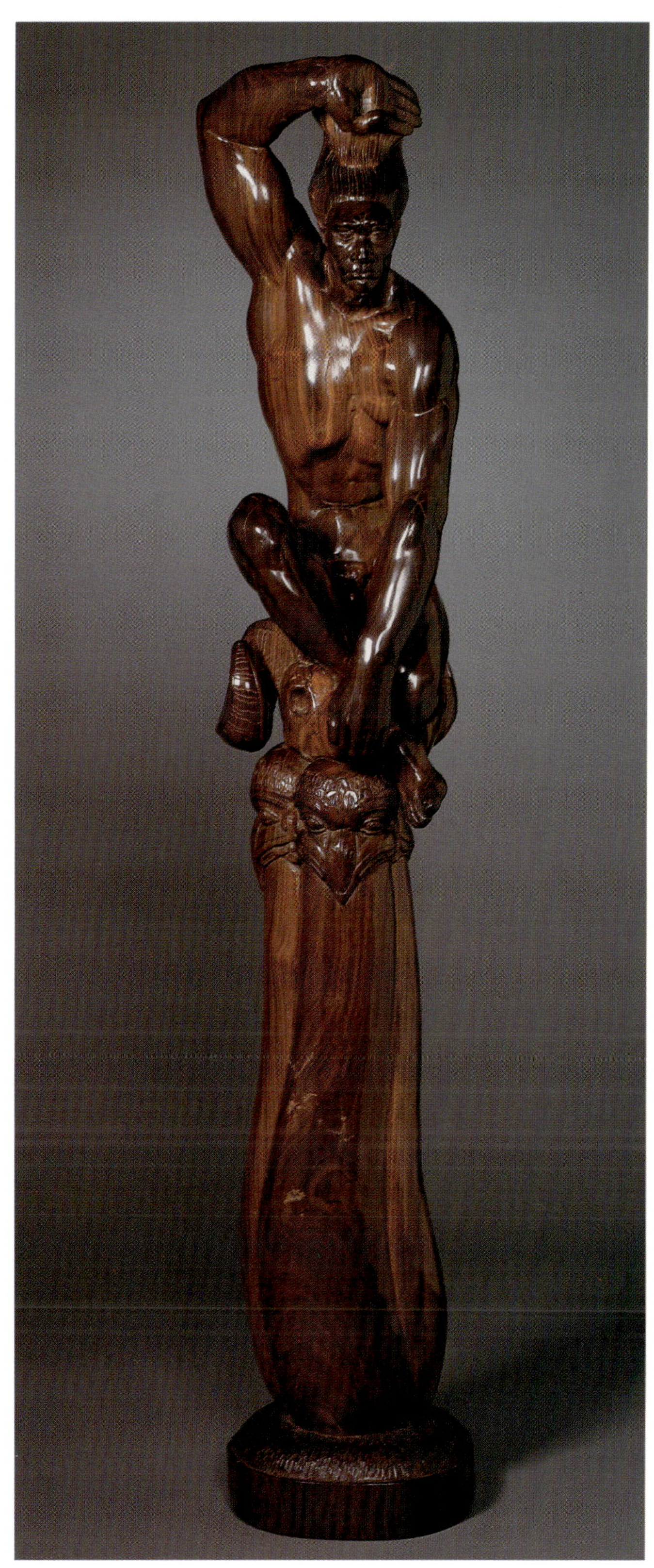

Midday Sun or *Noon Sun*
1942
Lignum Vitae
47 inches
Anonymous loan

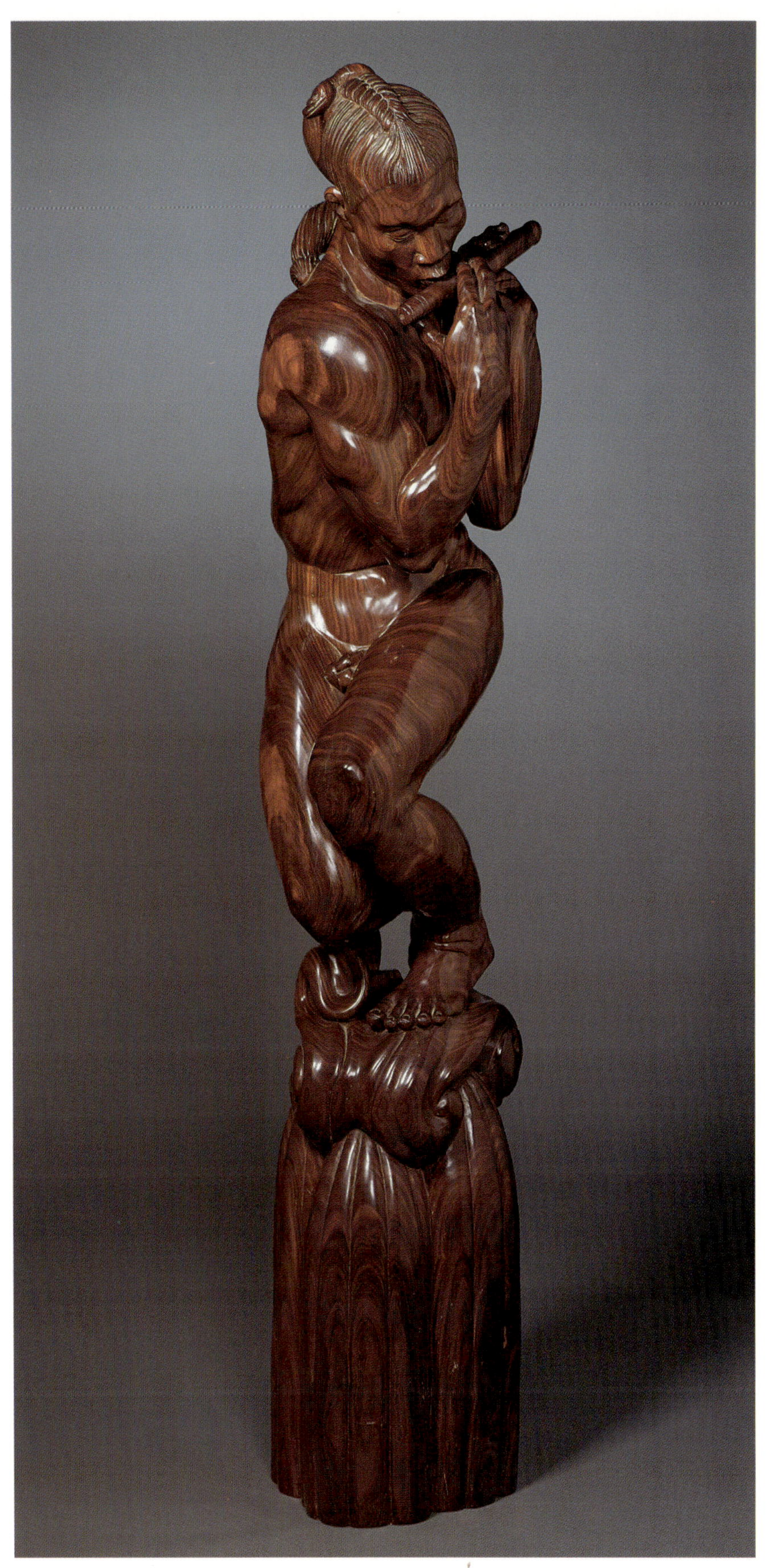

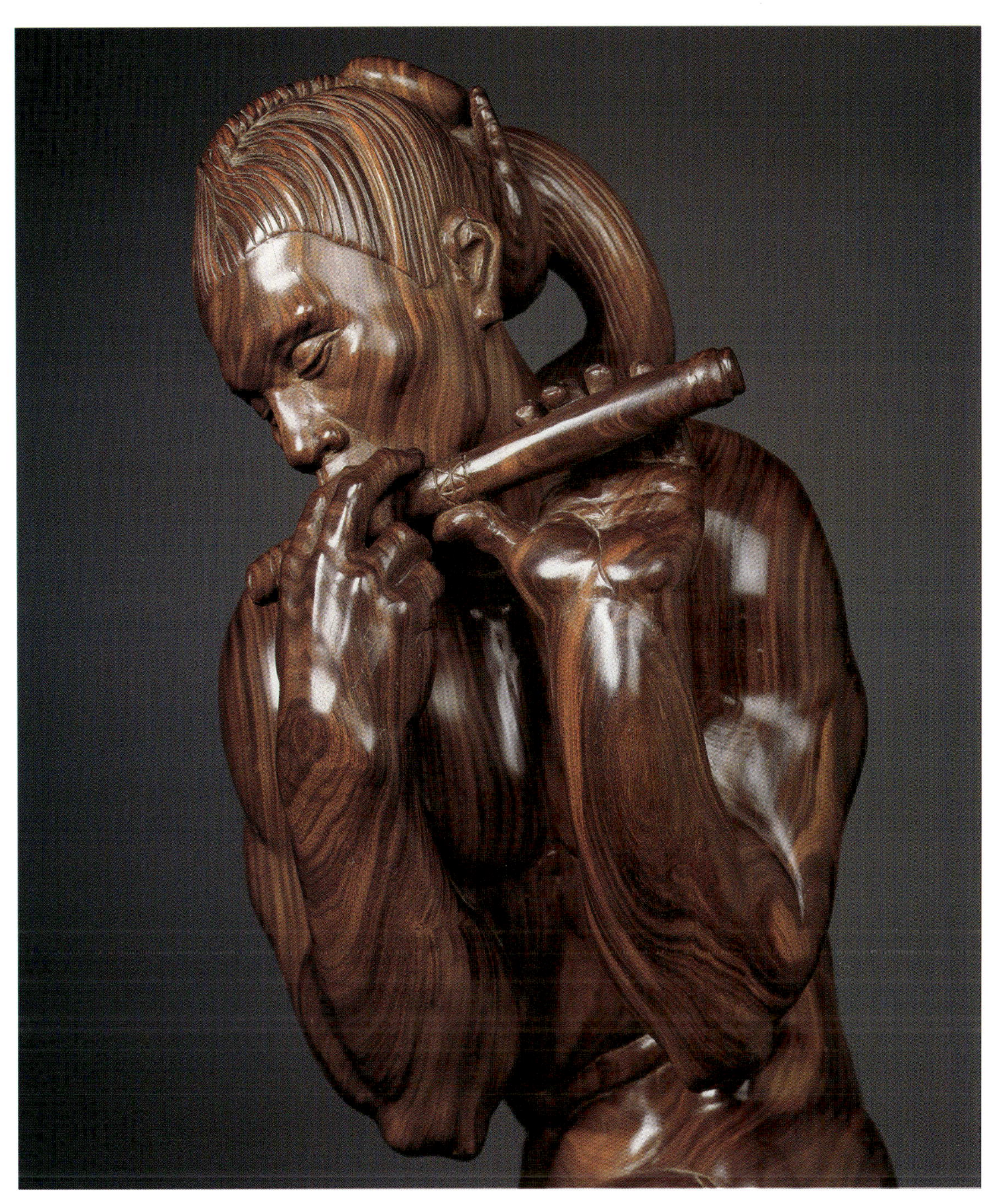

Desert Night, the Wind
1944
Lignum Vitae
43 inches
Anonymous loan

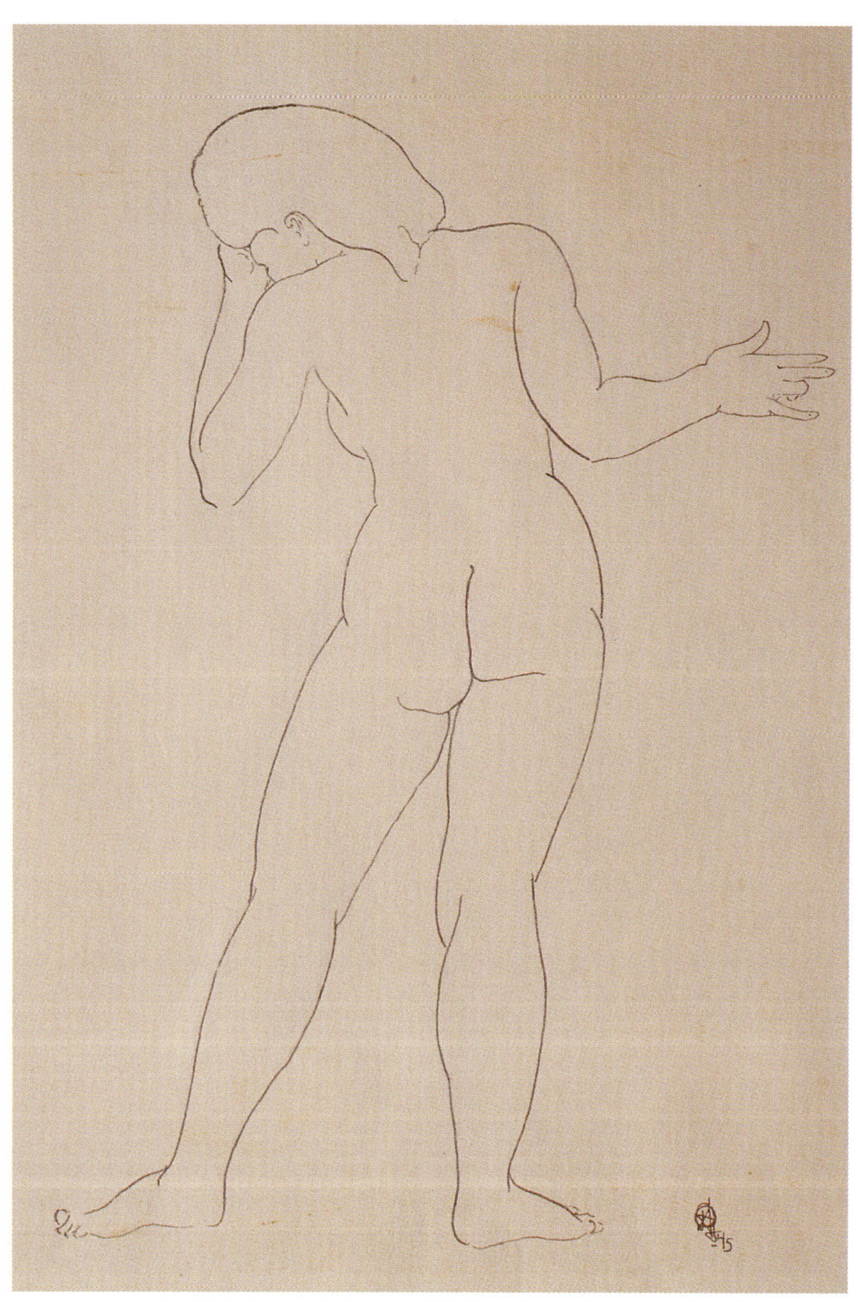

Nude Figure
1945
Pen on Paper
11 x 14 inches
Courtesy of San Diego Museum of Art

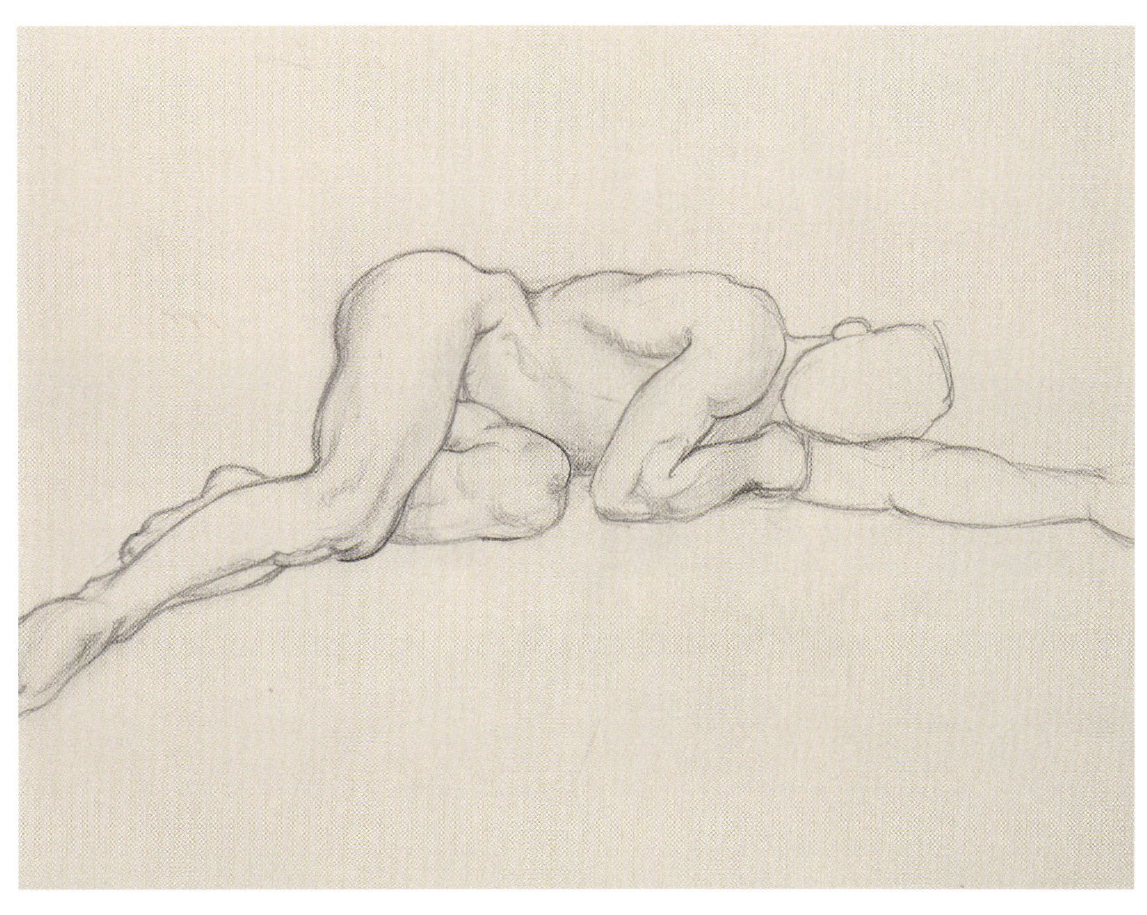

Nude Figure
1945
Pencil on Paper
11 x 14 inches
San Diego Historical Society
Gift of George A. Baker

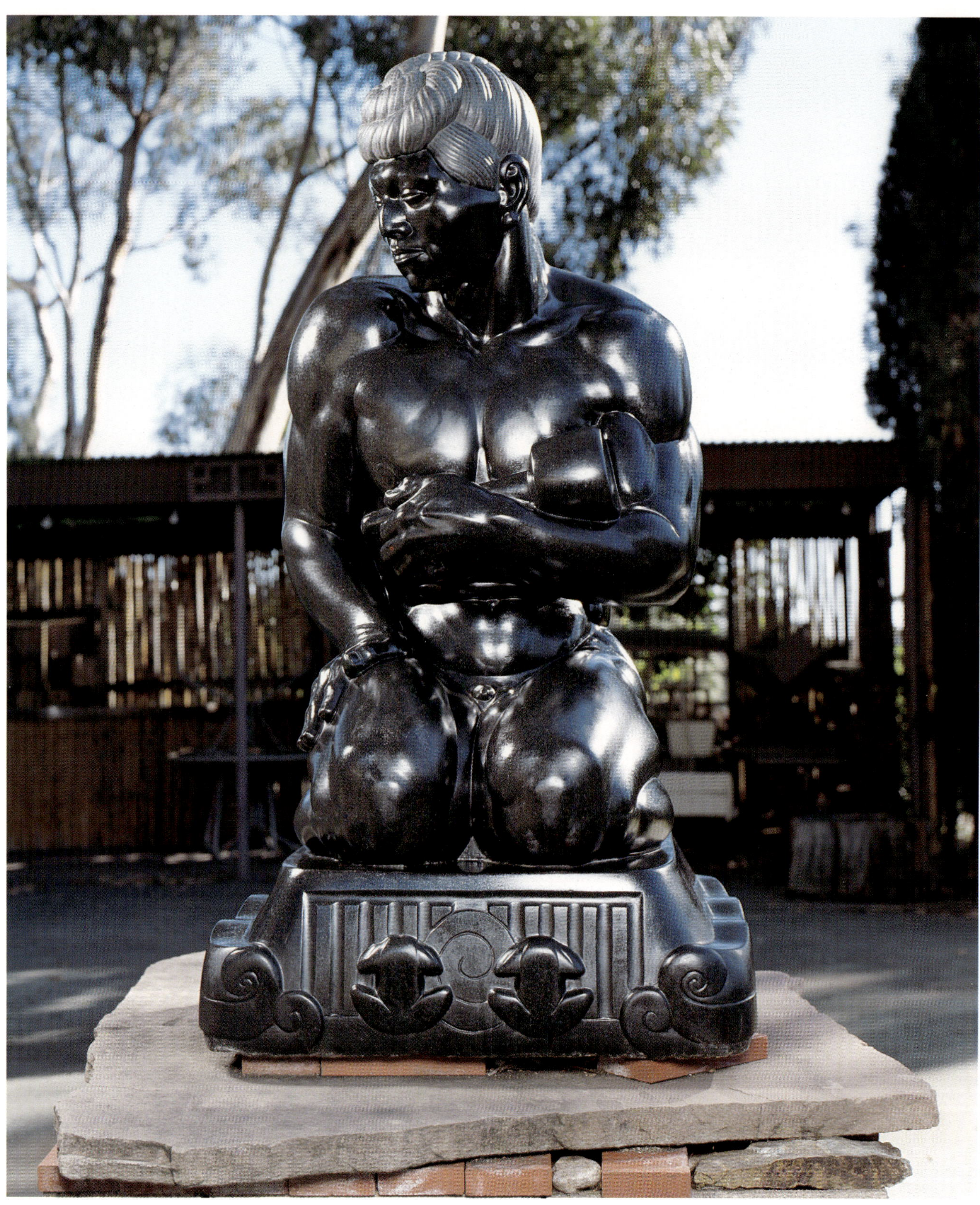

El Colorado, the Red One
1945
Diorite
53 inches
Courtesy of Bente and Gerald E. Buck
The Buck Collection

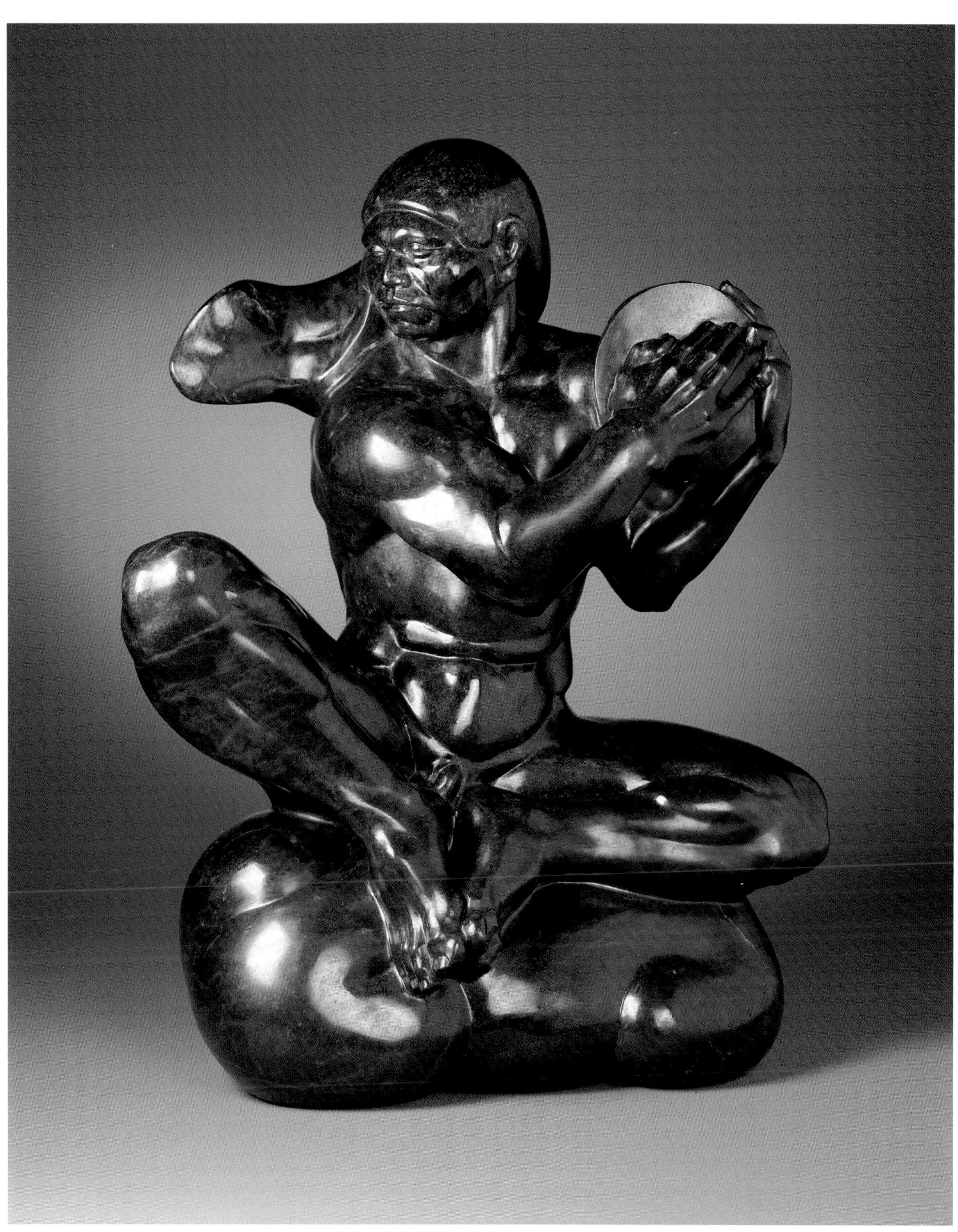

Thunder
1947
Spinach Green Nephrite Jade
20 x 16 inches
Courtesy of San Diego Museum of Art

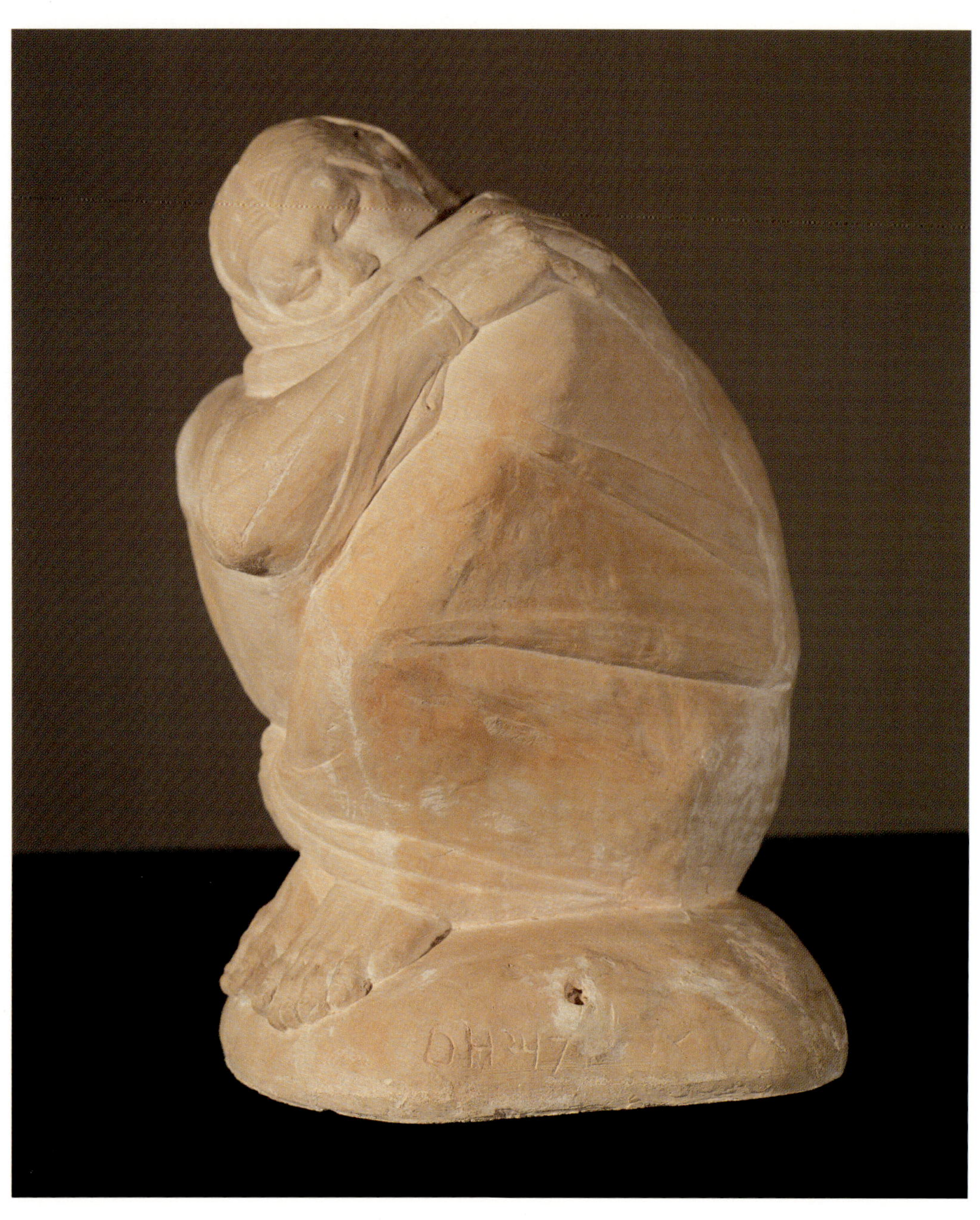

Spring Stirring
1947
Unfired Clay
13 inches
Courtesy of Bente and Gerald E. Buck
The Buck Collection

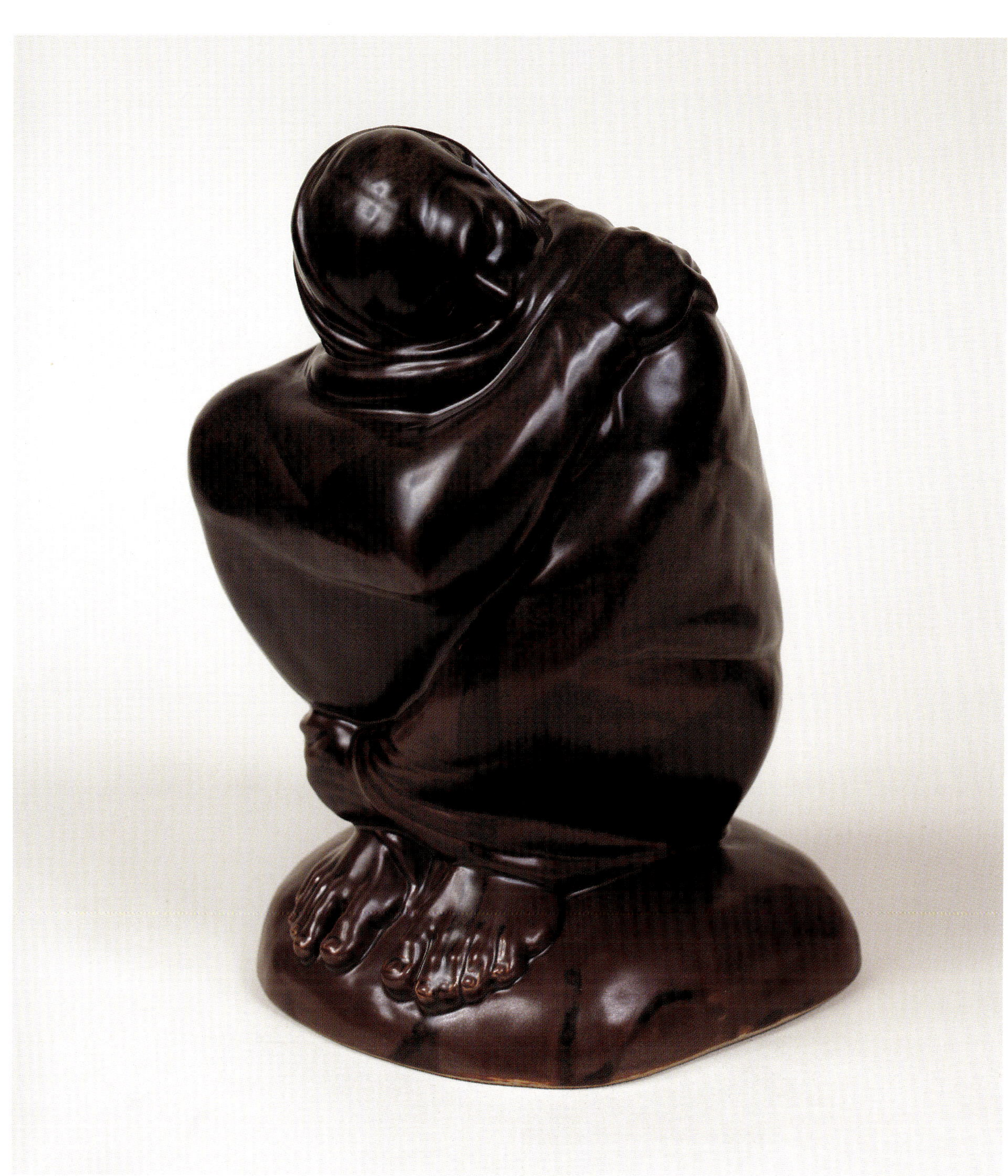

Spring Stirring
1947
Ceramic
11 ¼ inches
Courtesy of Bente and Gerald E. Buck
The Buck Collection

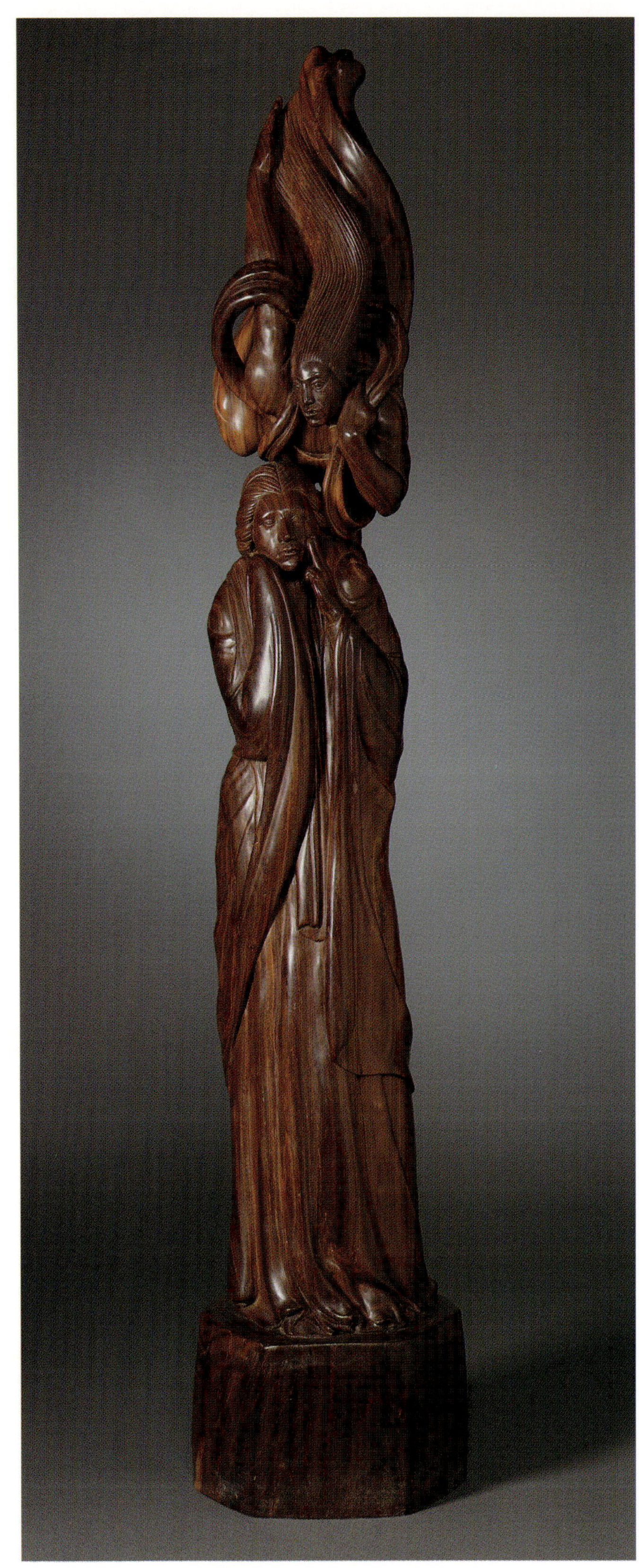

Annunciation
1949
Lignum Vitae
44 ½ inches
Courtesy of Ruth Chandler Williamson Gallery
Scripps College, Claremont, California

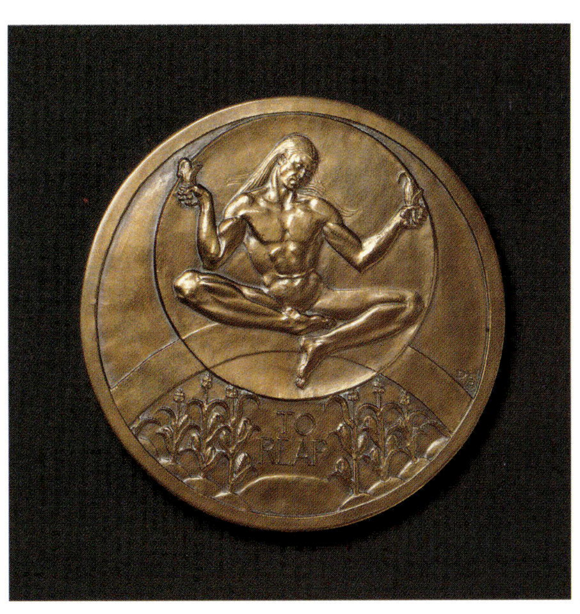

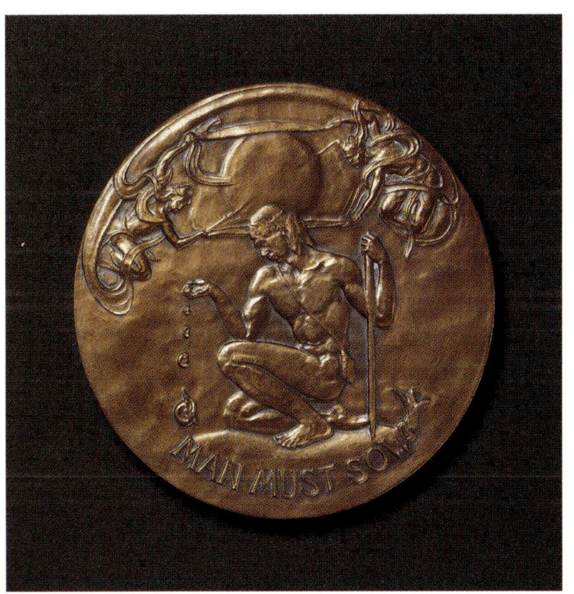

Man Must Sow – To Reap
1949 - 1950
Bronze
3 inches in diameter
Courtesy of San Diego Museum of Art

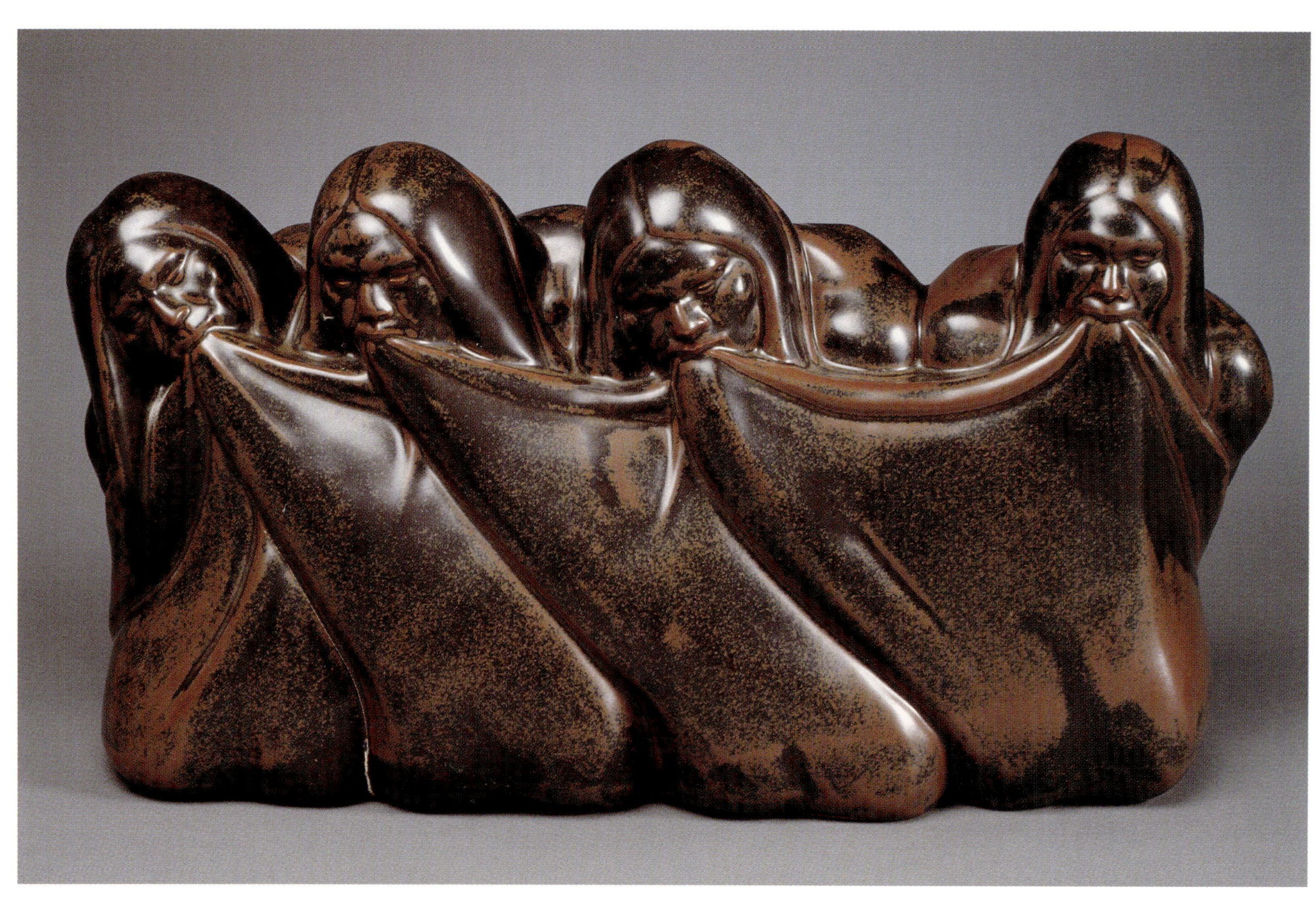

Peon Game Passers
1950
Plaster Stoneware
16 x 7 ½ inches
San Diego Historical Society
Bequest of Florence Hord

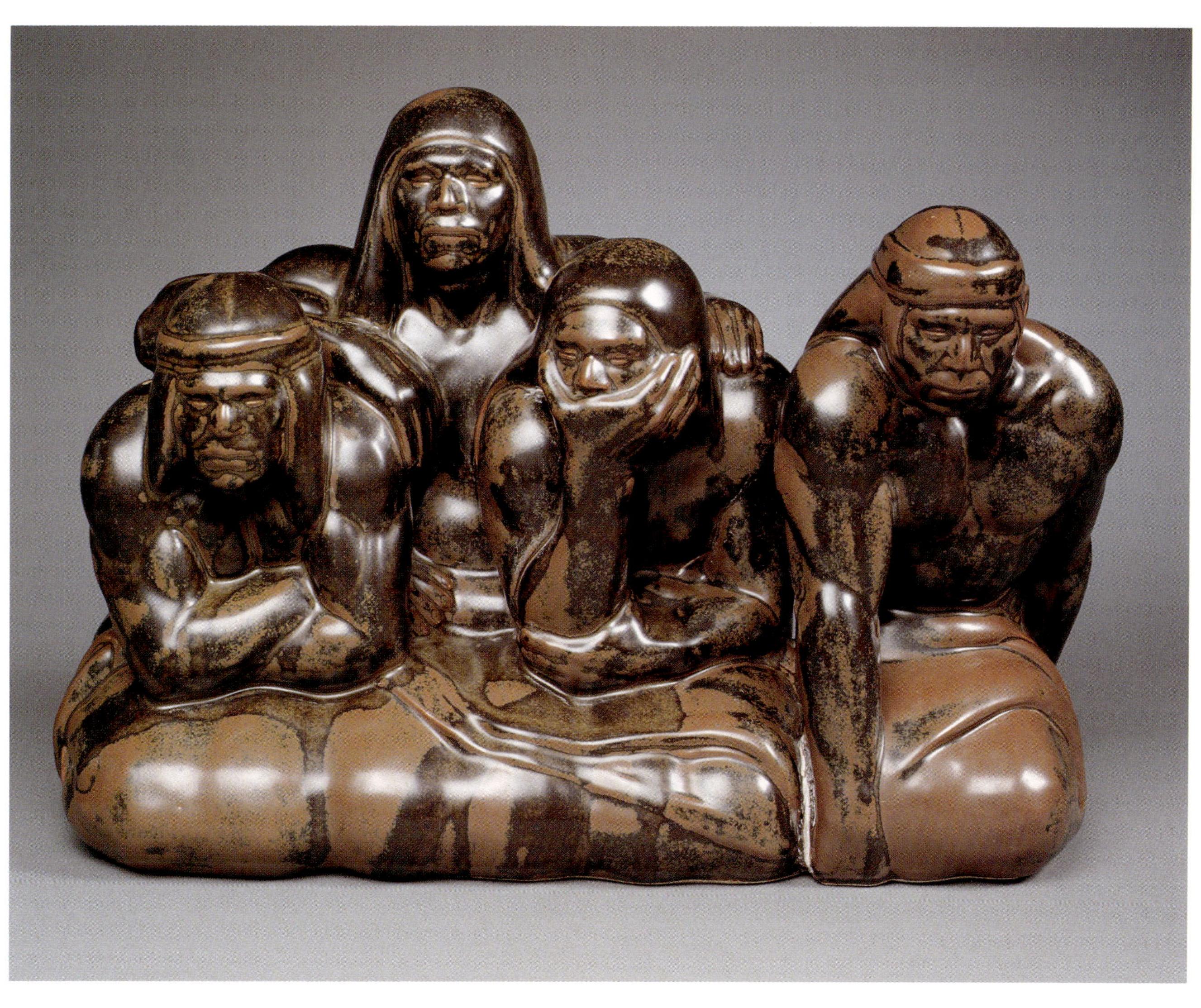

Peon Game Guessers
1950
Plaster Stoneware
14 ½ x 7 ½ inches
San Diego Historical Society
Bequest of Florence Hord

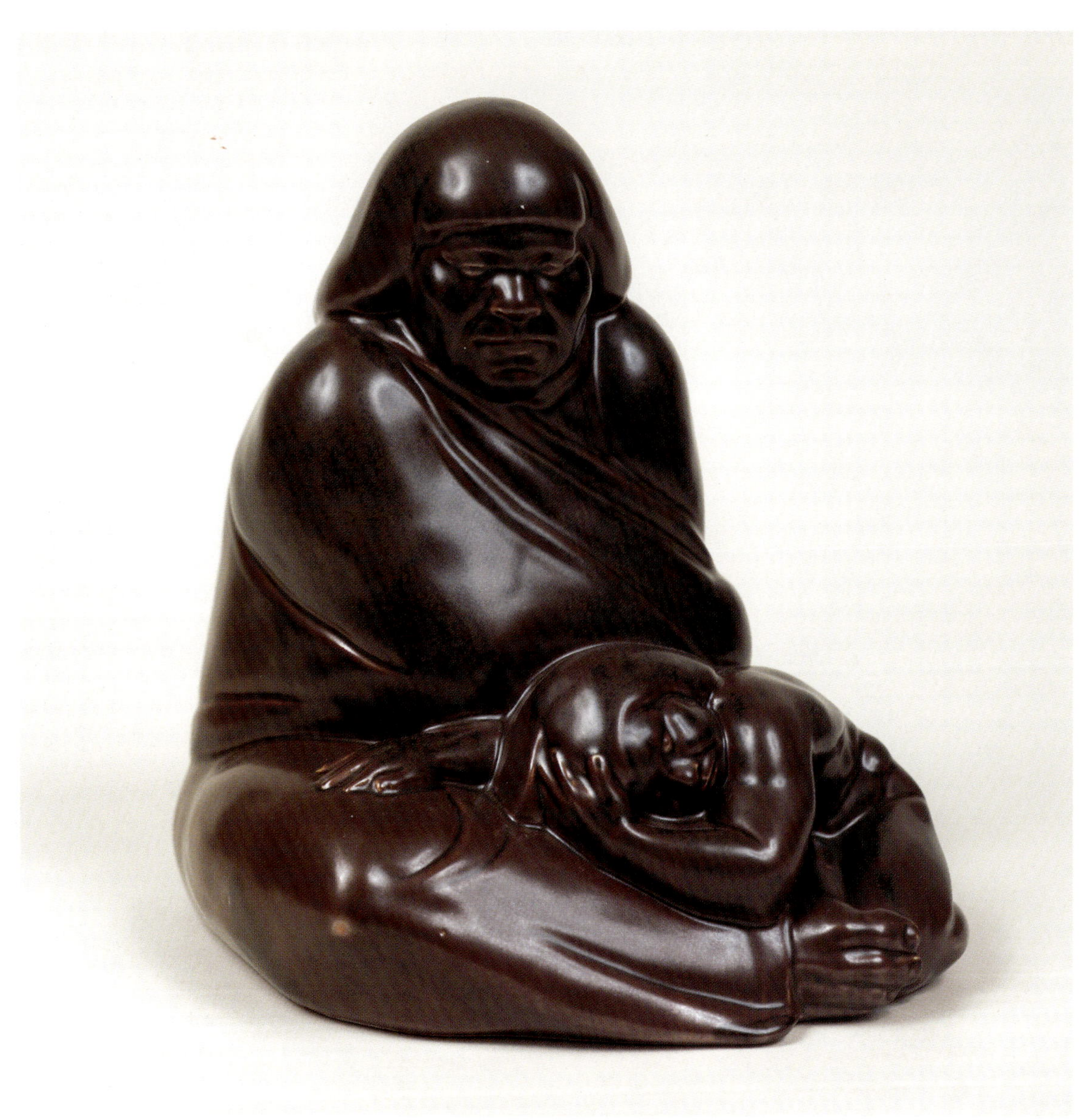

Peon Game Seated Woman
1950
Plaster Stoneware
9 1/4 inches
Courtesy of Bente and Gerald E. Buck
The Buck Collection

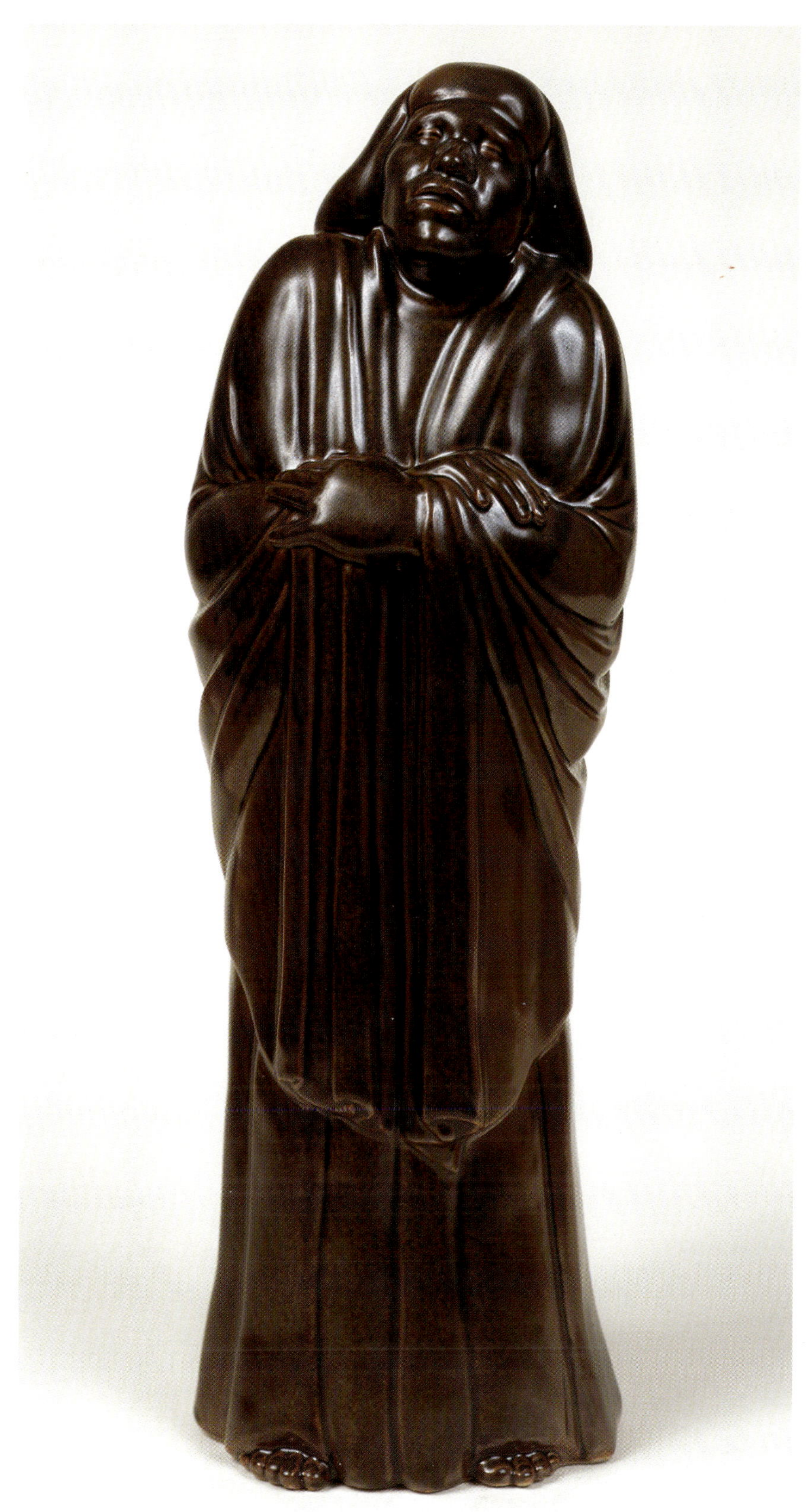

Peon Game Chanting Woman
1950
Plaster Stoneware
18 inches
Courtesy of Bente and Gerald E. Buck
The Buck Collection

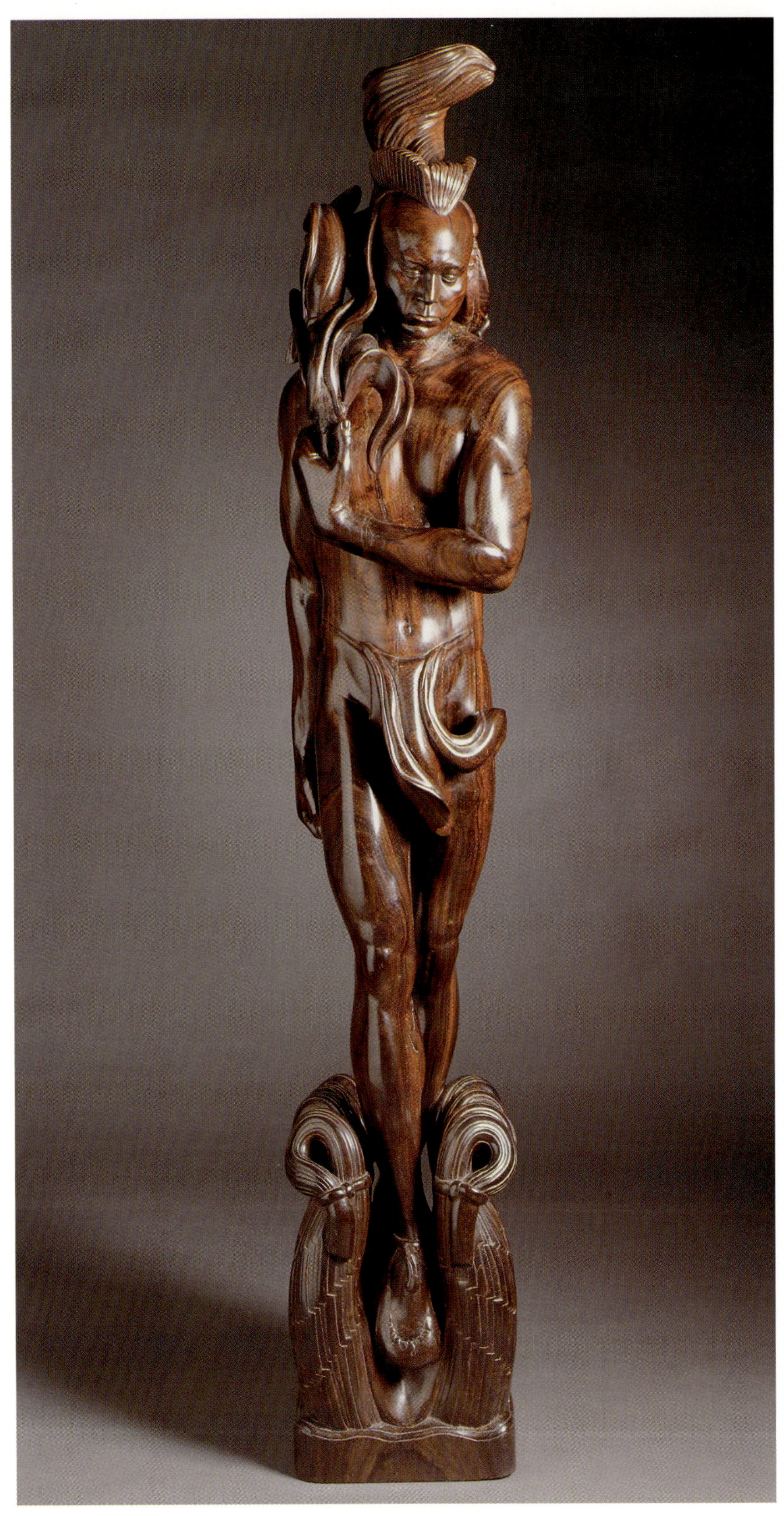

Harvest Spirit
1951
Rosewood
52 inches
Courtesy of San Diego Museum of Art

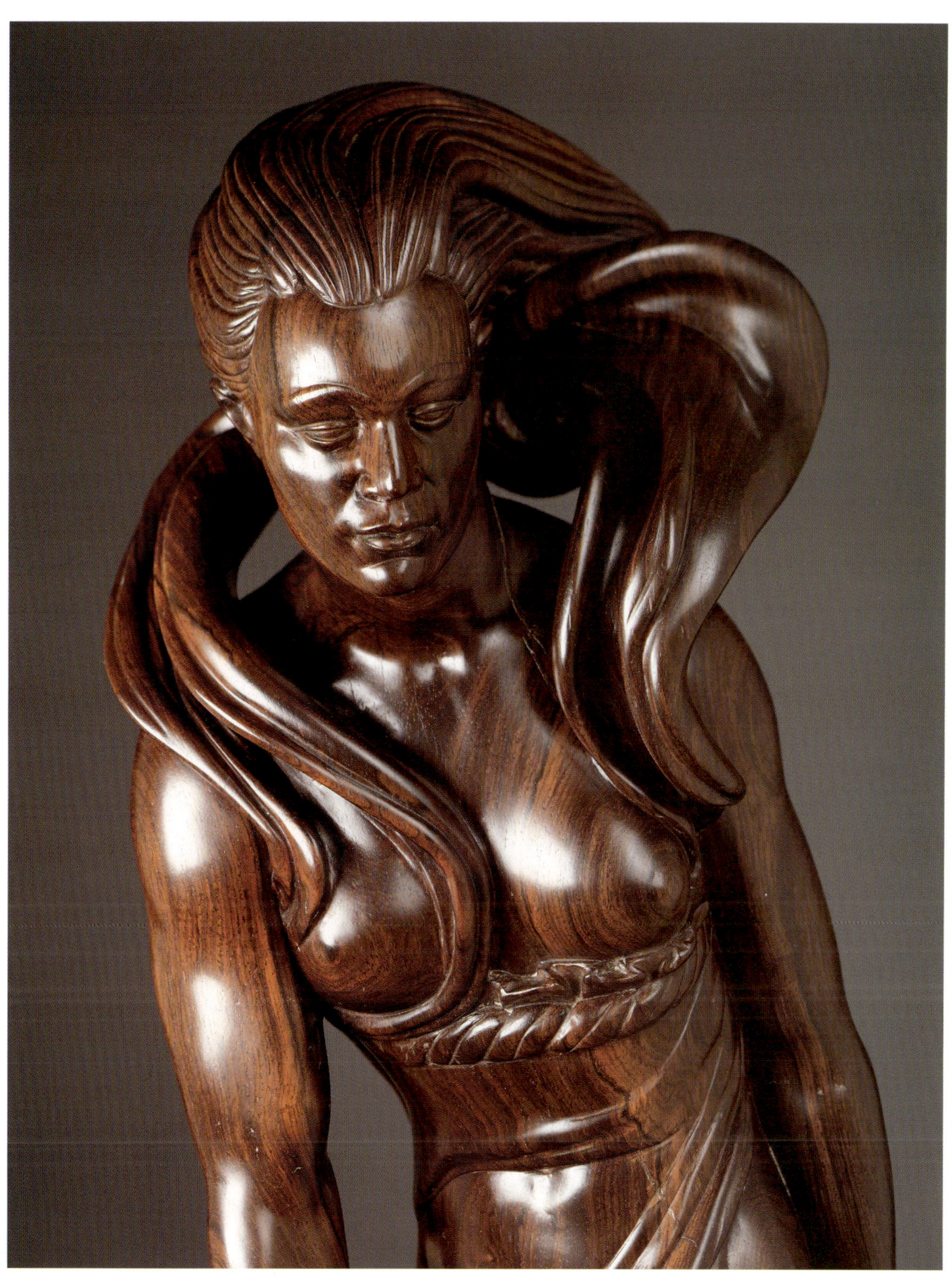

West Wind
1953
Rosewood
45 inches
Courtesy of San Diego Central Library

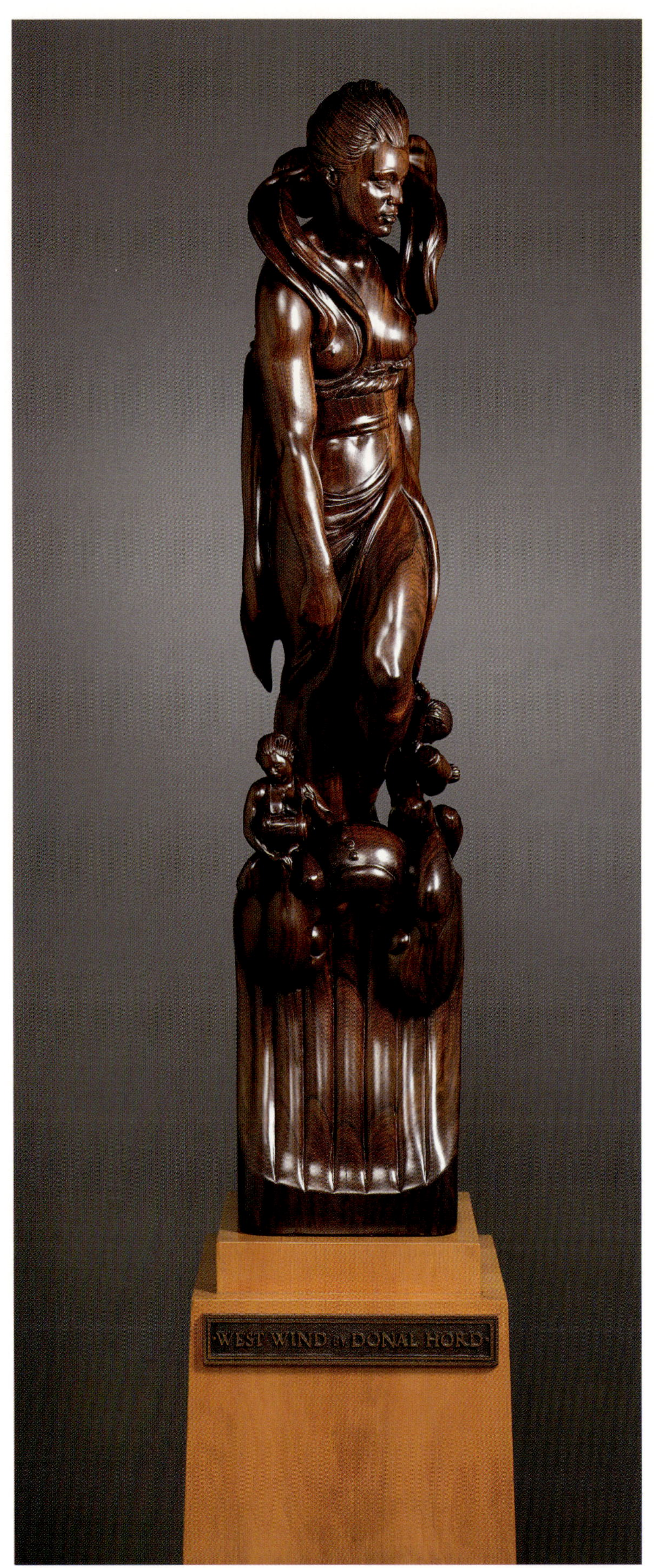
WEST WIND BY DONAL HORD

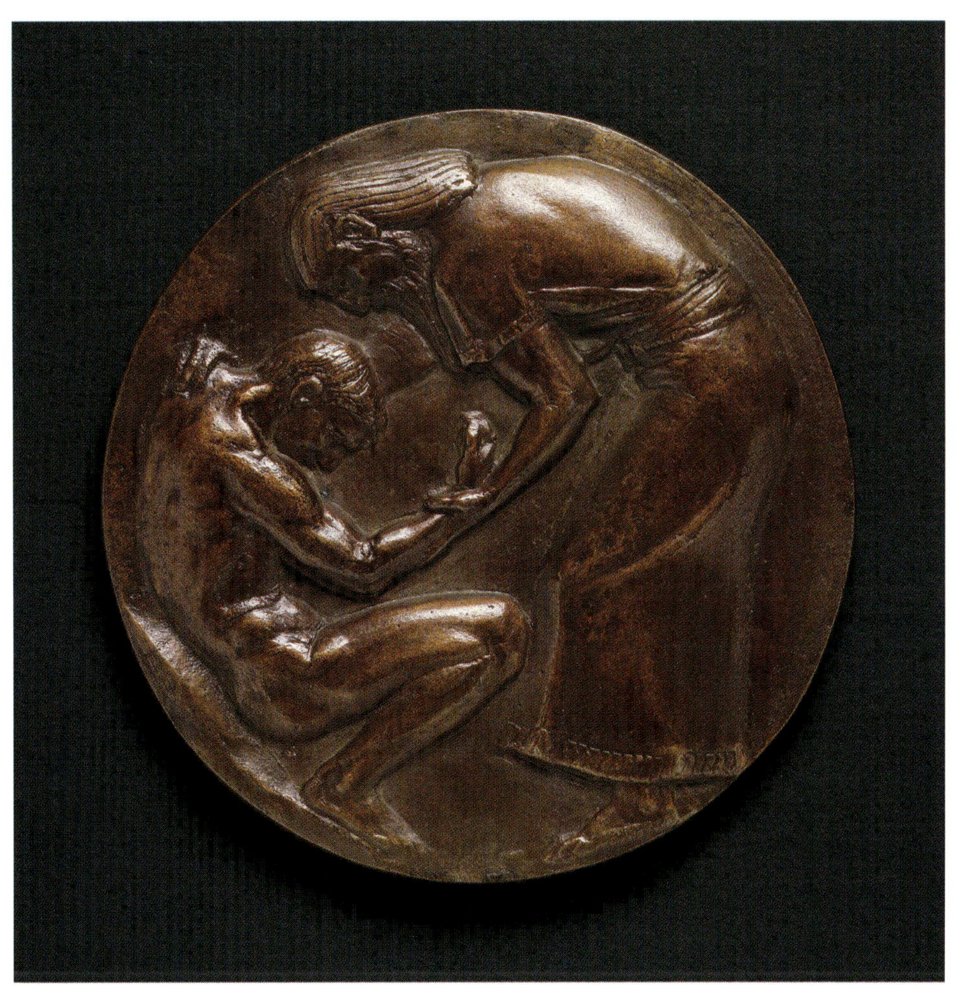

Good Samaritan
1955
Bronze
4 inches in diameter
Courtesy of San Diego Central Library

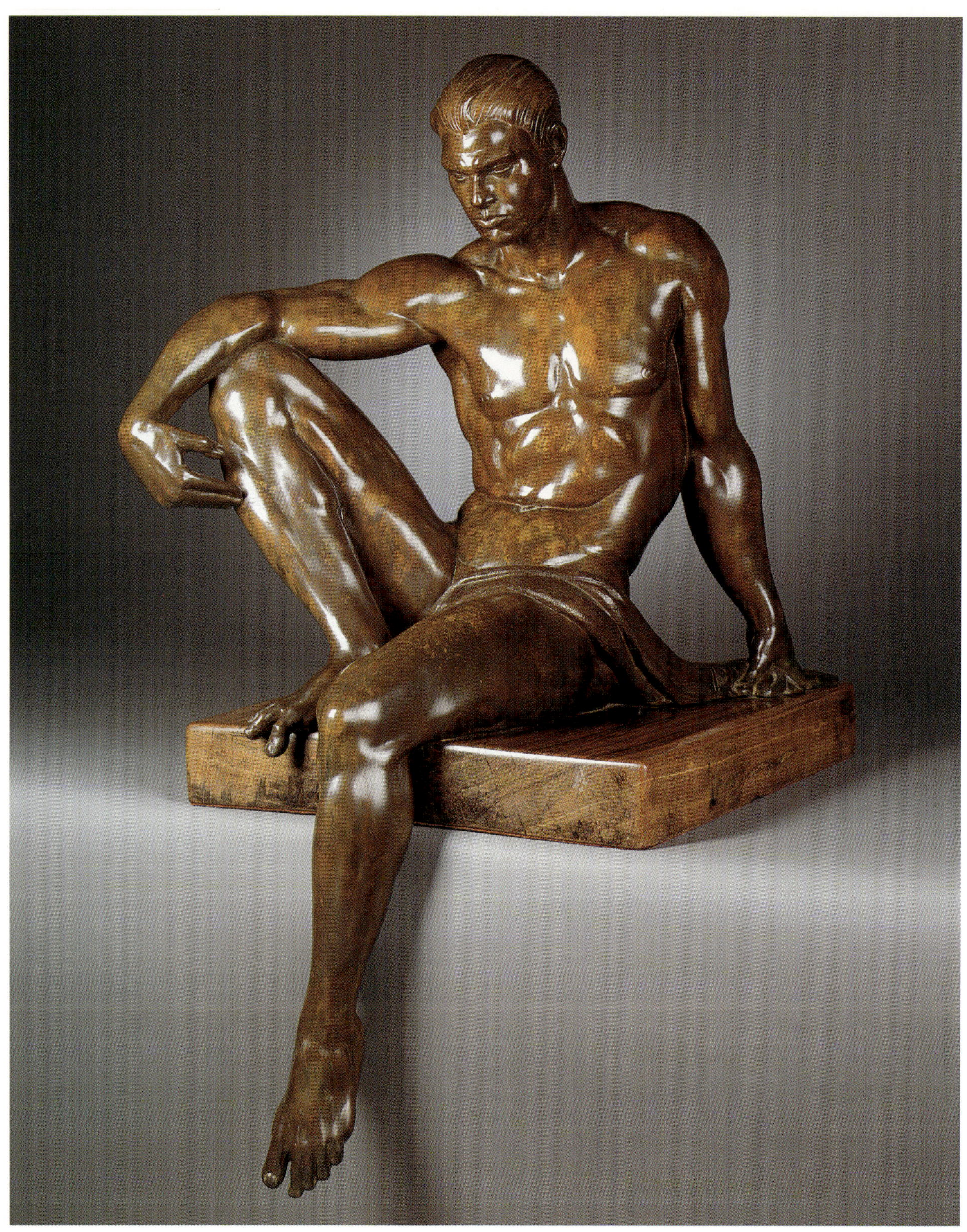

Young Bather
1955
Bronze
31 ½ inches
Anonymous loan

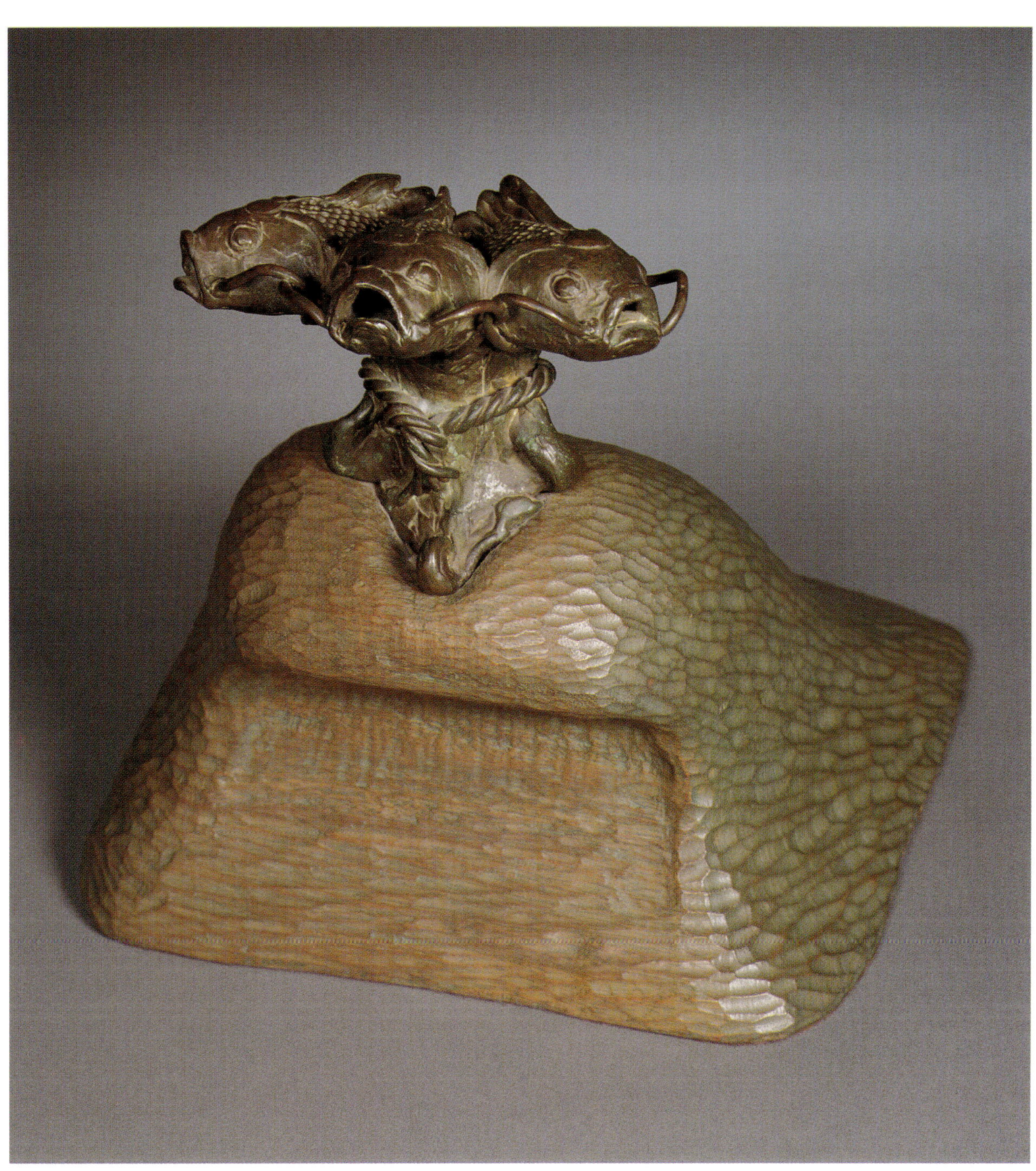

Fish Fountain Head for Young Bather
1955
Bronze
5 ½ inches
Anonymous loan

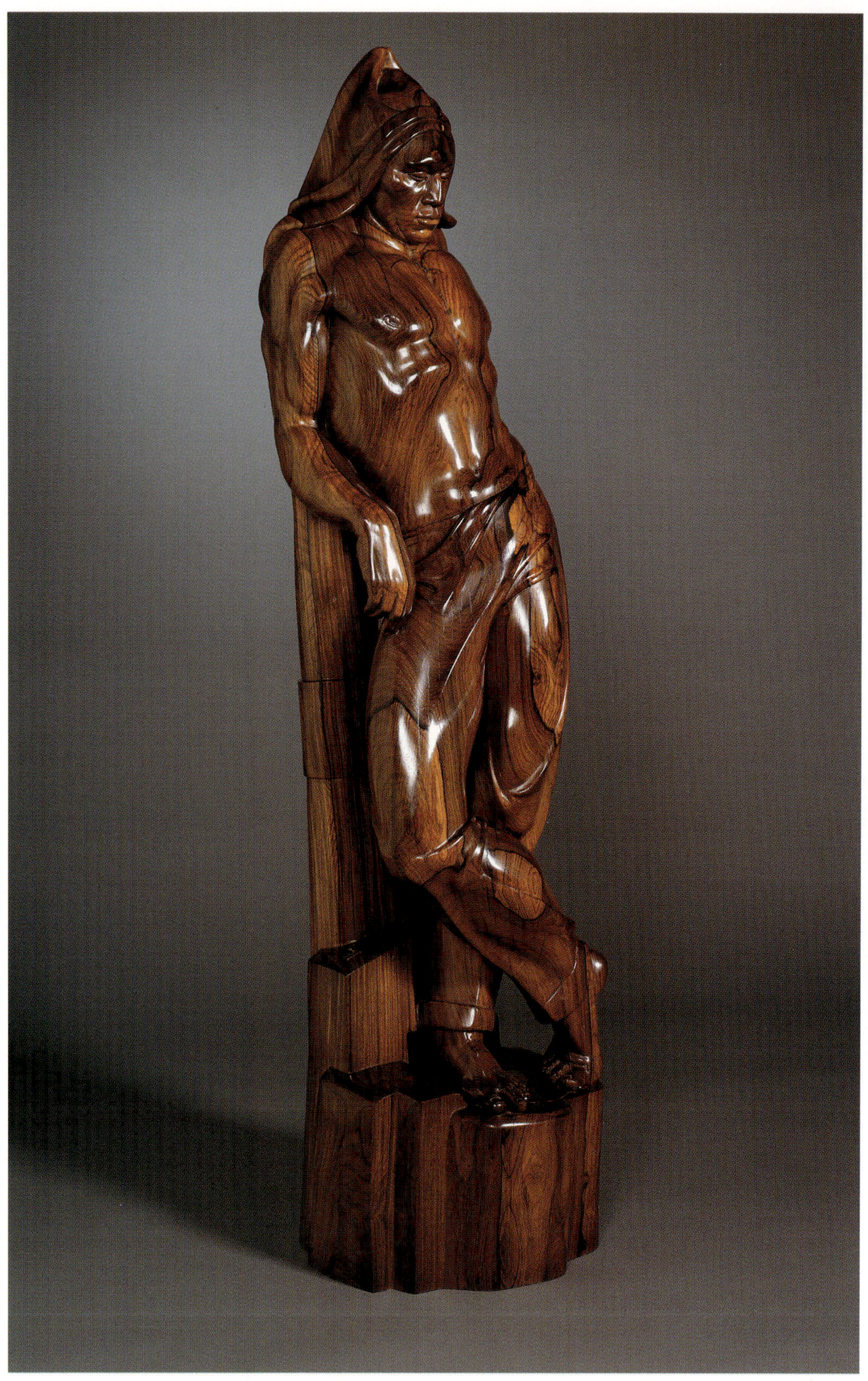

El Cargador
1956
Rosewood
45 inches
Anonymous loan

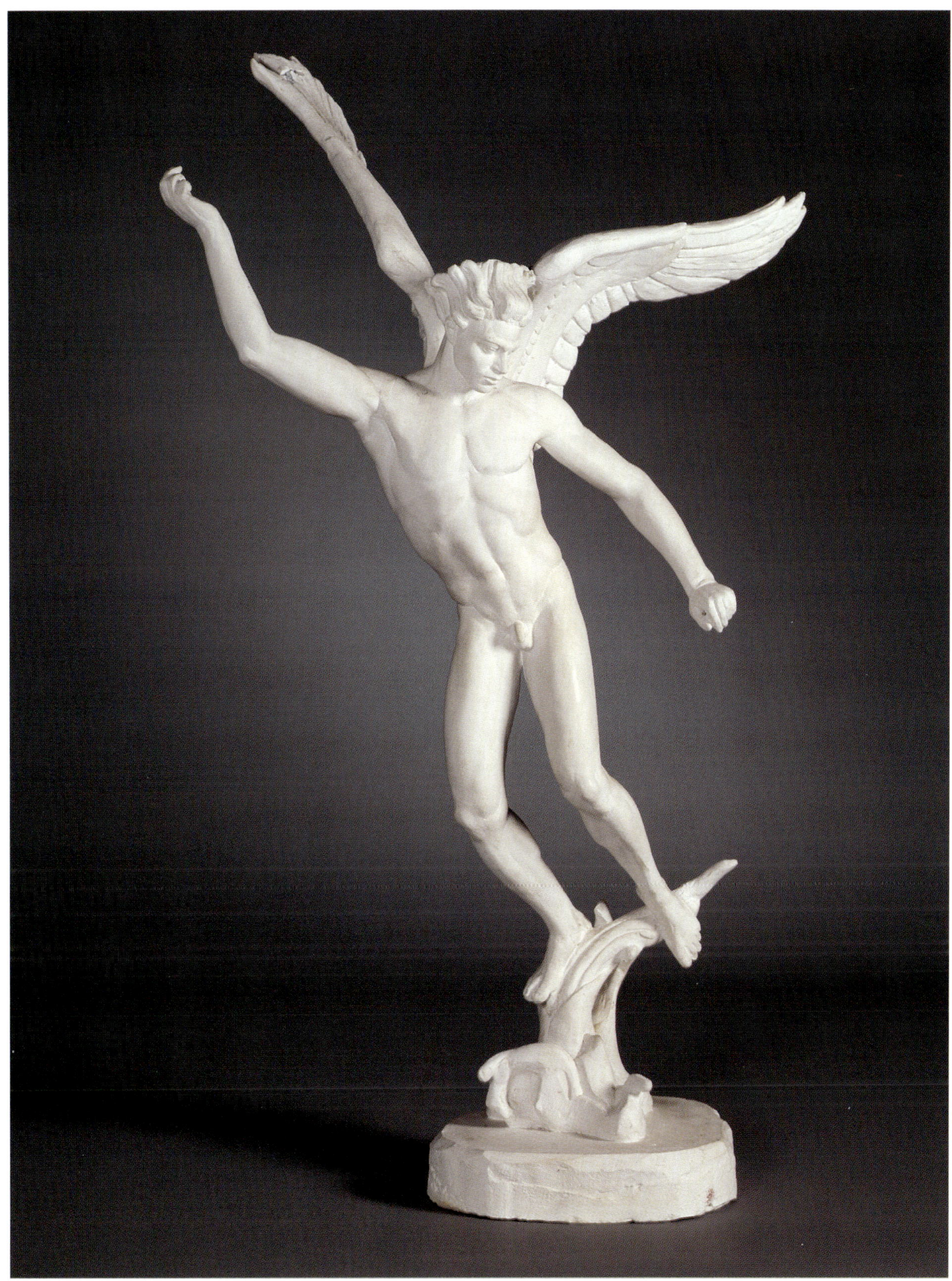

Angel of Peace maquette
1956
Plaster
31 inches
San Diego Historical Society
Gift of Florence Hord and Homer Dana

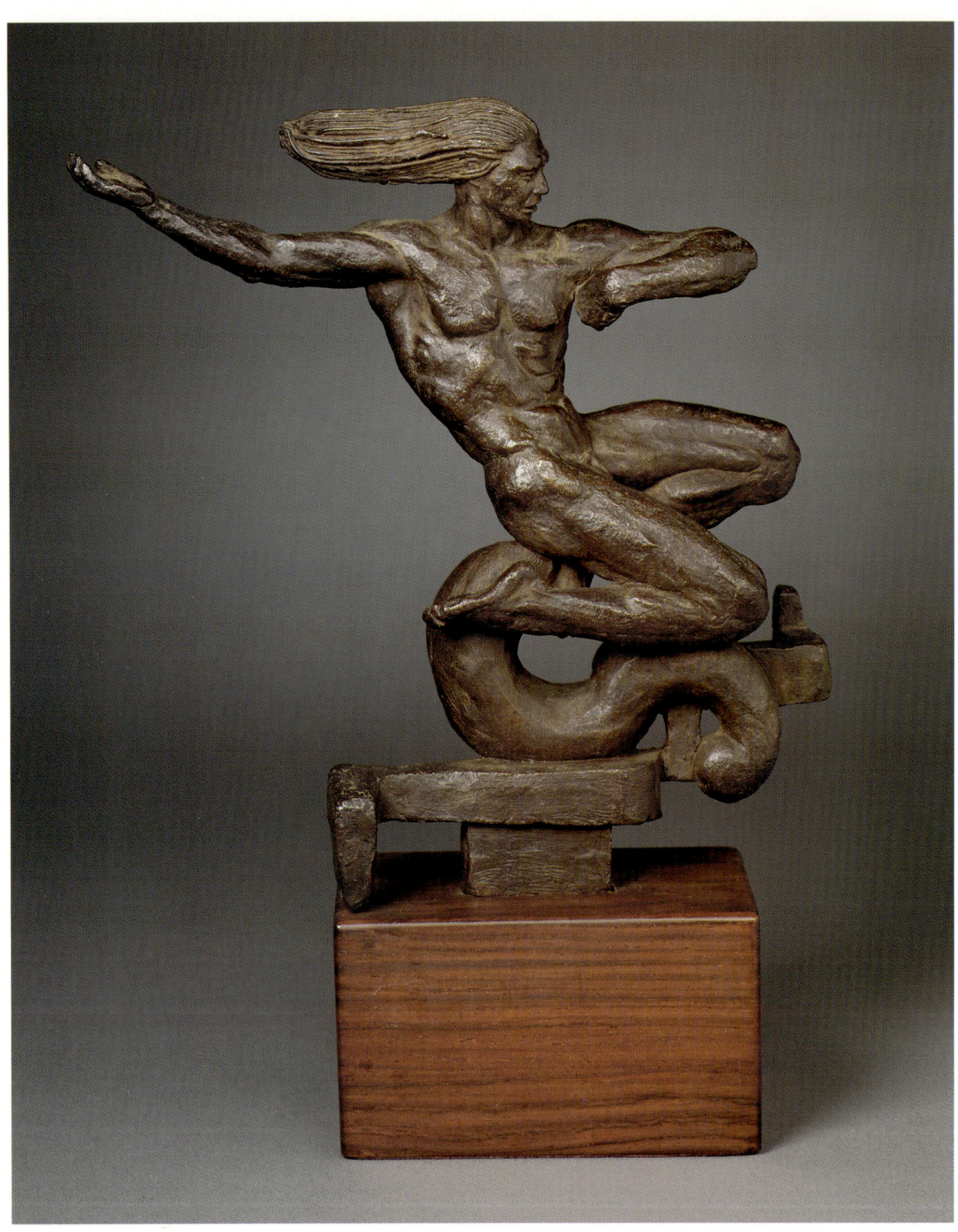

Kneeling Figure on a Cloud
1957
Bronze
10 ½ inches
Courtesy of Mandana Roe Harrison

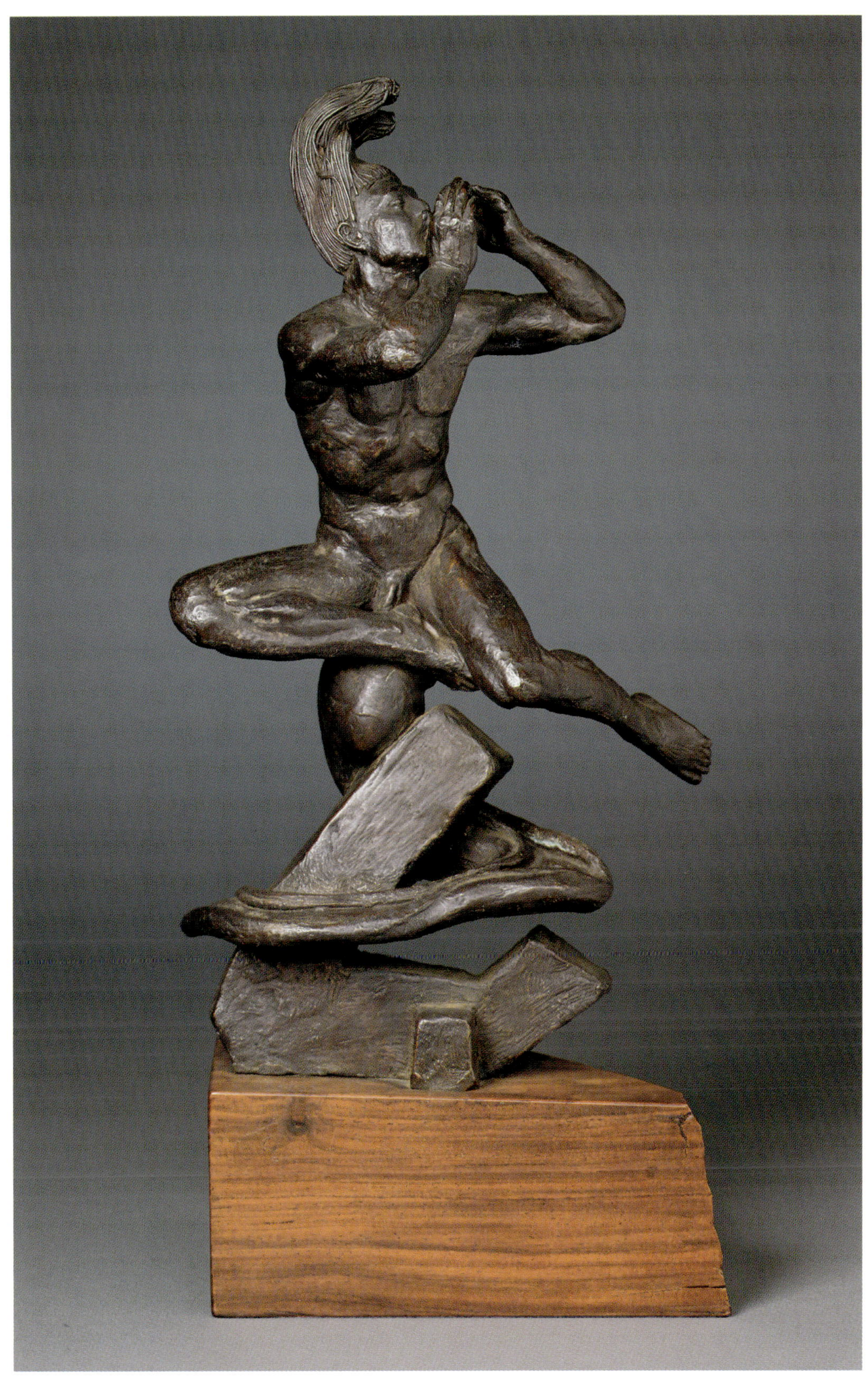

Wind Figure
1957
Bronze
10 ½ inches
Courtesy of Mandana Roe Harrison

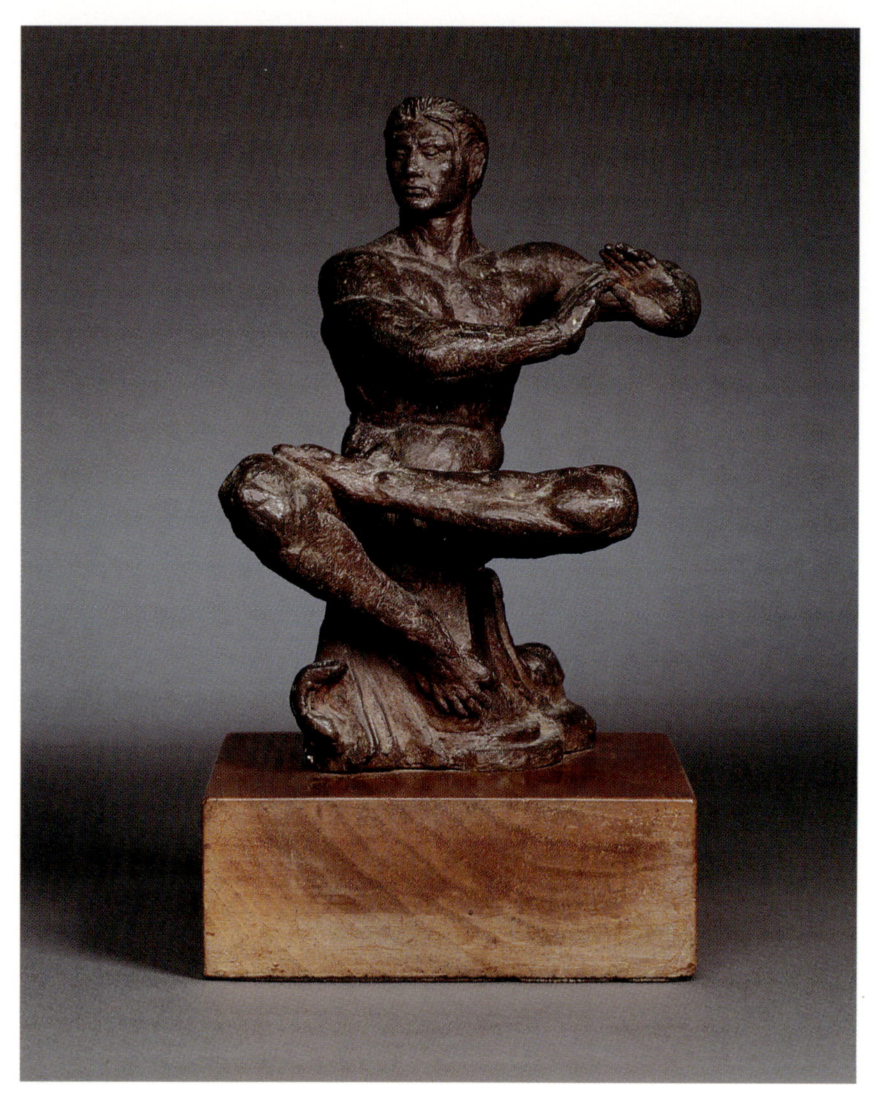

Seated Male Nude
1958
Bronze
9 inches
Courtesy of Walter and Judith Munk

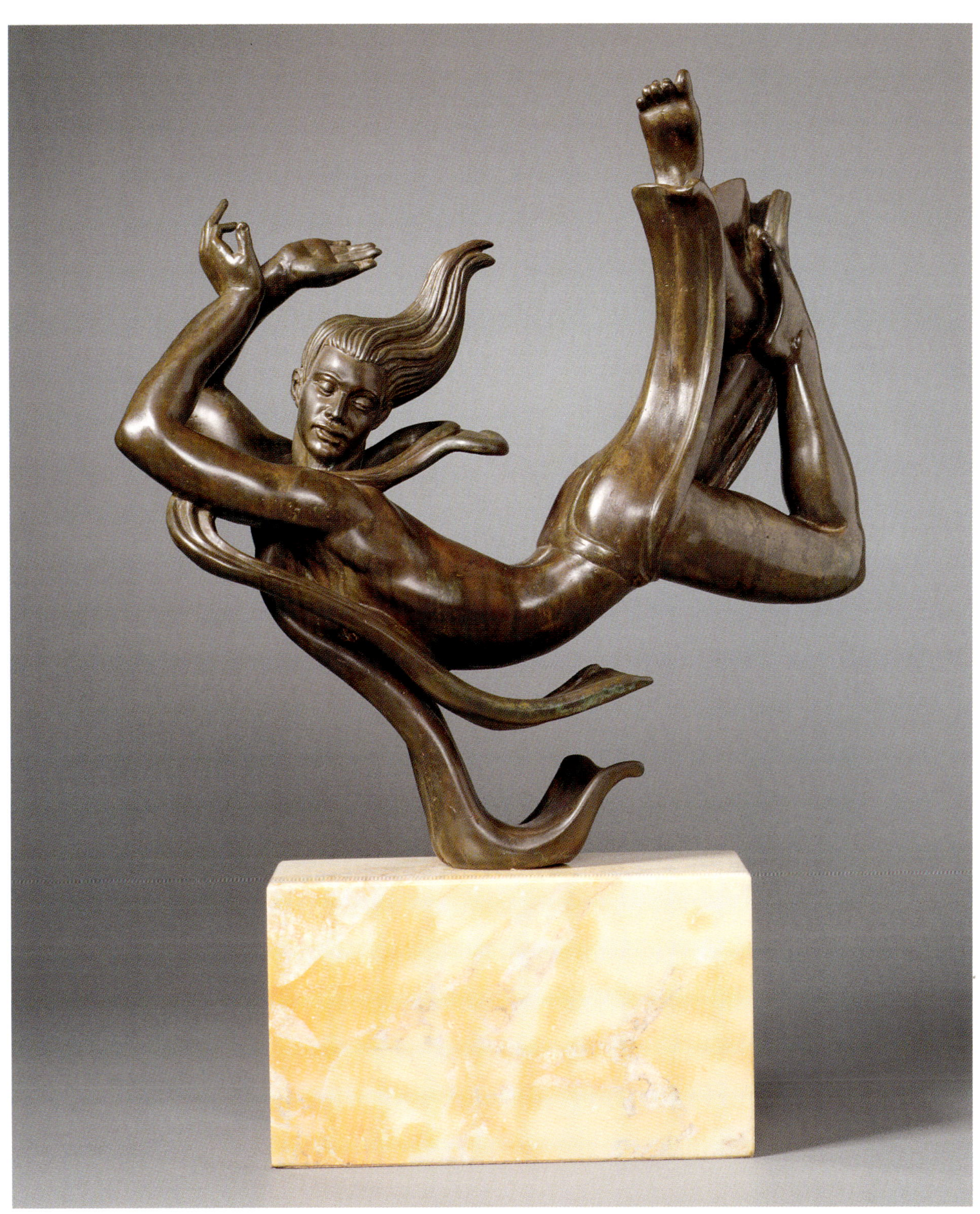

Sleeper in a Dream
1958
Bronze on Yellow Marble Base
12 inches
Anonymous loan

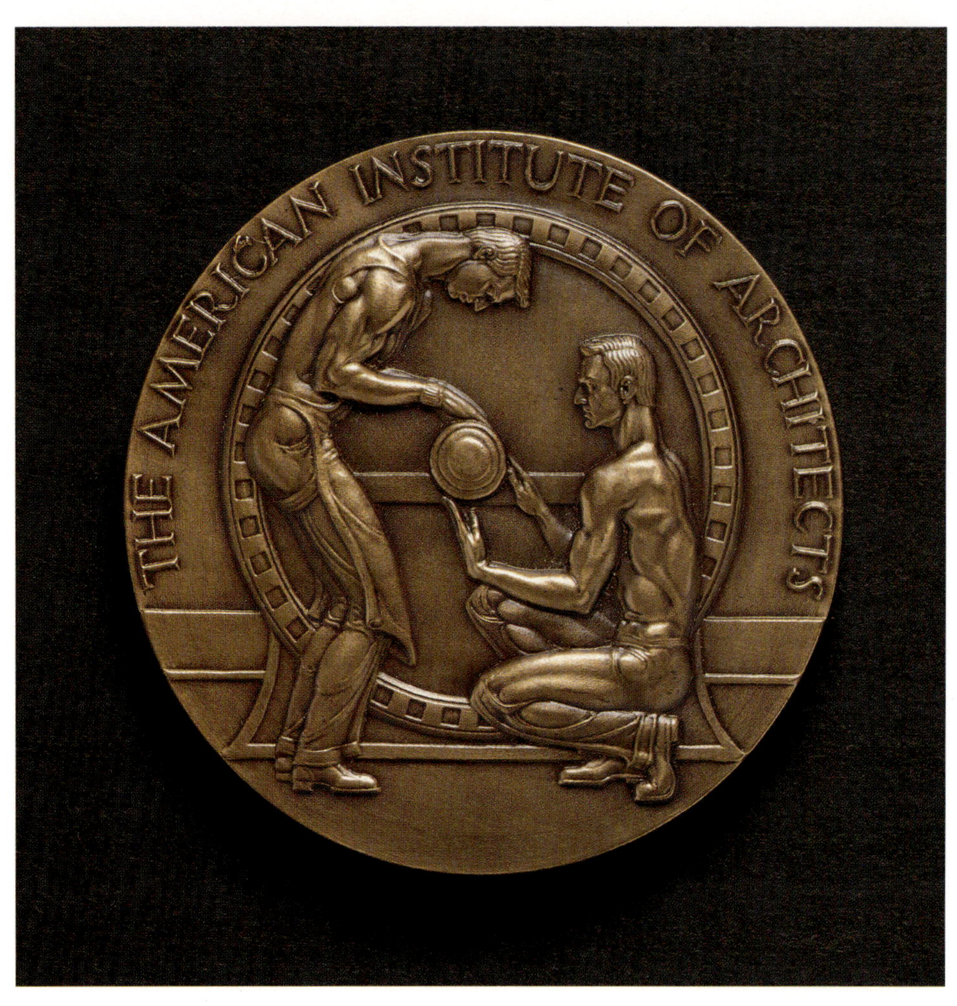

American Institute of Architects Medal for Industrial Arts
1959
Bronze
2 inches in diameter
Courtesy of San Diego Central Library

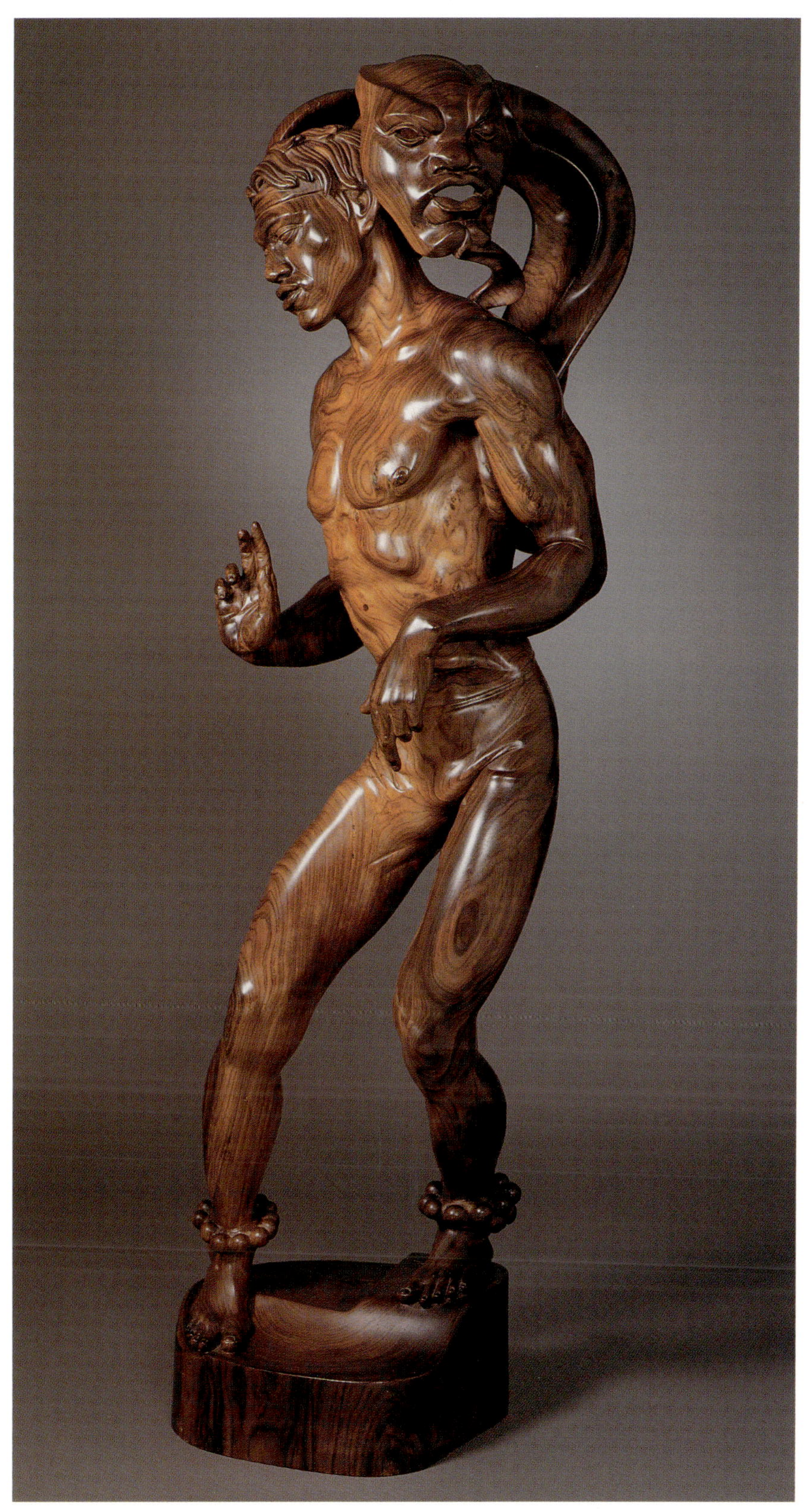

Feast Day of a Saint
1959
Rosewood
46 inches
Courtesy of Mr. and Mrs. William Smith

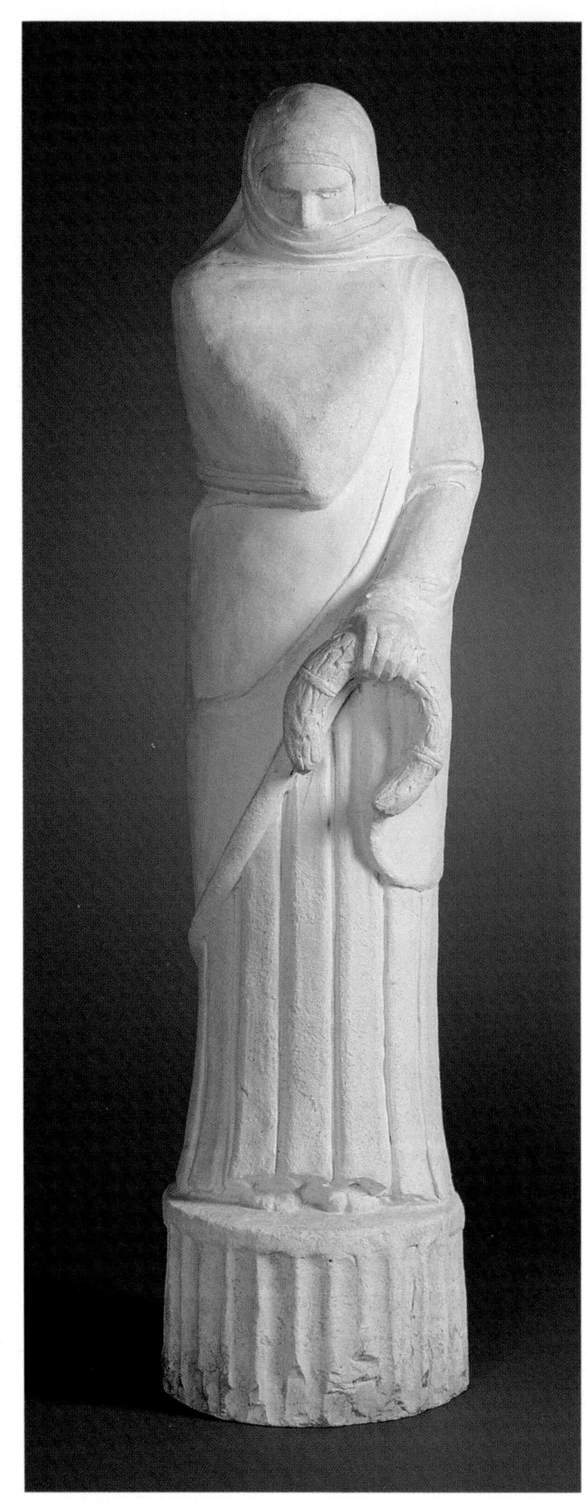

Mourning Woman maquette
1959
Terracotta
26 inches
Courtesy of Walter and Judith Munk

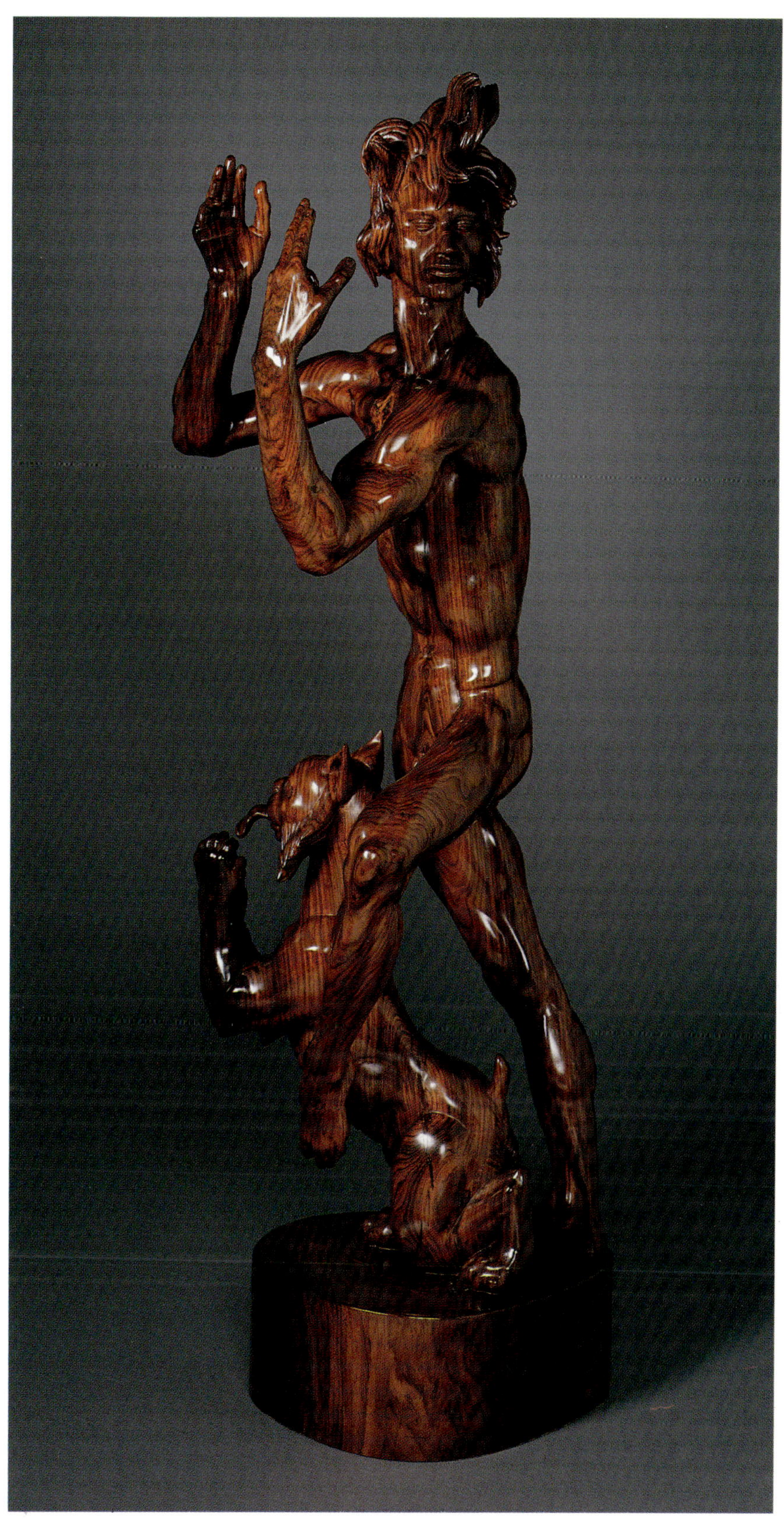

Nagual in Moonlight
1961
Rosewood
42 inches
Anonymous loan

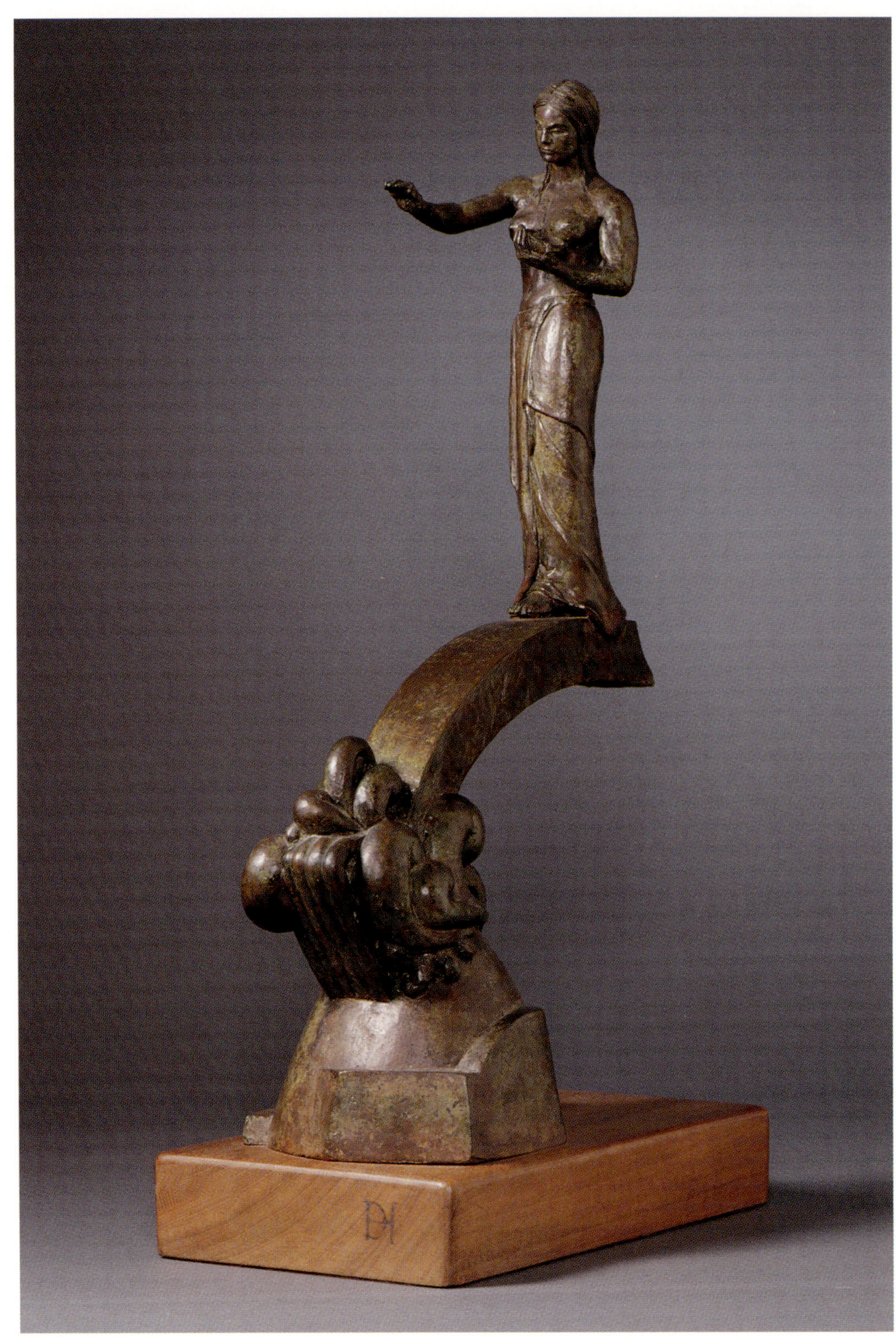

Spring Rain
1963
Bronze
9 inches
San Diego Historical Society
Bequest of Florence Hord

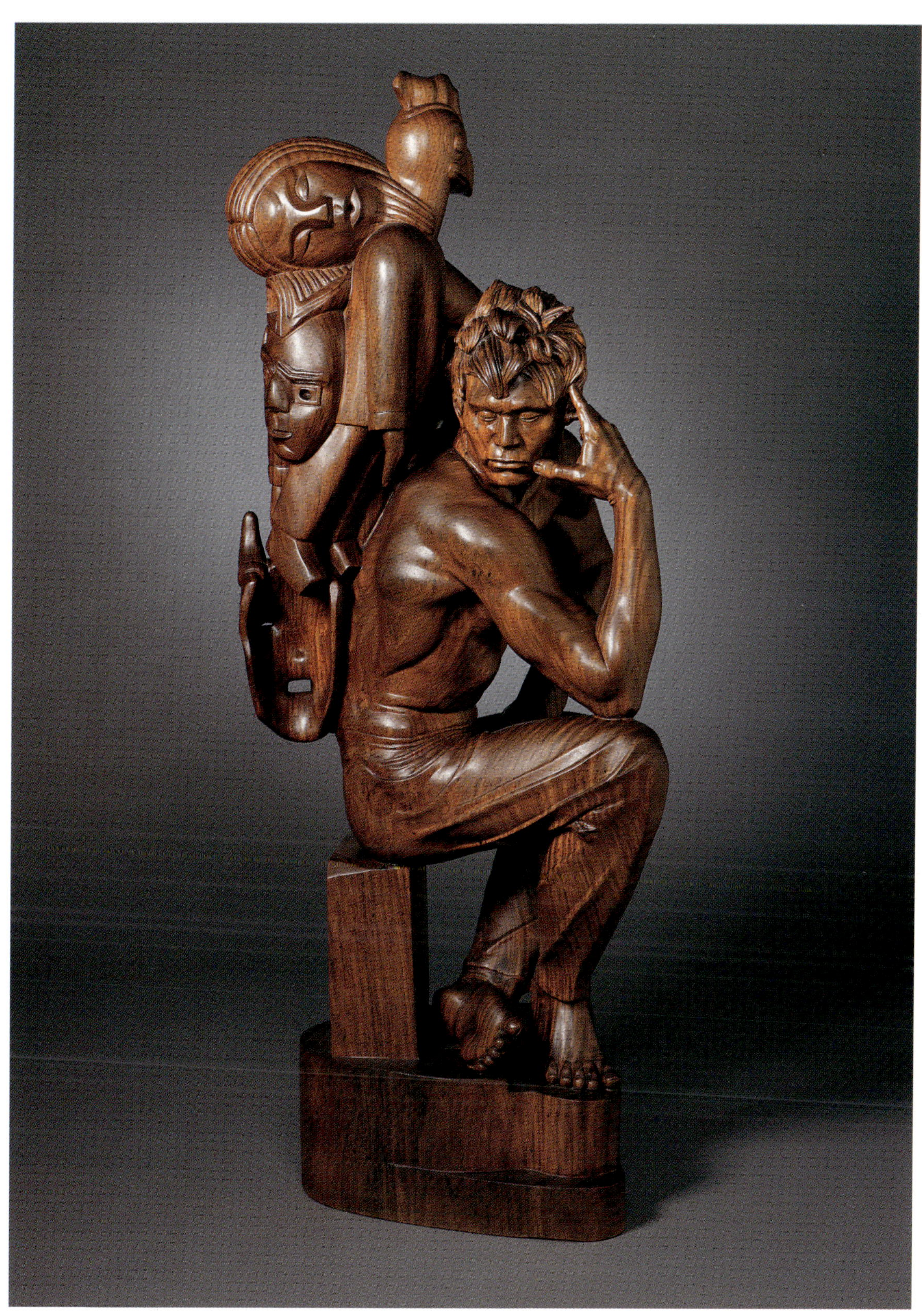

Day of the Judases
1963
Rosewood
40 inches
Courtesy of Museum of Western Art

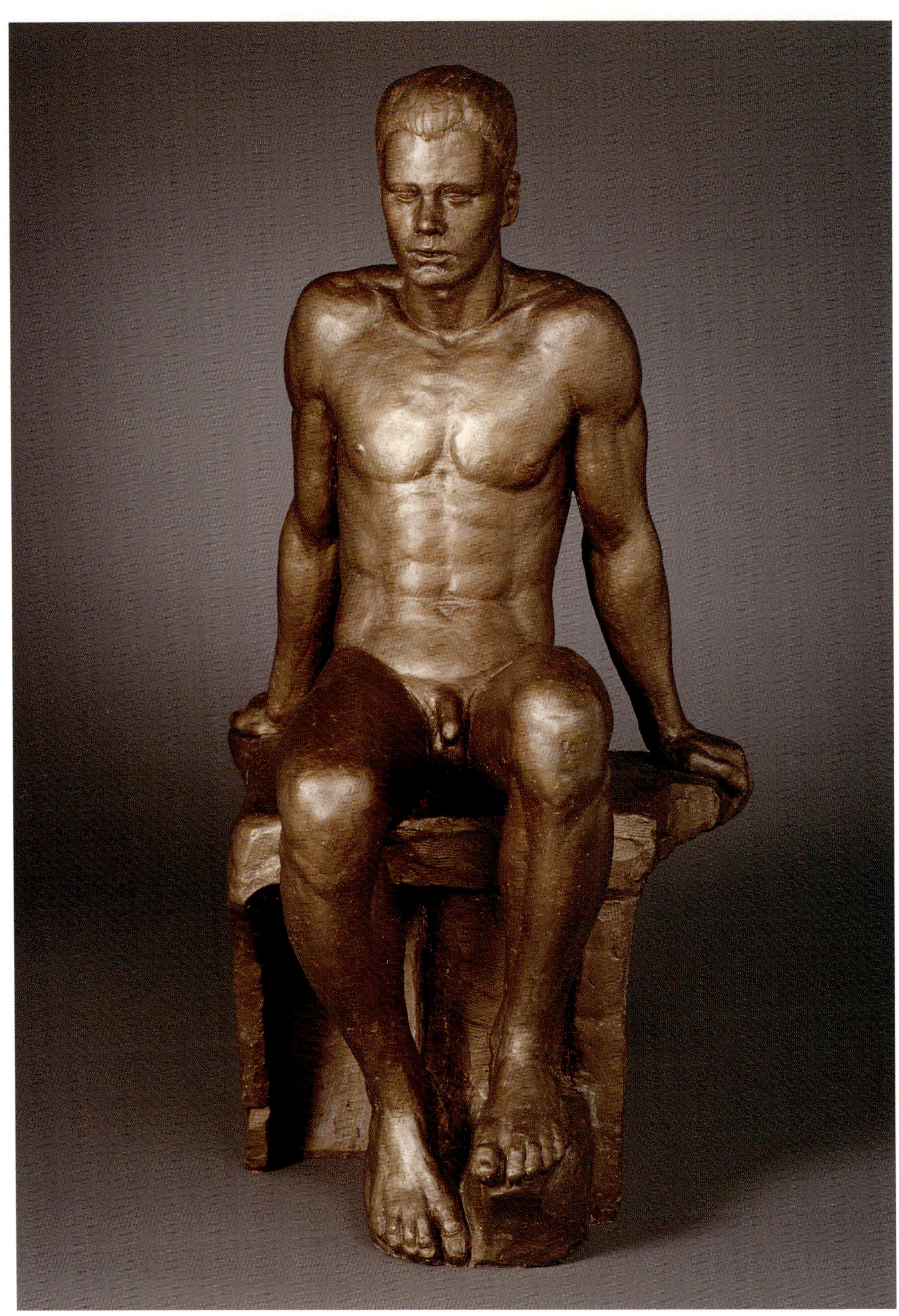

Seated Male Life Study
1964
Tinted Terracotta
24 ½ x 16 x 12 ½ inches
San Diego Historical Society
Anonymous gift

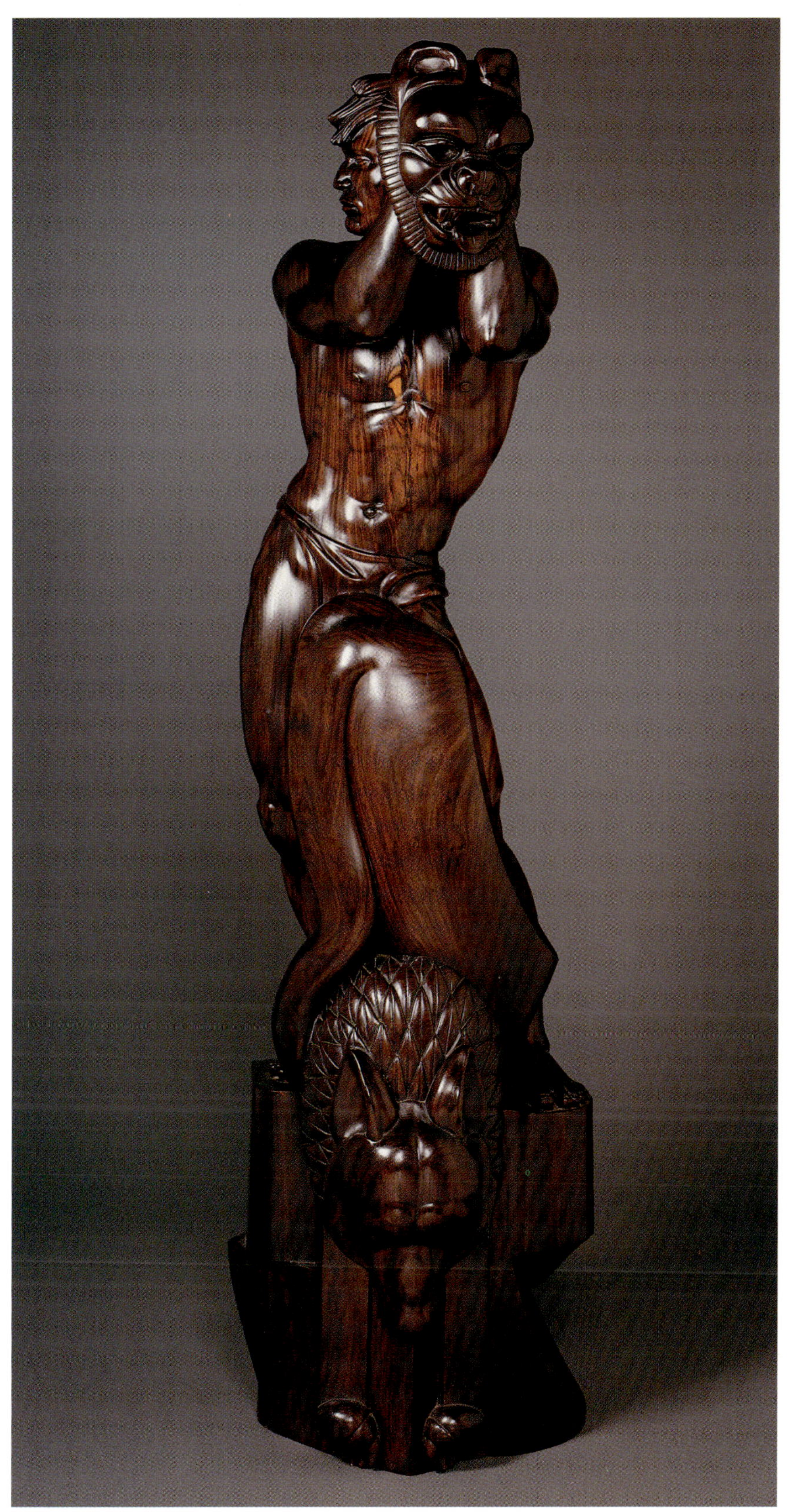

Daybreak
1965
Rosewood
43 inches
Courtesy of the Huckins Family

Notes to Exhibition Plates

Profile Relief of Woman's Head, page 51
Made while Hord studied with Anna Valentien. Both of their signatures are inscribed on the back.

Creeping Indian, page 52
The first piece Hord fired. It was made at San Diego High School and fired at the Rose Canyon Brickyard.

Laura, page 53
A bust portrait of Hord's mother.

Mike, page 54
Hord's mother suggested he sculpt monkeys to sell in gift shops. Dorr Bothwell painted them, however, they did not sell well and few were made.

El Cacique, page 56
Hord's first work done as a student at the Santa Barbara School of the Arts under the supervision of Archibald Dawson. The headdress was not present in the first casting. Hord later added a carved mahogany base.

El Cacique, page 57
The second casting was Hord's first piece to enter a museum collection.

Moon and Sea, page 60
The female figure represents the crescent moon and the male symbolizes a wave. Noted in *Contemporary American Sculpture*, 1929.

Tezcatlipoca or *Smoking Mirror Dance,* page 61
Tezcatlipoca means "smoking mirror" referring to obsidian glass used to foretell the future of the Gods. According to legend, Tezcatlipoca tried to devour the sun but was repulsed by the guise of the morning star.

Ome-Tochtli or *El dios del Maguey,* page 62
The figure represents intoxication from fermented juice of the maguey plant.

Tlaloc or *Thirst,* page 63
Meaning, "He who makes the plants sprout," was Hord's first sculpture in volcanic glass.

Channel Wind, page 67
The figure represents the forces of a Channel Island wind.

Hurakan, page 68
The title is derived from the language of the Taino people of the Bahamas. The word was later assimilated into the English language as "Hurricane".

Culna, page 69
Honored with the Merit Award in the Twelfth Annual Exhibition of American Painters and Sculptors at the Los Angeles Art Museum in 1931. This was Hord's first sculpture award.

Young Maize, page 71
The figure represents a tall corn stalk with sprouts at its base. *Young Maize* received the General Marshal O. Terry prize at the Sixth Annual Southern California Art Exhibition in 1931.

Desert Night, page 73
The figure was executed in painted gesso sottile. Photographs of it were used by Florence Hord to illustrate her Masters thesis on gesso formulas and their uses in sculpture.

Family on the Curb (Male and Female), page 75
Hord carved details in the pieces after the clay had partially hardened to achieve a crispness not possible in wet clay.

Mayan Mask, page 78
Also listed as *Aztec Warrior* and *Nahua Warrior*, the mask was carved thin enough to be worn.

Indigenas, page 79
Small panels at the top and the bottom of each door represent native plants.

Tropic Cycle, page 80
Represents the Mayan God of Spring emerging from a winter robe of jaguar skin. Carved from the same log as *Desert Sunrise.*

Transportation of the Mail, page 82
Five studies of architectural relief panels submitted for the Santa Barbara Post Office Competition. William O. Atkinson won the commission.

Portrait of Fred Sietz, page 87
Fred Sietz was the grandson of Hord's neighbor. The piece was fired by Wedgewood in Point Loma, however, it broke in the first processing. Wedgewood refired it a second time with black glaze to solidify it.

La Cubana, page 91
Exhibited for the first time at the New York World's Fair, 1939. The obsidian came from Coso Hot Springs in the Sierra Mountains. The volcanic glass contains reflective specks of fenocryst which were caused in the cooling process.

Rest on the Flight into Egypt, page 96
The stone was taken from the same quarry as that for *Aztec*. Hord and Dana had just installed *Rest on the Flight into Egypt* at the San Diego Fine Arts Gallery when the radio announced the attack on Pearl Harbor.

Corn Goddess, page 97
The female figure, whose hair represents sprouting corn, was first exhibited at the Metropolitan Museum in New York, 1942.

Silas St. John Memorial, page 98
Silas St. John was an early local stagecoach driver.

El Colorado, the Red One, page 104
Funded by a Guggenheim Award, the 2,400 pound sculpture represents a Mojave god who created the Colorado River and Grand Canyon.

Annunciation, page 108
Hord's depiction of Gabriel and the Virgin Mary focuses on her human consternation, unlike many earlier images, which depict her as serene.

Harvest Spirit, page 114
Depicts an Algonquin Indian with wild rice at his base and corn on his shoulder. Cumulus clouds rise above him, symbolic of those that often hang over Wisconsin lakes at harvest time.

Young Bather and *Fish Fountain Head,* pages 118 and 119
These companions were the first of three cast in Italy in 1955. Two more casts followed in 1964. The fountain was designed to shower the bather.

El Cargador, page 120
Cargados were men who hauled charcoal in Mexico. They wore sacks as hoods to keep their hair from getting covered with soot.

Sleeper in a Dream, page 125
The figure, modeled in Pietra Santa, Italy, depicts effortless flight.

Feast Day of a Saint, page 127
The figure has bells on his trousers as a mark of celebration.

Nagual in Moonlight, page 129
The figure is unusually slender for Hord's work. After he had begun, he discovered the piece had a bad heartcheck, or crack down the center. The figure was then carved toward the outside of the log to avoid this flaw.

Spring Rain, page 130
Cast in Italy, the female figure intimates a gentle Spring rain.

Daybreak, page 133
Bruce A. Kamerling described this piece as: *The coyote howls just before the sun comes up and then stops and becomes skin only as the night dies.*

Photograph Credits:

pages 62 and 78: Courtesy of Steve Turner Gallery
page 79: Courtesy of Tobey C. Moss Gallery
pages 85, 87, 89, and 90: Courtesy of Bente and Gerald E. Buck
page 96: Homer Dana
page 97: Courtesy of Los Angeles County Museum of Art
pages 106, 107, 112, and 113: Courtesy of Bente and Gerald E. Buck

List of Life's Work

1	*Sphinx*	1916	Sandstone
2	*Relief of Woman's Head*	1916	Plaster
3	*Bust of a Bearded Man*	1918	Plaster
4	*Creeping Indian*	1918	Terracotta
5	*Laura*	1919	Bronze
6	*Tenochtitlan*	1919	Terracotta
7	*Earnest Hill*	1920	Unfired Clay
8	*Mike*	1922	Plaster
9	*Two Wrestlers*	1920	Terracotta
10	*Captives*	1920s	Terracotta
11	*Gargoyle*	1920s	Terracotta
12	*Takquitch*	1920s	Terracotta
13	*Sleeping Figure*	1920s	Terracotta
14	*Standing Figure*	1920s	Terracotta
15	*Salome*	1920s	Terracotta
16	*Kneeling Male Figure*	1920s	Terracotta
17	*Bearded Head*	1920s	Terracotta
18	*El Cacique*	1926	Bronze
19	*Nahua*	1926	Bronze
20	*Stand with Kneeling Indians*	1926	Bronze
21	*Stand with Female Figures*	1926	Bronze
22	*Chalchuihnetzin*	1927	Bronze, Eucalyptus
23	*Dying Warriors*	1927	Bronze
24	*Study of a Chumash*	1927	Clay
25	*Plaque and Oil Lamp*	1927	Bronze
26	*Pair of Flower Vases*	1927	Bronze
27	*Flower Pot Holder*	1927	Bronze
28	*Cuy-a-ho-mar*	1928	Bronze
29	*Ku-Kul-Kan*	1928	Bronze
30	*Chaup*	1928	Tinted Plaster
31	*Standing Indian*	1928	Bronze
32	*Rhesus Monkey*	1928	Bronze
33	*Relief Panel*	1928	Eucalyptus
34	*Moon and Sea*	1928	Mahogany
35	*Wotan*	1928	Teak
36	*Woman and Child*	1928	Black Walnut
37	*Chumash Shaman*	1928	Mahogany
38	*Vieja*	1928	Mahogany
39	*Tezcatlipoca*	1928	Tropical Hardwood
40	*Ome-Tochtli*	1928	Tropical Hardwood
41	*Tlaloc*	1928	Obsidian
42	*Canec*	1929	Rosewood

43	*Desert Sun*	1929	Mahogany
44	*Frio*	1929	Ebony
45	*Swordfish Dancers*	1930	Mahogany
46	*Chumash Fisherman*	1930	Mahogany
47	*The Sprit of the Whirlwinds*	1930	Mahogany
48	*The Spirit of the Hills*	1930	Mahogany
49	*Channel Wind*	1930	Mahogany
50	*Hurrakan*	1930	Rosewood
51	*Culna*	1930	Rosewood
52	*Anthropological Heads*	1930	Terracotta
53	*Young Maize*	1931	Rosewood
54	*Noon*	1931	Rosewood
55	*Burden of Earth*	1931	Hardwood
56	*Dream of Summer*	1931	Rosewood
57	*Ramiletta*	1932	Mahogany
58	*Desert Night*	1932	Mahogany
59	*Desert Sunrise*	1932	Hardwood
60	*Oracion*	1932	Mahogany
61	*Family on the Curb*	1932	Terracotta
62	*Peon Praying*	1932	Terracotta
63	*Figure*	1933	Rosewood
64	*Aztec Bride*	1933	Mahogany
65	*Mayan Mask*	1933	Mahogany
66	*Indigenas*	1933	Mahogany
67	*Four Praying Figures*	1933	Mahogany
68	*Tropic Cycle*	1933	Mahogany
69	*Carbonero*	1933	Ceramic
70	*C.C.C. Workers*	1934	Plaster
71	*Man With a Sheaf of Wheat*	1934	Ceramic
72	*Wheel of Industry*	1934	Cast Stone
73	*Rhumba Dancers*	1935	Mahogany
74	*La Tehuana*	1935	Limestone
75	*Virgin of Guadaloupe*	1935	Ebony
76	*Dr. Edward Hardy*	1935	Bronze
77	*Indian Father and Son*	1935	Rosewood
78	*Father Serra*	1935	Plaster
79	*Three Ornamental Monkeys*	1936	Redwood
80	*Siesta at Noon*	1936	Rosewood
81	*Transportation of the Mail*	1936	Sketches
82	*Aztec*	1936	Black Diorite
83	*Study of Sam Lewis*	1937	Terracotta

84	*Portrait of Fred Sietz*	1937	Glazed Ceramic
85	*Men Working on a Road*	1937	Mahogany
86	*Guardian of the Waters maquette*	1937	Plaster
87	*Guardian of the Waters*	1937	Granite
88	*La Cubana*	1937	Obsidian
89	*Unfinished piece*	no date	Obsidian
90	*Mexican Mother and Child*	1938	Marble
91	*Mexican Beggar Woman*	1938	Marble
92	*Veiled Figure*	1938	Marble
93	*Swordfish Dancer*	1939	Lignum Vitae
94	*Fruits of the Earth*	1939	Tapestry
95	*Legend of California*	1939	Limestone
96	*Rest on the Flight into Egypt*	1939	Black Diorite
97	*Girl Reading*	1940	Mexican Onyx
98	*Sad Woman*	1941	Limestone
99	*Kit Carson Elementary School*	1942	Incised Concrete
100	*Corn Goddess*	1942	Lignum Vitae
101	*Kneeling Male Figure*	1942	Plaster
102	*Silas St. John Memorial*	1942	Bronze
103	*Vernal Sun*	1942	Lignum Vitae
104	*Midday Sun*	1942	Lignum Vitae
105	*Descending Sun*	1943	Lignum Vitae
106	*Desert Night, the Wind*	1944	Lignum Vitae
107	*Primavera*	1944	Tennessee Marble
108	*Desert Sand Wind*	1945	Lignum Vitae
109	*El Colorado*	1945	Diorite
110	*Study of Wally Silberhorn*	1945	Terracotta
111	*Summer Rain*	1946	Lignum Vitae
112	*Thunder*	1947	Nephrite Jade
113	*Spring Stirring*	1947	Black Diorite
114	*Annunciation*	1949	Lignum Vitae
115	*Man Must Sow – To Reap*	1949	Bronze
116	*Yang Kwei Fei*	1949	Nephrite Jade
117	*Peon Game*	1950	Plaster
118	*Autumn Wind*	1950	Rosewood
119	*Harvest Spirit*	1951	Rosewood
120	*Pastoral*	1951	Rosewood
121	*San Diego Central Library Panels*	1953	Cast Concrete
122	*West Wind*	1953	Rosewood
123	*Baby Chris*	1954	Bronze

124	*The Spring*	1955	Bronze
125	*Young Bather*	1955	Bronze
126	*Good Samaritan*	1955	Bronze
127	*Rhumba Dancers*	1955	Bronze
128	*St. Francis*	1955	Bronze
129	*Morning*	1955	Black Diorite
130	*Justice*	1956	Glazed Ceramic
131	*El Cargador*	1956	Rosewood
132	*Angel of Peace*	1956	Bronze
133	*Kneeling Figure on a Cloud*	1957	Bronze
134	*Wind Figure*	1957	Bronze
135	*Aeolus*	1957	Bronze
136	*Seated Male Nude*	1958	Bronze
137	*Winds Around the Moon at Tule Mountain*	1958	Bronze
138	*Leaping Figure*	1958	Bronze
139	*Sleeper in a Dream*	1958	Bronze
140	*Industrial Arts Medal*	1959	Bronze
141	*Feast Day of a Saint*	1959	Rosewood
142	*Marston Testimonial*	1959	never executed
143	*Mourning Woman*	1959	Terracotta
144	*American Eagle*	1959	Sketch
145	*Noctambulist*	1959	Rosewood
146	*Nagual in Moonlight*	1960	Rosewood
147	*Confederate Memorial Model of Robert E. Lee*	1961	Plaster
148	*Spring Rain*	1963	Bronze
149	*Man With a Mask*	1963	Bronze
150	*Day of the Judases*	1963	Rosewood
151	*Descending Sun*	1964	Bronze
152	*Award of Swedish Swimming Federation*	1964	Bronze
153	*Seated Male Life Study*	1964	Tinted Terracotta
154	*Reclining Life Study*	1964	Plaster
155	*Standing Life Study*	1964	Terracotta
156	*Daybreak*	1965	Rosewood
157	*Summer Rain*	1966	Bronze

Chronology

1902 February 26-born Donald Albert Horr at Prentice, Wisconsin, son of Riley Merton Horr and L'Aurore "Laura" Beaudin Horr

1909 Parents separate, taken by mother to Seattle, Washington; spelling of last name changed

1915 Studies watercolor in Seattle

1916 Winter-develops rheumatic fever, permanently damaging heart; Summer-arrives in San Diego on steamship *Congress*

1917 Studies sculpture under Anna Valentien, San Diego Evening High School

1920 Meets Homer Dana

1926 September through June 1928-studies bronze casting at the Santa Barbara School of the Arts with Archibald Dawson

1928 September through June 1929-Gould Scholarship study in Mexico

1929 Fall-Gould Scholarship allows one semester study at the Pennsylvania Academy of Fine Arts

1930 Winter-Gould Scholarship allows one semester study at the Beaux Arts Institute, New York. Returning from New York, visits father in Lemmon, South Dakota, who gives money to build Pascoe Street studio

1931 *Culna* receives Merit Award at the Los Angeles County Museum Annual Exhibit; *Young Maize* receives Purchase Award at the Southern California Art Exhibit of the San Diego Fine Arts Gallery

1932 June 19-marries Dorr Bothwell in San Diego; makes three month trip to Mexico with Francis Cooke

1933 April-first one-man show, Dalzell Hatfield Gallery, Los Angeles

1934 Completes first work for Federal Art Project; October 23-separates from Dorr Bothwell

1935 Completes fountain figure for California Pacific Exposition and exhibits *Mayan Mask*, *Tropic Cycle*, *Young Maize*, *Man with a Sheaf of Wheat*; awarded Gold Medal for Sculptural Excellence at California Pacific International Exposition; July-moves to new studio in Pacific Beach; October-begins writing Art & Artists column for the *San Diego Sun*

1936 August 20-final divorce from Dorr Bothwell

1939 December 16-marries Florence Silberhorn Norse in Salome, Arizona

1942 Elected Associate of the National Sculpture Society; exhibits five pieces in the *1942 Americans* Show at the Museum of Modern Art, New York

1943 February 15-named Associate of the National Academy of Design; suffers heart attack, urged by doctors to stop sculpting

1944 Named Fellow of the National Sculpture Society

1945	Receives Guggenheim Fellowship, begins to work in diorite
1947	Summer-begins teaching at the Coronado School of Fine Arts; receives second Guggenheim Fellowship
1948	May 21-receives Award of Merit Medal from the American Academy of Arts and Letters
1949	Exhibits *Spring Stirring* at the Philadelphia Museum of Art
1950	May 26-named Member of the National Institute of Arts and Letters
1951	April 25-named Full Academician of the National Academy of Design; Fall-begins teaching at the Art Center in La Jolla – *Thunder* exhibited at the National Sculpture Show, Metropolitan Museum of Art, New York
1952	January 21-elected Honorary Member of the San Diego Chapter of the American Institute of Architects
1953	June 16-receives Fine Arts Medal from the American Institute of Architects; October 17-receives Fine Arts Award from the California Council of Architects
1954	Fall through July 1955-first trip abroad (London, Paris, Rome, Florence, Egypt, Istanbul, Athens)
1956	Commissioned by the American Battle Monuments for *Angel of Peace* in the American Cemetery at Henri-Chapelle, Belgium
1957	May-leaves for Italy to model figure for *Angel of Peace*
1959	Designs Industrial Arts Medal for the American Institute of Architects
1960	Concrete replica of *Guardian of the Waters* sent to Yokohama, Japan, as part of the Sister Cities program. Sculptor not consulted about replica and disapproves
1962	One of three finalists in the competition for the Stone Mountain Memorial in Georgia. Walker Hancock awarded commission
1964	Receives commission for the *Swedish Swimming Federation.* Returns to Italy in Spring to supervise casting of figure
1965	Finishes what would be his last wooden figure, *Daybreak*
1966	June 9-suffers fatal heart attack before final work, enlarged version of *Summer Rain*, is cast in bronze. Passes away on June 29
1968	Dana returns to Italy to supervise bronze casting of *Summer Rain*

San Diego Historical Society & Research Archives, Junipero Serra Museum, Villa Montezuma, and Marston House Staff

Rose Arndt, *Staff Assistant*
Lynn Basquez, *Site Interpreter*
Frank Bennett, *Admissions*
Tammie Bennett, *Registrar*
Barry Blake, *Custodian*
Linda Canada, *Education Coordinator*
Elvira Chavez, *Staff Assistant*
Richard Crawford, *Archives Director/Journal Editor*
Eric Christiansen, *Exhibits Designer*
Carol De Bellas, *Development/Membership Secretary*
Patricia Dolton, *Site Interpreter*
Kathleen Eckery, *Special Events Coordinator*
Laura Finster, *Membership Director*
Melody Gilkeson, *Assistant to Executive Director*
Buddy Horne, *Site Interpreter*
Nik Kendziorski, *Curatorial Assistant*
Cynthia Richert Krimmel, *Assistant Photograph Archivist*
Betsy Loureiro, *Staff Assistant*
Jennifer Luksic, *Curator of Collections*
Carrie Miller, *Site Interpreter*
Carol Myers, *Photograph Archivist*
Waynette Newlin, *Receptionist*
Anne Sawin, *Public Relations Officer*
Dennis Sharp, *Archives Assistant*
Sarah Slaughter, *Financial Officer*
Candida Stauss, *Development Director*
Shelley Stefanyszyn, *Marketing Director*
Denny Stone, *Costume and Textiles Curator*
Donna Van Ert, *Museum Stores Manager*
Sally West, *Assistant Archivist*
Gregory Wilkerson, *Facilities Maintenance Manager*
Greg Williams, *Curator of Photographs*
Robert M. Witty, *Executive Director*